CliffsTestPrep®

Praxis II®: English Subject Area Assessments (0041, 0042, 0043, 0048, 0049)

CliffsTestPrep®

Praxis II®: English Subject Area Assessments (0041, 0042, 0043, 0048, 0049)

by

Diane E. Kern, Ph.D.

WILEY

Wiley Publishing, Inc.

About the Author

Diane E. Kern, Ph.D. (Wakefield, RI), is Assistant Professor of Education at the University of Rhode Island. She serves on the School of Education's ad hoc committee on licensure tests.

Publisher's Acknowledgments

Editorial

Acquisitions Editor: Greg Tubach

Project Editor: Matthew McClure

Composition

Proofreader: Henry Lazarek

Wiley Publishing, Inc. Composition Services

CliffsTestPrep® Praxis II®: English Subject Area Assessments (0041, 0042, 0043, 0048, 0049)
Published by:
Wiley Publishing, Inc.
111 River Street
Hoboken, NJ 07030-5774
www.wiley.com

Library of Congress Cataloguing-in-Publication data is available from the publisher upon request.

ISBN-13: 978-0-471-78506-4
ISBN-10: 0-471-78506-7

Printed in the United States of America

10 9 8 7 6 5 4

1O/SS/QY/QW/IN

WILEY

Table of Contents

PART I: PREPARING FOR THE FORMAT OF THE PRAXIS II

PART II: PREPARING FOR THE CONTENT OF THE PRAXIS II

PART III: FULL-LENGTH PRACTICE TESTS

PART IV: CLOSING THOUGHTS

Author's Acknowledgments

Special thanks go to the following people:

Kristyn Hill, a senior at North Kingstown High, and her English teacher, Melissa Waterman, for sharing their work and their passion for English.

Matt McClure, my project editor.

Jimmy and Tory Kern, my very own student writers, and Jim, my supporter and best friend.

Introduction

As you know, teaching English to middle or secondary school students is a rewarding and challenging profession. One way you will demonstrate that you are ready for your teaching license is to pass your state's required Praxis II English Subject Area Assessment test. To show that you *definitely* are ready for your teaching career, use this book to thoroughly prepare for your teaching licensure test. Successful teachers like you do their homework, so let's get started.

Format of the Test

This book contains information about the five tests that make up the Praxis II English Subject Area Assessment series. Each of these tests has a different test registration code, testing time, and format, as detailed in the following table.

Test	Registration Code	Time	Format
English Language, Literature, and Composition: Content Knowledge	0041	2 hours; about 1 minute per question	120 multiple-choice questions
English Language, Literature, and Composition: Essays	0042	2 hours; about 30 minutes per question	4 essay questions
English Language, Literature, and Composition: Pedagogy	0043	1 hour; about 30 minutes per question	2 constructed-response questions
Teaching Foundations: English	0048	4 hours; about 1 hour for each constructed-response question and 2 minutes for each multiple-choice question	50 multiple-choice questions and 2 constructed-response questions
Middle School English Language Arts	0049	2 hours; about 1 minute for each multiple-choice question and 15 minutes for each constructed-response question	90 multiple-choice questions and 2 constructed-response questions

The tests that include constructed-response questions require you to read a passage—about a literary work or a teaching situation, for example—and respond to a short-answer question. Chapter 1 of this book offers sample constructed-response questions and responses, as well as specific strategies to help you prepare for this type of test question.

Multiple-choice questions appear on three of the five Praxis II English Subject Area Assessment tests. These questions require you to quickly read a portion of a literary work, a synopsis of a teaching situation, or a question about teaching English and then choose the "credited response." The credited response is the answer that gets you points on the Praxis II. Chapter 2 provides suggested strategies for approaching the multiple-choice questions.

Only one of the Praxis II English Subject Area Assessments (test 0042, English Language, Literature, and Composition: Essays) requires you to respond to essay questions. If you must take this exam, Chapter 3 is dedicated to essay questions and strategies for success on the essay questions.

When you take your Praxis II test, the proctor will give you a test booklet, and you will determine how much time you spend on each item during the test. In other words, the sections of each test are not independently timed, so you can work on any part of the test at any time you choose. As a result, you most likely will want to work on your pacing for the specific format of your test. This opportunity is provided in Part III of this book, which contains full-length practice tests for each of the Praxis II English Subject Area Assessment tests.

Content of the Test

Now that you've got a general idea of the format and pacing of the test, let's take a closer look at the test's content. Each of the Praxis II English Subject Area Assessment tests is designed to measure your knowledge of a broad range of topics related to the teaching of English. Your knowledge of these topics is usually developed in undergraduate or teacher-certification teaching methods courses, as well as in English courses. Each test covers specific content categories with which you'll want to become familiar.

First, let's take a look at the four broad content categories: Reading and Understanding Text, Language and Linguistics, Composition and Rhetoric, and Teaching English. The following table shows you the frequency of each content category on your Praxis II English test. As you can see, Reading and Understanding Text and Composition and Rhetoric are assessed on every Praxis II English Subject Area Assessment test. Clearly, you will want to study these two content categories carefully to assess your areas of strength and weakness.

Test Number	Reading and Understanding Text	Language and Linguistics	Composition and Rhetoric	Teaching English
0041	X	X	X	
0042	X		X	
0043	X		X	X
0048	X	X	X	X
0049	X	X	X	

In the next section, we'll take a closer look at the specific content categories covered on each of the Praxis II English Subject Area Assessment tests to help you better understand what will be assessed on the specific test you must take.

Specific Praxis II English Test Descriptions

This section provides you with an overview of the content covered on your Praxis II English Subject Area Assessment test in order to help you acquaint yourself with the specific content categories in relation to the broad content categories. This will be helpful to know as you assess what content you need to study. In addition, I'll share the number of questions usually asked in each content category, as well as the approximate percentage of the test each content category comprises. This information will help you anticipate the question types and length of the exam, while also helping you feel more prepared for your test.

English Language, Literature, and Composition: Content Knowledge (0041)

This teaching licensure test is intended to measure the broad base of your knowledge and competencies related to those required of a beginning teacher of English in a secondary school. Test 0041 contains 120 multiple-choice questions that you must answer in a two-hour period. The following table provides an overview of this test's specific content categories, the related broad content categories and chapters in this book that can help you study this content, the approximate number of questions from each category, and the overall percentage of questions usually presented in each category.

Specific Content Category	Broad Content Category	Chapter to Help You Study This Content	Typical Number of Questions from This Category	Approximate Percentage of the Test
Reading and Understanding Text	Reading and Understanding Text	Chapter 4	66	55%
Language and Linguistics	Language and Linguistics	Chapter 5	18	15%
Composition and Rhetoric	Composition and Rhetoric	Chapter 6	36	30%

English Language, Literature, and Composition: Essays (0042)

This teaching licensure test is designed to assess the knowledge of future teachers of English at the secondary school level. Test 0042 is comprised of four essay questions that you must answer in a two-hour period. Of the five tests discussed in this book, this test is the only one that requires essay responses. The following table provides an overview of this test's specific content categories, the related broad content categories and chapters in this book that can help you study this content, the approximate number of questions from each category, and the overall percentage of questions usually presented in each category.

Specific Content Category	Broad Content Category	Chapter(s) to Help You Study This Content	Typical Number of Questions from This Category	Approximate Percentage of the Test
Interpreting Literature: Poetry	Reading and Understanding Text	Chapter 4	1	25%
Interpreting Literature: Prose	Reading and Understanding Text	Chapter 4	1	25%
Issues in English: Understanding Literary Issues	Composition and Rhetoric, Reading and Understanding Text	Chapters 4 and 5	1	25%
Issues in English: Literary Issues and Literary Texts	Composition and Rhetoric, Reading and Understanding Text	Chapters 4 and 5	1	25%

English Language, Literature, and Composition: Pedagogy (0043)

This teaching licensure test is designed for beginning teachers of English in a secondary school. It measures two areas required of English teachers—teaching literature and responding to student writing. Test 0043 contains two constructed-response questions that you must answer in a one-hour period. The following table provides an overview of this test's specific content categories, the related broad content categories and chapters in this book that can help you study this content, the approximate number of questions from each category, and the overall percentage of questions usually presented in each category.

Specific Content Category	Broad Content Category	Chapter to Help You Study This Content	Typical Number of Questions from This Category	Approximate Percentage of the Test
Teaching Literature	Reading and Understanding Text	Chapter 4	1	50%
Responding to Student Writing	Composition and Rhetoric	Chapter 6	1	50%

Teaching Foundations: English (0048)

This teaching licensure test assesses English teacher candidates' knowledge of teaching foundations, human development, modifying instruction for learning differences and special needs, teaching students whose primary language is not English, teaching reading, assessing students' progress, managing a classroom, and teaching methods in the English language arts middle- and secondary-school classroom. Test 0048 contains 50 multiple-choice questions and two constructed-response questions to be completed in a four-hour period. The following table provides an overview of this test's specific content categories, the related broad content categories and chapters in this book that can help you study this content, the approximate number of questions from each category, and the overall percentage of questions usually presented in each category.

Specific Content Category	Broad Content Category	Chapter(s) to Help You Study This Content	Typical Number of Questions from This Category	Approximate Percentage of the Test
Human Development	Teaching English	Chapter 7	8 or 9 multiple-choice questions	5-6%
Addressing Differences and Special Needs	Teaching English	Chapter 7	8 or 9 multiple-choice questions	5-6%
Working with English Learners	Teaching English	Chapter 7	8 or 9 multiple-choice questions	5-6%
Reading Instruction	Reading and Understanding Text	Chapter 4	8 or 9 multiple-choice questions	5-6%
Assessment of Student Progress	Teaching English	Chapter 7	8 or 9 multiple-choice questions	5-6%
Classroom Management Techniques	Teaching English	Chapter 7	8 or 9 multiple-choice questions	5-6%
Teaching Methods in English, Middle/ Junior High Level	Reading and Understanding Text, Composition and Rhetoric, Teaching English	Chapters 4, 6, and 7	1 constructed-response question	33%
Teaching Methods in English, High School Level	Reading and Understanding Text, Composition and Rhetoric, Teaching English	Chapters 4, 6, and 7	1 constructed-response question	33%

Middle School English Language Arts (0049)

This teaching licensure test measures the knowledge and competencies required of a beginning teacher of English at the middle school level. Test 0049 contains 90 multiple-choice questions and two constructed-response questions that must be answered in a two-hour period. The following table provides an overview of this test's specific content categories, the related broad content categories and chapters in this book that can help you study this content, the approximate number of questions from each category, and the overall percentage of questions usually presented in each category.

Specific Content Category	Broad Content Category	Chapter to Help You Study This Content	Typical Number of Questions from This Category	Approximate Percentage of the Test
Reading and Literature	Reading and Understanding Text	Chapter 4	37	31%
Language and Linguistics	Language and Linguistics	Chapter 5	16	13%
Composition and Rhetoric	Composition and Rhetoric	Chapter 6	37	31%
Constructed Response: Literary Analysis	Reading and Understanding Text	Chapter 4	1	12.5%
Constructed Response: Rhetorical Analysis	Composition and Rhetoric	Chapter 6	1	12.5%

Frequently Asked Questions

You've already started on the path to success by orienting yourself with the format of the questions, planning to pace yourself, and becoming familiar with the content covered on the Praxis II English Subject Area Assessment tests, but you probably still have several questions about your test. In this last section of the chapter, I'll answer some frequently asked questions about the Praxis II English Subject Area Assessment tests.

Q. How do I register for a Praxis II Subject Assessment test?

A. Contact the Educational Testing Service (ETS) at www.ets.org/praxis. My students and I have found that online registration is the easiest and least expensive way to register.

Q. How do I know which Praxis II test to take?

A. Contact the department of education for the state in which you seek teacher licensure. If you are enrolled in a school of education, the education department or office of teacher certification also may be able to help, so check their website or contact your advisor. I recommend that you use your favorite Internet search engine to locate your state department of education's teaching certification office. For example, for Rhode Island's teacher licensure information, I would search by the keywords "Rhode Island Department of Education." Once you know which test you need to take, go to the ETS website and select the Praxis II. At this time, the Praxis II tests are available only in paper-and-pencil format, not on the computer.

Q. How much does it cost to take the Praxis II tests?

A. There is both a registration fee and a testing fee. For the current cost of your test, visit the ETS website. At the time of publication, the registration fee for a Praxis II test is $40. Each test has its own additional fee schedule based on the format of the test, the complexity of the scoring process (for example, multiple-choice questions are less expensive to score than essay questions), and the testing time. Note that each Praxis II English Subject Area Assessment test has a 1, 2, or 3 before the test code. This number relates to the cost of the test and is required when you register. Below, you'll find the testing fees (at the time of this book's publication) by test code:

Test Number	Test Title	Fee
10041	English Language, Literature, and Composition: Content Knowledge	$75
20042	English Language, Literature, and Composition: Essays	$90
30043	English Language, Literature, and Composition: Pedagogy	$90
10048	Teaching Foundations: English	$115
10049	Middle School English Language Arts	$85

Q. What score do I need to earn my teaching license?

A. Each state department of education sets its own passing score. Contact your state department of education for this answer.

Q. Why do I need to take a teaching licensure test?

A. The No Child Left Behind Act (NCLB) is a federal education policy that calls for teachers to be "highly qualified" to teach in their area(s) of teacher certification. One way teachers can demonstrate that they are highly qualified to teach English is to earn a passing score on one or more of the Praxis II English Subject Area Assessment tests. While the federal government sets the requirements for federal funding for education programs, each state government is responsible for the education of its schoolchildren. Your state has determined which teaching licensure tests and/or other requirements are required to obtain a teaching license in that state. Your state's department of education also has set the passing score for any teaching licensure test required.

Q. Do all states require the Praxis II for teacher licensure?

A. No, but several states do. Some states have created their own teaching licensure tests. Some states use other Praxis II tests. Again, contact your state department of education for specifics. States that require the same Praxis II test you take will accept your Praxis II scores no matter where you take the test, provided that you meet that state's passing score requirement and that you did not take the test too long ago (usually five or more years).

Q. How long does it take to get my scores back?

A. ETS usually mails your scores to you in four to six weeks. You can also pay a fee to ETS to be able to phone for your scores about a week earlier than the date you would receive them by mail. The fee schedule is available at www.ets.org.

Q. Are any accommodations available to test-takers?

A. Yes. Test-takers with disabilities and those whose primary language is not English may apply for test-taking accommodations. More information is available at www.ets.org/praxis or in the Praxis series registration booklet. The general procedure is to complete a form documenting your learning difference or status as a person whose primary language is not English and to include a document from an individual (there are specific rules as to whom you can request this documentation from) who can attest to your learning difference or status as a person whose primary language is not English. A variety of appropriate accommodations are available to test-takers with learning disabilities or differences. The one accommodation available to test-takers whose primary language is not English is 50 percent more testing time. A word of advice: Look into this information three months before you plan to take your Praxis II test to allow yourself time to complete the appropriate documentation and ensure that registration at a test center that allows for these accommodations is available to you.

Q. What do I need on the day of the test?

A. You need

   1. A photo identification with your name, photograph, and signature
   2. A second form of identification with your name, photograph, and signature—just to be safe!
   3. Your admission ticket, printout of your registration, letter of authorization, mailgram, or telegram showing your test registration

4. Several #2 pencils and an eraser

5. Two blue or black pens for constructed-response or essay questions

6. A watch without calculator functions (optional, but advised)

    You are *not* allowed to bring a calculator to any of these tests.

Q. **What's the best way to prepare for the Praxis II English Subject Area Assessment tests?**

A. Do just what you're doing. Become familiar with the format, types of questions, and content of the test. After you're familiar with what will be on the test, complete several practice tests, correct them yourself, and study the content related to the questions you answered incorrectly.

Suggestions for Using This Study Guide

This book offers various levels of support to make your test preparation efforts more successful.

Part I: Preparing for the Format of the Praxis II

This section provides step-by-step instruction and specific strategies for each of the three question types—constructed response, multiple choice, and essay—on the five Praxis II English Subject Area Assessment tests.

Part II: Preparing for the Content of the Praxis II

As you know, the Praxis II English Subject Area Assessment tests have four broad categories of content: Reading and Understanding Text, Language and Linguistics, Composition and Rhetoric, and Teaching English. In this part of the book, detailed outlines have been prepared to save you time (no need to go through all those methods and English textbooks!) and offer a concise overview of the key theories and practices used in teaching English today. Each practice test question from Part III is linked to a chapter in Part II to provide the information you need to learn to be more successful on the actual test.

Part III: Full-Length Practice Tests

This part offers you the opportunity to apply all that you've learned—in this book and in your English teacher education coursework. Complete the practice test for your specific Praxis II English Subject Area Assessment test, check your answers, and then study the detailed explanations. You can even practice your pacing for the Praxis II—be sure to know whether your test is a one-hour, two-hour, or four-hour session. If you'd like, you can make the most of your studying by completing any of the other four full-length practice tests to give yourself additional practice on the English content covered on your test.

Part IV: Closing Thoughts

The last part of this book offers you study-planning options to guide you to successful and efficient test preparation for your teaching licensure test. In addition, you will find a list of resources and literary works that will give you a sense of the content covered on your test and where to get more information if you need it.

PART I

PREPARING FOR THE FORMAT OF THE PRAXIS II

This part of this book is divided into three chapters that are aligned with the three question formats found on the Praxis II English Subject Area Assessment tests: Constructed-Response Questions, Multiple-Choice Questions, and Essay Questions. After reading the introduction to this book, you will know which of the three formats appear on your Praxis II teaching licensure test. Remember, only one of the tests—Test 0042, English Language, Literature, and Composition: Essays—requires the essay-question format. All the other tests are comprised of multiple-choice and/or constructed-response questions. I suggest that you study only the chapters in Part I that pertain to your test.

Constructed-Response Questions

This chapter provides specific examples and helpful strategies that you can use to approach the constructed-response questions on three of the five Praxis II English Subject Area Assessment tests. Constructed-response questions appear on the following Praxis II tests:

- Test 0043: English Language, Literature, and Composition: Pedagogy
- Test 0048: Teaching Foundations: English
- Test 0049: Middle School English Language Arts

If you are required to take one of these tests, you will benefit from a careful review of this chapter. If not, you may want to skip this chapter and turn to Chapter 2 or Chapter 3 to learn more about the types of questions you'll find on your specific test.

How to Approach the Constructed-Response Questions

The constructed-response format requires that you carefully and quickly read a short passage and then write a short-answer response to one or more questions about the passage. Let's take a look at a generic constructed-response question:

Directions: For this question, you will read an excerpt from a novel and then write a brief response.

Passage:

The remainder of my schooldays were no more auspicious than the first. Indeed, they were an Endless Project that slowly evolved into a Unit, in which miles of construction paper and wax crayon were expended by the State of Alabama in its well-meaning but fruitless efforts to teach me Group Dynamics.

Question:

Chapter 4 of *To Kill a Mockingbird,* a novel by Harper Lee, opens with these lines. Explain how the author uses metaphor and word choice to help us better understand Scout, the narrator of the novel.

As you can see, a constructed-response question is made up of three parts: directions, a passage, and one or more questions about the passage. In the next section, I suggest specific strategies for you to try out on the sample constructed-response questions that appear later in this chapter and again on the practice tests in Part III.

Strategies for the Constructed-Response Questions

Here are some suggested strategies that I recommend you employ as you approach the constructed-response questions:

1. **Read the question(s) first.** Most test-takers would naturally read the passage first and then move to the question(s). I did! But remember, you are reading the passage in order to get the answers to the questions right. Before you spend time reading the passage, read the question(s) you'll be required to answer so that you can think about *why* you are reading it. Reading specialists call this practice "setting purpose for reading." I suspect that you'll find this a more efficient and effective approach than reading the passage first.
2. *Actively* **read each passage.** As you read the passage, take notes, keep your mind on the question(s) you'll have to answer, and think about your response as you read. It's fine for you to make notes, underlines, or other marks in your test booklet.

3. **Reread each question and then make a brief plan or sketch of the points of your response.** For example, a brief plan for the sample question above might look like this:

   - *Metaphor:* Formal schooling is a never-ending unit plan.
   - *Meaning:* Scout views her formal school experience as unchallenging, ineffective, and boring. In addition, her school experiences have not taught her how to get along with others.
   - *Word choice:* Auspicious, expended, fruitless.
   - *Meaning:* Word choice demonstrates that Scout is bright, literate, and clever and suggests that she is clearly learning to think critically outside of her formal school experiences.

4. **Review the passage and question(s).** Make sure that you have referred specifically to the passage and have addressed all the question requirements with examples and details.

5. **Review your response.** Were you clear, concise, specific, and accurate? Did you base your response on principles of learning and teaching English? Did you answer all parts of the question?

   Here is a sample response to our generic question on *To Kill a Mockingbird*:

   Harper Lee opens Chapter 4 of <u>To Kill a Mockingbird</u> with the metaphor that school is a never-ending unit plan. By this, the author is showing the main character's view that formal schooling is pointless drudgery. The narrator, Scout, sees formal schooling as ineffective in its attempts to teach her to get along with others—in her words, "Group Dynamics." Furthermore, the author's word choices, such as auspicious, fruitless, and expended, provide the reader with the idea that Scout may be finding her formal experiences ineffective and unchallenging because she is learning more outside of school than during school. Lee presents our young narrator as a character who appears to be a bright, reflective, and critical thinker.

   Of course, I have the opportunity to use spell-check and word-processing tools to edit and revise this sample response. You will not have this opportunity, and the test scorers will take this into account. You may have noticed that I underlined the title of the novel. You can't italicize when you handwrite your answers, but you can underline book titles to show that you know this convention of written English. As you'll see when we look at the scoring guide for your particular test in the last section of this chapter, you will need to demonstrate "facility with conventions of standard written English," but not perfection.

6. **Beware of the multiple-part constructed-response questions!** These questions have two or more parts rather than just one, and you need to make sure that your response addresses all parts of the question.

7. **Remember that this is not an essay test.** In general, you will write a one- to two-paragraph response for each part of the question, although the length of your response will vary depending on the question as well as on the amount of testing time you have allotted to each question. This is not an essay-test format, so it is okay for you to use bulleted lists or brief examples. You do not have to have "perfect paragraphs" or use essay format to earn a high score. The most important aspect of your response is the content you write and the accuracy of the examples you provide.

8. **Be mindful of your testing time.** Depending on which Praxis II test you take, you will have between one and four hours to complete your test. Each test-taker will need a different amount of time to respond to a constructed-response question accurately and thoroughly, so I cannot give you a specific time to spend on each constructed-response question. I have provided general guidelines in the Introduction to this book to give you the test publisher's suggested pacing. You'll have to practice your timing before the actual exam. Many of my students report that their timing was more of a problem than content knowledge was, especially on the constructed-response questions. Several of my students simply ran out of time to fully answer one or more questions. Constructed-response questions are likely to take more of your testing time, so practice the full-length tests at the back of this guide with your watch in hand. Be sure to check your watch at the start of the test and then every 30 minutes into the testing session. Remember, you are in charge of your pacing on the entire test. The sections of the Praxis II are not independently timed by the proctor.

How to Read the Passage

Now that you better understand the format of the constructed-response questions, let's take a closer look at the passage itself and develop a strategy for reading the passage actively and efficiently.

The remainder of my schooldays were no more auspicious than the first. Indeed, they were an Endless Project that slowly evolved into a Unit, in which miles of construction paper and wax crayon were expended by the State of Alabama in its well-meaning but fruitless efforts to teach me Group Dynamics.

1. **Remember to read the questions first.**

2. **Read the passage carefully, closely, and actively.** By *carefully,* I mean read slowly enough to comprehend what you've read. By *closely,* I suggest that you consider the literary elements the author uses. By *actively,* I mean to make margin notes, underline key points, and think about why this information is included. As you can see in the passage from *To Kill a Mockingbird* above, some recollection of this literary work is expected if you are to earn a higher score on this question.

3. **Ask questions as you read.** What issues about teaching and learning English language arts does this passage raise? How might the teacher help the student(s) achieve a learning goal or understand this passage? What literary elements does this passage feature? Keep in mind that all information in the passage is included on the test for a reason. Reading and knowing the questions *before* you read the passage really pays off here. You can read the passage actively and efficiently to get ideas for your constructed response. This should save you time as well.

As you know, three of the five Praxis II tests use the constructed-response question format, but each of the tests contains a slightly different topic for the passage and constructed-response question. In the next section, we'll look at sample constructed-response questions test by test. When you're finished reviewing the format of *your test's* constructed-response questions, I suggest that you practice completing your answer to the question using notebook paper. I have included answers and explanations at the end of this chapter for you to review after you complete your responses.

English Language, Literature, and Composition: Pedagogy (0043)

There are two types of constructed-response questions on test 0043: Teaching Literature and Responding to Student Writing.

Teaching Literature—Sample Question

Directions: Assume that you are teaching literature to a tenth-grade class. Your overall goal is to help your students recognize and understand key literary features of the works they read. Your choices of literary works to use as parts of this unit are listed below.

- Ray Bradbury, *Fahrenheit 451*
- Tennessee Williams, *The Glass Menagerie*
- J. D. Salinger, *The Catcher in the Rye*
- F. Scott Fitzgerald, *The Great Gatsby*
- Nathaniel Hawthorne, *The Scarlet Letter*
- William Shakespeare, *Macbeth*

1. Choose ONE of the works in the preceding list. Choose a work that you know well enough to identify and to cite examples of its key literary features. For example, you may identify and cite examples of specific characterization and narration methods, characteristics of the genre or subgenre, specific literary devices, or specific poetic techniques. Once you have chosen one of the literary works, answer the following three-part question.

2. Identify and describe TWO literary features key to the work that you have chosen for your tenth-grade literature unit. In your response:
   - Be specific about what you want your students to know about each literary feature.
   - Include specific examples from the literary work that are relevant to each feature.
   - Describe how knowledge of these literary features is appropriate to teach in a tenth-grade classroom.

3. Identify and describe TWO challenges to understanding this work that you anticipate your tenth-grade students might have. In your response:

   ■ Explain why each challenging aspect of this text is likely for tenth-grade students.

   ■ Include specific examples from the literary work that are relevant to each challenging aspect.

4. Describe TWO instructional activities that you would use to teach this literary work to your tenth-grade literature students. Be sure to incorporate either the literary features you described in part 2 and/or the challenging aspects you described in part 3. In your response:

   ■ Offer clear, well-formulated activities that actively involve students.

   ■ Explain how each activity helps students understand the literary features (from part 2) and/or the challenging aspect of the work (from part 3).

   ■ Describe activities that are appropriate for tenth-grade students.

Responding to Student Writing—Sample Question

Directions: In this exercise, you will answer questions about a student's writing sample. Some questions will ask about strengths, weaknesses, and errors in conventions of standard written English. Below are some examples of how you should understand these terms for the purpose of this test question. You may find it helpful to refer to these examples when you write your response, although you may introduce your own examples.

Examples of strengths and weaknesses in writing:

■ Sense of voice
■ Paragraph organization
■ Essay organization
■ Sentence variety and complexity
■ Sense of audience

Examples of errors in conventions of standard written English:

■ Misplaced semicolons or commas
■ Unparallel construction
■ Run-on sentences
■ Sentence fragments
■ Subject-verb agreement errors
■ Verb tense inconsistency
■ Pronoun-antecedent agreement errors

Question

A ninth-grade English class was assigned to write a personal narrative from another person's point of view. What follows is a student response to this assignment. It is a final draft. Read this response carefully.

Broken Bones

I'm good friends with Jimmy. I live right next to him and on days school is canceled we usually hang out. On this day, school was cancelled due to too much snow on the roads. So I called Jim and we came to consensus that we would go to the mall at about 11:00 am. He came down to my house and we were ready to go at 11:15.

The snow that has fallen slowly last night had continued into the morning. The sky was filled with gray clouds. Jim said he wanted to go sledding too. *We live right near Monsignor Clark School, and they have a good sledding hill.* I said I wanted to go to the mall, so we made an agreement to go to the mall first and then the sledding hill second. *I got my way.*

Jim didn't have a sled, and he liked using his boogie board as a sled anyway, so he brought that. He took some other snow gear with him to stay warm. I had a sled, but really wasn't planning on going sledding. Jim was way into this stuff.

We walked over the hill toward the mall, saw Monsignor Clark School, and kept walking towards the Wakefield Mall. Jim jumped down a small hill near the Paul Baileys' car dealership. He was laughing the whole time. He sprung up and looked at me with the biggest smile on and his eyes were as wide the night sky. Then Jim sprinted to a hill that a snow plow had made on the side of the road. The plow had come to a little three-way intersection and just went straight, right up to the grass. All I could see was a mound of snow about 10 or 12 feet high and Jim disappear over it. I walked a bit further so I was parallel with the hill and could see that on the other side it was straight down and lead to a hill that was more like 15 or 16 feet high.

Jim did a "dropping in" motion two or three times on his stomach and said this was the coolest ever. Then he said what I figured he would eventually say, "You think I'll do it standing up?" and of course I said that I didn't think he would. *I knew he would get up there but I wasn't sure if he would actually drop in.* He got on top with boogie board in hand, and tried to place it under his feet and almost fell. He finally got his feet set and leaned forward. He was all good, going straight down the slope very fast. That's until he hit the bottom. At that moment the sky turned even grayer.

It looked like Jim was going to try to stand up when he slipped violently to his left side. Jim hit the ground with way too much force, and to make things worse, he didn't get up. I couldn't discern what had happened. Then Jim yelled, "I didn't know the ground was that hard!"

Jim picked up his boogie board and walked away to leave, without the smile on his face. Jim's face was hard to read, no expressions, which is how he usually is. He was quiet on the walk home, and then he said he couldn't move this left arm. When we got back to my house, my mom, who is a nurse, helped him get his coat off and looked at his arm. Jim's elbow was sticking out. "It's not supposed to look like that, huh?" Jim said. "No, Jim, ha-ha, it's not" my mom mumbled with a nervous laugh.

Jim's dad took him to the hospital. He had broken his ulna, and would have to wear a cast for awhile. I thought of how ironic it was that on a day we planned to have lots of fun sledding, Jim ended up breaking his arm. At least I will get to sign his cast! I hope he is resilient and bounces back soon. I think the lesson he learned is not to be a fool and do something zany without the proper equipment and protection. Maybe next time he'll replace the boogie board with a sled!

1. Identify ONE significant strength (give specific examples and line references) and explain how this strength contributes to the paper's effectiveness. Do NOT discuss the student's ability with conventions of standard written English (e.g., grammar, punctuation).

2. Identify ONE significant weakness (give specific examples and line references) and explain how this weakness interferes with the paper's effectiveness. Do NOT discuss the student's ability with conventions of standard written English (e.g., grammar, punctuation).

3. Identify TWO specific errors in the conventions of standard written English in the student's writing (quote from the narrative and give specific line references). For each error, identify the type of error being made.

4. Based on this student's writing sample, describe ONE follow-up assignment you would give to help improve this student's writing ability. Explain how you would address the strength (from part 1 of this question) and/or the weakness (from part 2) of this question. Your follow-up assignment should NOT address errors in conventions of standard written English (e.g., grammar, punctuation).

Teaching Foundations: English (0048)

There are two types of constructed-response questions on test 0048: Teaching Methods for the Middle/Junior High Level English classroom and Teaching Methods for the High School Level English Classroom.

Teaching Methods for Middle/Junior High Level English Classroom—Sample Question

Directions: There are FOUR parts to this constructed-response question. Given the student learning goal and grade level indicated, you are to develop an appropriate instructional sequence (i.e., lesson plan) and then analyze specific elements of your lesson plan. The suggested amount of time for this constructed-response question is 80 minutes.

Student learning goal: Evaluate the structural elements of the plot (e.g., subplots, parallel episodes, climax), the plot's development, and the way in which conflicts are (or are not) addressed and resolved across multiple literary works (Grade 8, Reading, 3.2).

Grade level: Grade 8

The class is made up of 26 students: 13 boys and 13 girls.

Part 1: Instructional sequence

Describe a lesson plan that you would use to help students meet the student learning goal stated above. You can use a bulleted list or outline form. Be certain that the content and the instructional approaches you suggest are appropriate for the grade level stated above. Your instructional sequence can be structured for a single class day or for a span of a few days. In your lesson plan:

- Include one group activity that requires active student participation.
- Identify one reading skill or strategy that students must use to be successful in the lesson, and include an activity in your lesson plan to help students improve this reading strategy or skill.
- Include three assessment activities: 1) prior to instruction, 2) during instruction, and 3) after instruction to evaluate whether students achieved the learning goal.

Part 2: Group activity

Describe ONE of the group activities from your lesson plan. Be sure to provide sufficient detail in your description and to explain what the teacher will do, what the students will do, and why the activity contributes to the student learning goal.

Part 3: Strengthening reading abilities

Describe why you chose the reading skill or strategy included in your lesson plan. Be sure to explain why this reading strategy or skill is important to the students' achievement of the lesson goal and why your activity would be effective for improving the skill.

Part 4: Assessment

Describe ONE of the three assessment activities that you included in your lesson plan (prior to instruction, during instruction, after instruction). Be sure to describe how the assessment would provide evidence of the degree to which students have achieved the learning goal.

Teaching Methods for the High School Level English Classroom—Sample Question

Directions: There are FOUR parts to this constructed-response question. Given the student learning goal and grade level indicated, you are to develop an appropriate instructional sequence (i.e., lesson plan) and then analyze specific elements of your lesson plan. The suggested amount of time for this constructed-response question is 80 minutes.

Student learning goal: Students will structure their writing ideas and arguments in a sustained, persuasive, and sophisticated way and support ideas and arguments with precise and relevant examples (Grades 11–12, Writing, 1.3).

Grade level: Grade 11

The class is made up of 30 students: 15 boys and 15 girls.

Part 1: Instructional sequence

Describe a lesson plan that you would use to help students meet the student learning goal stated above. You can use a bulleted list or outline form. Be certain that the content and the instructional approaches you suggest are appropriate for the grade level stated above. Your instructional sequence can be structured for a single class day or for a span of a few days. In your lesson plan:

- Include one group or participatory activity that requires active student participation.

- Identify one writing skill that students must use to be successful in the lesson, and include an activity in your lesson plan to help students improve this writing skill.

- Include three assessment activities: 1) prior to instruction, 2) during instruction, and 3) after instruction to evaluate whether students achieved the learning goal.

Part 2: Group or participatory activity

Describe ONE of the group activities from your lesson plan. Be sure to provide sufficient detail in your description and to explain what the teacher will do, what the students will do, and why the activity contributes to the student learning goal.

Part 3: Strengthening writing abilities

Describe why you chose the writing skill included in your lesson plan. Be sure to explain why this writing skill is important to the students' achievement of the lesson goal and why your activity would be effective for improving the skill.

Part 4: Assessment

Describe ONE of the three assessment activities that you included in your lesson plan (prior to instruction, during instruction, after instruction). Be sure to describe how the assessment would provide evidence of the degree to which students have achieved the learning goal.

Middle School English Language Arts (0049)

There are two types of constructed-response questions on test 0049: Literary Analysis and Rhetorical Analysis.

Literary Analysis—Sample Question

Directions: This short-answer, or constructed-response, question requires you to interpret a piece of literary or nonfiction text. Plan to spend approximately 15 minutes of your testing time on this constructed response.

The Prologue

Enter Chorus.
Chorus. Two households, both alike in dignity,
In fair Verona, where we lay our scene,
From ancient grudge break to new mutiny,
Where civil blood makes civil hands unclean.
From forth the fatal loins of these two foes
A pair of star-cross'd lovers take their life;
Whose misadventur'd piteous overthrows
Doth with their death bury their parents' strife.
The fearful passage of their death-mark'd love,
And the continuance of their parents' rage,
Which, but their children's end, naught could remove,
Is now the two hours' traffic of our stage;
The which if you with patient ears attend,
What here shall miss, our toil shall strive to mend.
[Exit.]

In this prologue from Shakespeare's <u>Romeo and Juliet,</u> describe how the author uses imagery and poetic devices to introduce the play.

Rhetorical Analysis—Sample Question

Directions: This short-answer, or constructed-response, question requires you to discuss the rhetorical elements of a piece of writing. Plan to spend approximately 15 minutes of your testing time on this constructed response.

The following passage is an excerpt from "Incidents in the Life of a Slave Girl" by Harriet Jacobs (a.k.a. Linda Brent):

Such were the unusually fortunate circumstances of my early childhood. When I was six years old, my mother died; and then, for the first time, I learned, by the talk around me, that I was a slave. My mother's mistress was the daughter of my grandmother's mistress. She was the foster sister of my mother; they were both nourished at my grandmother's breast. In fact, my mother had been weaned at three months old, that the babe of the mistress might obtain sufficient food. They played together as children; and, when they became women, my mother was a most faithful servant to her whiter foster sister. On her death-bed her mistress promised that her children should never suffer for any thing; and during her lifetime she kept her word. They all spoke kindly of my dead mother, who had been a slave merely in name, but in nature was noble and womanly. I grieved for her, and my young mind was troubled with the thought who would now take care of me and my little brother. I was told that my home was now to be with her mistress; and I found it a happy one. No toil-some or disagreeable duties were imposed on me. My mistress was so kind to me that I was always glad to do her bidding, and proud to labor for her as much as my young years would permit. I would sit by her side for hours, sewing diligently, with a heart as free from care as that of any free-born white child. When she thought I was tired, she would send me out to run and jump; and away I bounded, to gather berries or flowers to decorate her room. Those were happy days—too happy to last. The slave child had no thought for the morrow; but there came that blight, which too surely waits on every human being born to be a chattel.

Describe the major organizational features of the paragraph. Refer directly to the excerpt to support your description of its organization.

Constructed-Response Scoring Guides

This section of the chapter helps you focus on how to earn the highest score. It also helps you better understand what makes a less effective response. You'll see that your answers need to be *complete, relevant, appropriate, thorough,* and *specific to the literary work or other works in the passage.* While an appropriate response must be legible and accurate, note that you are not required to use perfect spelling, grammar, or handwriting. Let's begin with a look at the scoring process itself, and then move to the specific scoring guides for the constructed-response items on your Praxis II test.

How Is an "Appropriate Response" Determined?

The Educational Testing Service (ETS) uses the term *appropriate* in its scoring guide. It's important that you consider how the ETS scorers determine "appropriate responses":

- Two or three education experts are asked to read case histories and answer the questions.
- Benchmark papers are selected from individuals who have agreed to participate in a pilot test. In other words, your test is not used to train scorers!
- The test writer uses the experts' "model answers" to develop a specific scoring guide for each case history and its questions. These models become examples of correct answers, not *the* correct answers.
- Next, the specific scoring guide is used to select model answers that serve as "benchmark papers" for training scorers for your exam.
- During the training session and when reading benchmark papers, scorers can add new answers to the scoring guide as they see fit.
- Training sessions are designed to train scorers to use benchmark papers and the specific scoring guide, not their own opinions or preferences.

While test experts generally agree that the ETS has set up a reliable and valid way to score test-takers' written responses, you may have concerns about how your own constructed responses are scored. If this is the case, you can request and pay for your score to be verified. See the website www.ets.org/praxis for more information about the score-verification process and fees.

How to Use the Scoring Criteria to Assess Your Own Practice Test Responses

As you'll see in this section, each of the Praxis II tests that includes constructed-response questions has different scoring criteria. This section presents each test's scoring criteria. After you review this section, you may want to share your constructed-response questions from the sample test items earlier in this chapter with an experienced teacher or educator and ask him or her to use the scoring guide to provide feedback to you. You also may want to compare your own constructed responses to the answers and explanations provided. This way, you are making sure that you are addressing all the important aspects of each question.

English Language, Literature, and Composition: Pedagogy (0043)

There are two constructed-response questions on test 0043 that are made up of three or four parts each. The scoring range for each question is between 0 and 6. While each test's scoring criteria may vary, the points are generally distributed as follows.

Teaching Literature

Part 1—2 points awarded for the identification of two key literary features and clear connections to specific examples in the text.

Part 2—2 points awarded for the identification of two challenges to understanding this passage and an accurate explanation as to why these challenges would likely pose a problem for student understanding. Specific examples from the text are included.

Part 3—2 points awarded for the description of two instructional activities that are appropriate for the given grade level and that address the literary features and/or challenges cited in parts 1 and 2. The activities are designed to help students understand specific elements of the knowledge.

Responding to Student Writing

Part 1—1 point for the identification of one significant strength and a detailed explanation of how it contributes to the paper's effectiveness.

Part 2—1 point for the identification of one significant weakness and a detailed explanation of how it interferes with the paper's effectiveness.

Part 3—2 points: 1 point for the correct identification of each of the two errors.

Part 4—2 points for a clear, concise discussion of the follow-up assignment that connects clearly to the strengths or weaknesses of the student's paper and also contributes to the student's development as a writer.

Teaching Foundations: English (0048)

There are two constructed-response questions on test 0048 that are made up of four parts. The scoring range for each constructed-response question on this test is between 0 and 4. Points are distributed as follows:

Score of 4

The candidate's response includes most or all of the following:

- Answers to all parts of the questions are clear and appropriate.
- Instructional activities are presented in a logical sequence related to the students' learning goal.

- Instructional activities are appropriate for the grade level.
- The response demonstrates strong understanding of subject matter and pedagogy.
- The response contains sufficient and well-chosen examples and supporting details.

Score of 3

The candidate's response includes most or all of the following:

- Answers to most parts of the questions are clear and appropriate.
- Instructional activities are appropriately sequenced and relate to the instructional goal.
- The response demonstrates adequate understanding of content and pedagogy.
- The response contains some appropriate examples and supporting details.

Score of 2

The candidate's response includes most or all of the following:

- Responses to some parts of the question are appropriate.
- Activities do not follow in a logical sequence and do not relate clearly to the instructional goals.
- Activities may be appropriate for the grade level but some may be clearly inappropriate.
- The response shows an incomplete understanding of subject matter and pedagogy.
- The response includes few appropriate examples and supporting details.

Score of 1

The candidate's response includes most or all of the following:

- Answers to very few parts of the question are appropriate.
- Activities do not flow in a logical sequence and do not relate clearly to the instructional goals.
- Activities, overall, are inappropriate for the given grade level.
- The response shows a weak understanding of subject matter and pedagogy.
- The response includes no appropriate examples or supporting details.

Score of 0

The candidate's response contains no strategies, examples, or details that appropriately address the question.

Middle School English Language Arts (0049)

There are two constructed-response questions on test 0049. The scoring range for each constructed-response question on this test is between 0 and 3. Points are distributed as follows:

Score of 3

The response is strong in the following ways:

- Candidate demonstrates the ability to analyze the constructed-response question thoughtfully and in depth.
- Candidate demonstrates strong knowledge of the subject matter relevant to the question.
- Candidate responds appropriately to all parts of the question.
- Candidate demonstrates facility with the conventions of standard written English.

Score of 2

An acceptable response demonstrates some understanding of the topic but is limited in one or more of the following major ways:

- Candidate indicates a misreading of the constructed-response question or material and/or provides superficial analysis.
- Candidate demonstrates only superficial knowledge of the relevant subject matter.
- Candidate responds to one or more parts of the questions inadequately or not at all.
- Response may contain significant writing errors.

Score of 1

An unacceptable response is seriously flawed in one or more of the following ways:

- Candidate demonstrates a weak understanding of the subject matter or of the writing task.
- Candidate fails to respond adequately to most parts of the question.
- Response may be incoherent or severely underdeveloped.
- Response may contain severe and persistent writing errors.

Answers and Explanations

English Language, Literature, and Composition: Pedagogy (0043)

Teaching Literature—Sample Response

The following response earned a score of 6 on a 6-point scale:

1. One literary feature of <u>Fahrenheit 451</u> is Bradbury's use of symbolism to convey meaning. The author uses book burning as a symbol of the power censorship holds in this futuristic society that employs "firefighters" who obediently set fire to books, not extinguish the fires, or censorship, in this society. Another symbol used throughout this novel is "the book," an enemy of the state. Books represent knowledge and intellectualism, which are forbidden in this culture. In this opening excerpt from the novel, Montag compares book pages to pigeon wings. This allusion symbolizes books as freedom, a theme the author will develop throughout the novel.

   Another important literary feature of <u>Fahrenheit 451</u> is the use of its genre, science fiction, as a vehicle for social criticism. The author suggests that an unchecked oppressive government causes irreparable damage to society. Written in the early 1950s, after WWII and during the rise of McCarthyism, the use of the science-fiction genre to raise apprehension about the United States becoming an oppressive, authoritarian society was incredibly popular and well-received. The notion of a dystopia, a futuristic and technocratic society that requires order, harmony, and obedience at the expense of personal rights and individuals' creative expression, is a specific element of the science fiction genre that Bradbury uses successfully in <u>Fahrenheit 451</u>.

2. One challenge to understanding this novel that I anticipate tenth-graders might have is identifying the themes in the text. Identifying theme requires high-level reading skills, such as analysis, synthesis, and evaluation. Not all tenth-graders are reading at grade level and some may be challenged to think critically, as required by this task. For example, one central theme in the novel is censorship. In the futuristic setting of this book, buying and owning books is illegal and if one is found with books, the books are burned and the owner is arrested. Another theme Bradbury develops is the dichotomy of knowledge and ignorance. In the novel, a main character, Montag who is a fireman, has the responsibility to burn books, or knowledge. As the story progresses, Montag finds himself questioning the status quo, and experiencing more satisfaction in his life when it is filled with knowledge.

   A second challenge to understanding that tenth-graders might experience is identifying and understanding the use of symbolism in <u>Fahrenheit 451</u>. Students at this grade level may miss the subtlety of the author's meaning by reading or even skipping sections of the text that include important symbols. For example, the Phoenix plays a key role and symbolizes fire and flight. A second symbol that tenth-graders may not immediately understand is the symbol of the Mechanical Hound that represents a manipulation of nature which causes death and destruction.

3. One instructional activity I would use to teach <u>Fahrenheit 451</u> to tenth-grade students is activating and developing prior knowledge. Prior to reading the novel, I would engage the students in a discussion about banned books, censorship, and the right to freedom of speech in the United States. After this discussion, I would provide the students

with an outline of the historical context of this novel and check for understanding of McCarthyism, communism, the First Amendment, WWII, Hitler, and post-WWII events, such as the Cold War. This activity would help students to more deeply understand the symbolism and to identify the major themes in the novel.

A second instructional activity I would use to teach this novel is cooperative learning. For example, the tenth-grade students would work in groups of four and take individual responsibility for finding the theme or symbolism in a portion of the text. Next, the group would discuss its findings and support each other in reaching higher level understanding of the novel. Finally, the group would present its interpretation of the novel's symbols and identified themes in the format of a poster presentation. This activity would help students to reach higher levels of understanding of literary features through active involvement, speaking and listening, as well as individual accountability.

Responding to Student Writing—Sample Response

The following response earned a score of 6 on a 6-point scale:

1. One significant strength of this student's writing is its sense of voice. The reader can imagine Jimmy's enthusiasm on a snow day with no school, as noted in lines 10–11, "Jim was way into this stuff," and in line 14, when the author describes Jimmy's smile "as wide as the night sky." The author's voice is that of an adolescent, perhaps one who is a bit older than Jim and sees Jim as a younger brother. This older adolescent voice is noted in line 10, "I had a sled, but really wasn't planning on going sledding," and lines 28–29, in which the narrator talks about Jim's expressions being hard to read "which is how he usually is." The sense of voice this young author creates draws the reader in to learn more about the broken bones incident and lets the reader know these adolescent boys have a brotherly, caring, yet competitive, relationship. This makes the reader wonder if the older friend causes the broken bones and how the boys will handle an accident. Voice is a significant strength of this piece.

2. One significant weakness of the student's writing is the inclusion of unnecessary events leading up to the "broken bones" incident in the story. Furthermore, the student author tends to overuse sequence of events as the rationale for inclusion of events. For example, the author includes details about why school was cancelled (line 3) and the snow gear that Jim brought (line 10). The result of this weakness is a loss of the reader's interest from time to time. In addition, the time order of going to the mall and then sledding seems important in the opening but is not clearly developed at the close of the piece. The narrator talks about the irony of the day's events, but misses the opportunity to revisit who got his way—Jimmy or the narrator (line 8), a more significant and subtle bit of irony in the piece.

3. One specific error in the conventions of standard written English is comma use. For example, in line 2, the author does not use a comma before a coordinating conjunction joining independent clauses. There are several other examples of not understanding this convention in line 14 ("He sprung up and looked at me with the biggest smile on and his eyes were as wide as the night sky.") and line 17 (I walked a bit further so I was parallel with the hill and could see that on the other side it was straight down and lead to a hill that was more like 15 or 16 feet high). The author appears to understand this convention in line 9 (". . . , so we made an agreement) and line 10 ("I had a sled, but . . ."). In addition, the author does not use a comma when needed in the nonrestrictive adjective clause in line 25 (It looked like Jim was going to try to stand up <u>when</u> he slipped violently to his left side.)

   A second specific error in the conventions of standard written English is verb tense. In line 5, the young author attempts to use rich, descriptive language to describe the snowy day, but these attempts are ineffective when an intrusive error in verb tense occurs in the sentence. "The snow has fallen slowly last night had continued into the morning." The student chooses the present perfect tense "has fallen," when he needed to choose the past perfect tense "had fallen" to agree with the tense in the remainder of the sentence "had continued into the morning."

4. One follow-up assignment I would give to this student writer is an author study of works that include sequential events that are important to the development of a narrative, as well as examples of other ways to organize a narrative, such as flashback, journal format or carefully selecting events to return to later in the narrative. <u>Flowers for Algernon</u>, <u>The Catcher in the Rye</u>, and <u>To Kill a Mockingbird</u> all could provide excellent models for this study. Next, I would ask the author to re-examine this piece of writing in order to suggest one paragraph to revise. Specifically, I will help the student see the inclusion of unnecessary events and contrast this with the inclusion of necessary events that are important to the piece.

Teaching Foundations: English (0048)

Teaching Methods in English, Middle/Junior High Level—Sample Response

The following response earned a score of 4 on a 4-point scale:

Part 1: This lesson plan is designed for eighth-grade learners' ability to evaluate the structural elements of plot, plot development, and the ways conflicts are resolved, or not resolved, in multiple literary works.

Opening: Tell the students that they are going to be viewing and reading texts to evaluate the important parts of a story's plot—climax, subplots, and conflicts. Explain that this is an important reading skill to help students remember the story line and to be able to write or to discuss a summary of a film or a text.

Show a film clip from <u>Holes</u> that demonstrates a climactic moment in the plot. Stop the film and discuss the key elements of the event. Students will be assessed prior to instruction during this opening section of the lesson to determine if they understand the structural elements of plot, subplot, conflicts, and climax. The teacher will ask the students what made the event exciting, interesting, or suspenseful and try to elicit students' prior knowledge of these story elements.

Next, read aloud the same plot event from the literary work. Ask the students to elaborate on the features of this climactic moment in the story. Next, collaboratively write a definition of climax and ask all to take notes.

Proceed in a similar way, alternating the use of film and literary work, to help students to identify, define, and describe subplots and conflicts.

Middle: Organize the students in small, heterogeneous groups to read one of four texts in a text set. Have each member of the group become an "expert of the day" on finding climax, main events, subplots or conflicts, and then alternate this role each day to ensure students have experience identifying each structural element. The students first read independently, taking margin notes (using stick-on notes) on examples of the structural elements. Then the students reconvene their small group to discuss, correct, or enrich understanding of today's reading. The teacher will conduct a "during reading" assessment by sitting in on small group discussions and evaluating individual student participation and level of understanding. In addition, she will randomly collect student books to review stick-on notes.

Closing: The class reconvenes whole group to plot the story's structural elements on a large, bulletin-board size graphic organizer.

The students continue with this sequence of activities until the story is read completely and all chapters have been charted on the graphic organizer. After the graphic organizer is complete, the students will work in their small groups to practice orally summarizing the plot of the literary work.

Follow-up activity: Students write a summary of the literary work. The students have been taught in previous lessons about the format of a summary. This summary will act as the summative assessment to determine if each individual student has achieved the learning goal.

Part 2: As briefly stated in the lesson plan, the eighth-graders will work in small, cooperative groups to read and identify structural elements of the plot in a literary work. The students will take turns becoming an "expert of the day" in identifying examples of the plot's climax, subplot, main events, and conflicts. The students will be held individually accountable by having to write margin notes, which will be randomly checked by the teacher. In addition, the student will be individually accountable to the group and the class when the group reports to the whole class at the end of the lesson. The teacher will also sit in to assess the level of performance of each group. The students will work simultaneously to read and identify structural elements of the plot and then discuss their findings with the small group. This activity contributes to the students' achievement of the learning goal by requiring reading, writing, speaking, listening, and thinking as individuals and as a group member. The cooperative nature of the group activity offers all students an opportunity to learn.

Part 3: The reading strategy—comprehending structural elements of plot in a literary work in order to summarize—was chosen because it is a real-life and important comprehension strategy adolescents must practice and master. In addition, this reading strategy was chosen because it usually still needs to be *taught* to eighth-graders. The inclusion of film to activate students' prior knowledge is designed to motivate and engage all adolescent readers to open them to examining more challenging literary works for the same structural elements.

Part 4: The assessment planned for the middle of the lesson occurs during reading and provides a formative assessment of the student learning goal. The teacher will observe the students' participation in their small, cooperative groups and evaluate each student's level of participation and accuracy of contributions. In addition, the teacher will randomly collect the students' books to more carefully review the margin notes on plot elements to assess students' individual contributions and content knowledge. This assessment helps to hold students individually accountable in the small groups, provides the students with ongoing feedback about their progress, and allows the teacher to plan for closing discussion questions and future lessons, as needed.

Teaching Methods in English, High School Level—Sample Response

The following response earned a score of 4 on a 4-point scale:

Part 1: This lesson plan is designed for 11th-grade learners' ability to structure their writing ideas and arguments in a sustained, persuasive, and sophisticated way. In addition, students will support ideas and arguments with precise and relevant examples.

Lesson instructional sequence:

Opening: Explain real-life connections and purpose for the lesson and why they are learning this writing strategy. Tell the students that they are going to be arguing in class for the next few weeks—reading arguments, critiquing arguments, engaging in arguments, and finally writing an argument. Clearly, we argue all the time in real life—in court we have closing arguments, at home we argue for more privileges or respect for our privacy, we criticize the President's argument for tax-hikes or engaging in war, and we read arguments on the editorial page in the newspaper.

Next, engage the whole class in a discussion about a recent policy change for professional athletes that requires them to wear "business dress" while traveling to games. The teacher will seek student prior knowledge (prior to instruction assessment) on this topic to provide more historical context for this policy, or she will provide information as needed. After discussion, the teacher will poll the class on its support or lack of support for this policy. Split the class based on its views (it's okay if it's not evenly divided) and have the students write as many reasons as they can in five minutes for their view on this issue. Reconvene the class and have student representatives of each view report their argument. The teacher will take notes on the students' points to be used in the middle of the lesson.

Middle: Using an overhead projector, blank overhead transparencies, and projector pens, the teacher will provide a brief lecture on the format of an argument essay and define premises, thesis, and conclusions. She will incorporate the views of the students on both sides of the "business dress for professional athletes" argument to demonstrate the variety of ways one can organize a cohesive and persuasive argument. Next, the teacher will provide photocopies of editorials from the newspaper that contain models for writing an argument. She will ask the students to work in pairs to identify and critique the arguments in published editorials, labeling the argument's conclusion, thesis, premises, weaknesses, and strengths. During this time, the teacher will circulate among the students to informally assess students' understanding of the elements of an argument during instruction assessment.

Closing: The class will reconvene and discuss the strengths and weaknesses of the arguments they have read in pairs. Last, the teacher will review the assignment for students to write their own argument with a sustained, persuasive, and sophisticated effort. This assignment will serve as the summative assessment of the learning goal. The teacher will provide assignment criteria and set deadline for topic, first draft, peer conference feedback, and final copy. In the next day's lesson (described in part 3), the teacher will provide explicit modeling and guiding practice on how to write an effective argument.

Follow-up assignment: Students will be encouraged to send their argument essays to the school or local newspapers for possible publication.

Part 2: One of the group activities in this lesson is designed for students to work in pairs to identify and critique the written arguments in published editorials. This activity is designed to help students see multiple models of arguments and the real-life purposes for writing an argument. During the students' work in pairs, the teacher will circulate among her students to assess students' individual ability to identify the arguments' premises, thesis, and conclusion. If students are experiencing difficulty, the teacher can provide instructional supports, as needed. This activity contributes directly to the students' achievement of the learning goal by giving the students opportunities to discuss written arguments and consider authentic purposes for writing their own arguments.

Part 3: The writing skill chosen for this lesson involves writing a persuasive essay in the form of an argument. During pre-writing, the students will review the editorials they read and what makes a persuasive argument and which topics interest the students. The teacher will write elements of a strong argument and topics of interest on the chalkboard and students discuss. Next, the teacher will ask the students to select one or two topics to research in order to gather details. The students will be encouraged to use credible Internet sources and reference materials. The students will bring detailed notes to class the next day and work in pairs to generate two or more opinion statements as possible thesis statements for their arguments. Then, students will be required to select one topic for their argument and to write an outline of the argument's premises and conclusion(s). Next, the students will write a draft in class so the teacher can monitor progress. The teacher will require students to share their arguments with their partners for peer review. Finally, students will write a final copy for a summative grade and for possible publication in a local newspaper.

Part 4: One assessment in this writing lesson plan for 11th-graders is the summative writing assessment—the final persuasive essay. This assignment demonstrates a student's individual ability to demonstrate the stated learning goal: to structure arguments in a sustained, persuasive, and sophisticated way. This assignment was modeled in class, taught with guided practice, and individually assessed in the format of an editorial. Students were given a rubric for scoring and criteria for successful completion of the task prior to assessment. Students who meet or exceed the standard for success on this assignment will be encouraged to submit this work for possible publication. Students who do not will be required to meet with a peer reviewer, read the teacher's comments, and resubmit the argument for a possible grade change and to demonstrate competency on this task.

Middle School English Language Arts (0049)

Literary Analysis—Sample Response

The following response earned a score of 3 on a 3-point scale:

Shakespeare uses imagery and the English sonnet form to set the context for the play <u>Romeo and Juliet</u>. Specifically, he uses imagery in the prologue to cleverly introduce the main characters as well as the primary conflict in the play. He also opens the tragedy with a poetic form traditionally used to express deep love.

The sonnet is performed by the Chorus, which tells the audience to attend carefully to this two-hour play, set in Verona. Two young lovers, from noble families that share a longstanding rivalry, take their lives, which serves only to deepen their families' rage and anger rather than help them learn from the deaths of their children. Shakespeare uses phrases such as "civil blood makes civil hands unclean" and "From forth the fatal loins of these two foes" to conjure images of two noble families responsible for their children's demise because of their longstanding feud. In the latter phrase, the author uses alliteration; in the former phrase, he uses repetition of the word <u>civil</u>. Each of these phrases contains poetic elements that raise the reader's level of interest in listening carefully to the performance.

Shakespeare uses the sonnet form to introduce this tragic play about two "star-cross'd" young lovers. The prologue, a sonnet, is written in iambic pentameter, comprised of three quatrains and one couplet, for a total of fourteen lines. The rhyming scheme is formal—each quatrain has its own rhyming pair (abab, cdcd, efef), and the two lines of the couplet contain the end rhyme pattern gg. This apparent contradiction of using a love sonnet to set the stage for a tragedy serves to heighten the reader's interest and to foreshadow the depth of love and loss about to be portrayed in the play.

Rhetorical Analysis—Sample Response

The following response earned a score of 3 on a 3-point scale:

This excerpt from Harriet Jacobs' essay is organized sequentially, in the context of personal and historical information. The author opens the essay with a seemingly contradictory statement in which she uses the phrase "unusually fortunate" to describe her childhood. She then describes her status as a six-year-old slave living in the home of her deceased mother's mistress. Next, the author offers personal context as to why her circumstances as a slave are unusually fortunate, describing activities such as sewing by her mistress' side and happily picking berries as one would expect a free white six-year-old would be allowed to do. Jacobs then begins to close the paragraph with foreshadowing: "Those were happy days—too happy to last." She steps out of her personal narrative and changes to the third-person perspective with her closing reflective statement, "The slave child had no thought for the morrow; but there came that blight, which too surely waits on every human being born to be a chattel." The reader can anticipate that the next years of Jacobs' life as a slave child will be filled with hardship and bleakness.

Multiple-Choice Questions

This chapter offers you specific examples and helpful strategies to approach the multiple-choice questions included on three of the five Praxis II: English Subject Area Assessment tests. Multiple-choice questions appear on the following tests:

- Test 0041: English Language, Literature, and Composition: Content Knowledge has 120 multiple-choice questions.
- Test 0048: Teaching Foundations: English has 50 multiple-choice questions.
- Test 0049: Middle School English Language Arts has 90 multiple-choice questions.

In this chapter, you will learn about the format and types of multiple-choice questions on the Praxis II tests. Multiple-choice questions require you to analyze passages, synthesize information, and apply knowledge, all of which takes time. Knowing the format of these questions will get your mind ready to recognize the patterns and answer each question quickly and efficiently. This chapter also includes helpful tips to help you achieve your goal—a passing score on your teaching licensure test!

How to Approach the Multiple-Choice Questions

There are five types of multiple-choice questions: Complete the Statement, Which of the Following, Roman Numeral, LEAST/NOT/EXCEPT, and Tables/Reading Passages. The Educational Testing Service also develops new formats occasionally, so if you see a question type not listed in this section, don't let it throw you off. Just read the directions and approach the question carefully. The following section gives you an example of each of the five types of multiple-choice questions.

Complete the Statement

Complete the Statement questions require you to read a short passage that remains incomplete at its close. You must choose one of the answer choices to complete the statement.

> **Example:** The meaning of the prefix *ab-* in the word *abduction* is
>
> A. With
> B. Into
> C. Out of
> D. Away from

Answer: **D**

Which of the Following

In this question type, you read a short question that includes the phrase "Which of the following?" This is the most frequent question type on the Praxis II.

> **Example:** Which of the following best describes the most significant feature common to both Orwell's *Animal Farm* and Bradbury's *Fahrenheit 451*?
>
> A. Oxymoron
> B. Parody
> C. Social criticism
> D. Apostrophe

Answer: **C**

Roman Numeral

Roman Numeral questions require you to read a short passage that includes several options to consider. The answer choices are presented as a list of Roman numerals. You must use your critical reasoning to determine which of the answer choices contains all of the correct options. These questions take more time than most other multiple-choice questions and appear infrequently on the Praxis II.

Example: Of the sentences below, which two contain a dangling modifier error?

   I.   Running and shouting for help, the dog bit the mail carrier while making her routine deliveries.

  II.   After successfully winning the gold medal, the Olympics was the skater's realization of her dream.

 III.   Although he was not found guilty of any crime, Randy was fired from his law firm for an ethics violation.

 IV.   Upon successful completion of the Praxis II exam, I obtained my teaching license and started my career as an educator.

   A. III, IV
   B. II, III
   C. I, II
   D. I, IV

Answer: **C**

LEAST/NOT/EXCEPT

A LEAST/NOT/EXCEPT question contains a short passage and then one of the three terms—LEAST, NOT, or EXCEPT. This type of question requires you to reverse your thinking and reason carefully, so take a bit more time on these!

LEAST Example: Which of the following works is LEAST likely to be described as a romance?

   A. *Le Morte d'Arthur*
   B. *Amadís of Gaul*
   C. *Sir Gawain and the Green Knight*
   D. *The Iliad*

Answer: **D**

NOT Example: Which of the following literary works was NOT written by William Shakespeare?

   A. *A Midsummer Evening*
   B. *Julius Caesar*
   C. *Hamlet*
   D. *All's Well That Ends Well*

Answer: **A**

EXCEPT Example: Each of the following accurately describes common features of ballads and hymns, EXCEPT that they are

   A. Oral forms meant to be sung rather than read
   B. Written in iambic or dactylic pentameter
   C. Usually written in quatrains
   D. Rhyming

Answer: **B**

Tables/Reading Passages

Reading Passage questions are more likely to appear on your Praxis II test; multiple-choice questions that require you to read and interpret a table are less common. I've included samples of both the Reading Passage format and the Table format to help you prepare for these types of questions.

Table Example: This sample question is based on the following table.

Literary Period				
Movement	*Formal Characteristic*	*Representative Author(s)*	*Representative Work*	*Time*
Modern	Open form, free verse	T. S. Eliot	*The Waste Land*	1900–1940
Realist	Objective, various voices	Twain	*The Adventures of Huckleberry Finn*	1855–1900
Romantic	Imagination, transcendence	Wordsworth, Coleridge	*Lyrical Ballads*	1750–1850
Renaissance	Order, humanism, imitation	Shakespeare	*Hamlet*	Late 14th–16th century

Poets from which of the following literary periods wrote about the supernatural, the exotic, and the medieval?

A. Realist
B. Renaissance
C. Modern
D. Romantic

Answer: **D**

Reading Passage Example: This sample question is based on the following excerpt from *Flowers for Algernon* by Daniel Keyes.

There was nothing more to say, to her or the rest of them. None of them would look into my eyes. I can still feel the hostility. Before, they had laughed at me, despising me for my ignorance and dullness; now, they hated me for my knowledge and understanding. Why? What in God's name did they want of me?

Which of the following themes from *Flowers for Algernon* helps to explain why the narrator, Charlie, was laughed at and despised by his bakery coworkers?

A. The importance of redemption and forgiveness
B. Miscommunication based on cultural differences
C. Mistreatment of the mentally disabled
D. Persistence of the past in the present

Answer: **C**

Strategies for the Multiple-Choice Questions

You now know that there are either 50, 90, or 120 multiple-choice questions on your Praxis II test, and you know to look for five basic types of multiple-choice questions. In this section, you will review a systematic approach to the multiple-choice questions and then practice the strategy.

1. **Read the question stem.** The bold part of the question below is the question stem:

   Each of the following accurately describes **common features of ballads and hymns,** EXCEPT that they are

   A. Oral forms meant to be sung rather than read
   B. Written in iambic or dactylic pentameter
   C. Usually written in quatrains
   D. Rhyming

2. **Read all the answer choices.** Don't be too quick to select the answer choice you think is correct without carefully considering all the answer choices. Remember, one key thing that this test assesses is your critical reasoning skills, so each test question has at least one "distracter." This is an answer choice that appears correct in some way—either it's related to the topic, it has a similar spelling or meaning, or it is almost correct, but not as good as the credited response. The credited response is the answer choice that will get you the points on the Praxis II, so clearly this is the one you want!

3. **Use the process of elimination.** Cross out any answers that you know are incorrect. It's fine to write in your test booklet. Underline key words and phrases if you find it helpful. Analyze the situation and apply your knowledge to the question. If you do not know the correct answer, your goal is to find the best two choices of the four. If you can use the process of elimination to get this close to the credited response, you have a 1 in 2 chance of choosing the right one. If you simply guess, you have a 1 in 4 chance. Your odds are clearly better when you use the process of elimination!

4. **Insert each of the answer choices into the question stem.** Try out the best two answer choices to find the credited response.

5. **Mark your bubble sheet carefully.** Because you can skip questions or start at any point on the Praxis II that *you* would like, it is important for you to mark your bubble sheet carefully so that each answer choice refers to the correct question. Also, make sure to fill in the bubbles completely and do not make any stray marks on the sheet, since a computer will be scoring the multiple-choice responses that you record.

A Few More Tips

- Remember, your goal is to *pass* the Praxis II, not to compete with another's score or to set Praxis II test-taking records. Norm-referenced tests are designed for you *not* to know all the answers, particularly in the multiple-choice format. Be prepared for several difficult questions, and do not worry about your score as you work.

- Don't let difficult words or unfamiliar passages throw you. Use the context of the question to help you infer the answer on difficult test questions.

- You can work on the multiple-choice questions in any order. In other words, you can skip the ones you're having difficulty with. If you do so, be sure to mark your bubble sheet carefully and accurately.

- Write in your test booklet if it helps you. Underline, circle key words, and make note of any items you skipped. Just be sure to mark your final choice on the answer sheet. Your test booklet is not scored, but it is collected at the end of the test session.

- Remember that there are no patterns to the order in which questions are posed or to the credited responses.

- There is no penalty for guessing. Don't leave any multiple-choice questions blank! Remember to use the process-of-elimination strategy if you have the time to do so.

- Monitor your testing time. Don't rely on the proctor or your general sense of time. Bring a watch and make sure that you are working quickly but carefully.

- Read all the answer choices before choosing the credited response.

- If time permits, check your answers. Yes, it's okay to change your answer if you have taken the time to analyze the question and determine that your initial thought was incorrect.

Preview and Practice: Apply the Strategies

Now it's your chance to practice the strategies for the multiple-choice questions. Remember to read the question stem first, skim all the answer choices, and use the process of elimination to get to the credited response. In this practice section, you will work on 12 multiple-choice items made up of all five types of multiple-choice questions: Complete the Statement, Which of the Following, Roman Numeral, LEAST/NOT/EXCEPT, and Tables/Reading Passages.

After you complete these 12 questions, review the answers and explanations, paying particular attention to the types of questions you got correct and the types you got incorrect. In addition, I have included the broad categories tested on each of these tests—Reading and Understanding Text, Language and Linguistics, Composition and Rhetoric, and Teaching English—to help you diagnose any strengths or weaknesses in your English content knowledge. You will find Part II of this book particularly helpful in closing any gaps in content knowledge that you may discover.

Sample Multiple-Choice Questions

Directions: Questions 1–12 are multiple-choice questions similar to those found on the Praxis II: English Subject Area Assessment tests 0041, 0048, and 0049. Circle the letter that corresponds to the credited response. After you complete these sample multiple-choice questions, look in the next section of this chapter for an answer key and explanations.

1. Phrases such as "physical persuasion" and "downsizing" are known as

    A. Personification
    B. Metaphors
    C. Similes
    D. Doublespeak

2. Which of the following sentences contains the correct use of the word *whom*?

    A. When lifesaving gear is scarce, the fishermen must give the resources to whomever has the best chance of surviving.
    B. Matthew was a young man whom knew his goals and future plans.
    C. Whom will be invited?
    D. You will student teach with our finest English teacher, whom you will meet later in the day.

3. Language minority students who experience academic difficulties because of a lack of proficiency in English are more likely to experience which of the following?

    I. Assignment in special education
    II. Single-parent families
    III. Inclusion in a "tracked" program of bilingual learners
    IV. Low intelligence scores on tests

    A. I, II, IV
    B. I, III, IV
    C. I, III
    D. II, III, IV

4. Each of the following phrases is an example of onomatopoeia EXCEPT

    A. kicking and screaming
    B. mooing and baaing
    C. beep, beep
    D. drip, drop, drip, drop

Questions 5–6 are based on the following excerpt from Edgar Allan Poe's poem "The Raven."

> [1] Once upon a midnight dreary, while I pondered, weak and weary,
> [2] Over many a quaint and curious volume of forgotten lore,
> [3] While I nodded, nearly napping, suddenly there came a tapping,
> [4] As of some one gently rapping, rapping at my chamber door.
> [5] "'Tis some visitor," I muttered, "tapping at my chamber door—
> [6] Only this, and nothing more."

5. The meaning of this stanza can best be interpreted as

   A. The speaker is dozing and thinking of Lenore when he falls asleep.

   B. A man is reading in bed and dozing when he is awakened by a knock on his door.

   C. A man is dreaming of his lost love, Lenore.

   D. The speaker is startled by the sound of wind and then falls asleep.

6. In the passage above, lines 1 and 3 contain

   A. Personification

   B. Internal rhyme

   C. Metaphor

   D. Free verse

Question 7 is based on the following excerpt from The Giver *by Lois Lowry.*

With the chant, Jonas knew, the community was accepting him and his new role, giving him life, the way they had given it to the new child Caleb. His heart swelled with gratitude and pride.

But at the same time he was filled with fear. He did not know what his selection meant. He did not know what he was to become.

Or what would become of him.

7. Which of the following literary elements is used in the passage above?

   A. Foreshadowing

   B. Metonymy

   C. Apostrophe

   D. Hyperbole

8. Which of the following authors are known for their writing during the Harlem Renaissance?

   I. John Donne

   II. Zora Neale Hurston

   III. Langston Hughes

   IV. Countee Cullen

   A. I, II, IV

   B. I, III, IV

   C. II, III, IV

   D. I, II, III

9. Which of the following is NOT an appropriate activity in the prewriting stage of writing?

    A. Reading for background information
    B. Listing ideas
    C. Brainstorming
    D. Editing for grammar

Questions 10–11 are based on the following excerpt from The Scarlet Letter *by Nathaniel Hawthorne.*

But there was a more real life for Hester Prynne here, in New England, than in that unknown region where Pearl had found a home. Here had been her sin; here, her sorrow; and here was yet to be her penitence. She had returned, therefore, and resumed,—of her own free will, for not the sternest magistrate of that iron period would have imposed it,—resumed the symbol of which we have related so dark a tale. Never afterwards did it quit her bosom. But . . . the scarlet letter ceased to be a stigma which attracted the world's scorn and bitterness, and became a type of something to be sorrowed over, and looked upon with awe, and yet with reverence, too.

10. The scarlet letter is an example of which of the following literary elements?

    A. Rhetoric
    B. Free verse
    C. Symbolism
    D. Simile

11. In the sentence "Here had been her sin; here, her sorrow; and here was yet to be her penitence," a semicolon is used to connect which of the following?

    A. Prepositional phrases
    B. Dependent clauses
    C. Independent clauses
    D. Coordinating conjunctions

12. Which of the following is an example of holistic scoring of a student essay?

    A. A score of 5 for exemplary content, use of conventions, and cohesiveness
    B. A score of 4 based on the number of errors in conventions with no consideration of content
    C. A score of 100% based on the number of items correct
    D. A score of 25 based on the number of points earned for correct responses

Answers and Explanations

Answer Key			
Question	*Answer*	*Content Category*	*Question Type*
1.	D	Language and Linguistics	Complete the Statement
2.	D	Language and Linguistics	Which of the Following
3.	C	Language and Linguistics	Roman Numeral
4.	A	Language and Linguistics	LEAST/NOT/EXCEPT
5.	B	Reading and Understanding Text	Tables/Reading Passages
6.	B	Reading and Understanding Text	Complete the Statement
7.	A	Reading and Understanding Text	Which of the Following
8.	C	Reading and Understanding Text	Roman Numeral
9.	D	Composition and Rhetoric	LEAST/NOT/EXCEPT
10.	C	Composition and Rhetoric	Tables/Reading Passages
11.	C	Composition and Rhetoric	Which of the Following
12.	A	Composition and Rhetoric	Which of the Following

1. **D.** Doublespeak, also known as doubletalk, is the intentionally evasive or ambiguous use of language.

2. **D.** *Whom* is the direct object of the verb of the subordinate clause, *will meet.* Be sure to rephrase the sentence to help you see that *whom* is the best choice: *you will meet whom.* You may have chosen A, which appears to be correct if *whomever* is the object of the preposition *to.* This is not correct, though, because the object of the preposition is the entire subordinate clause *whoever has the best chance of surviving.* The verb of the clause is *has,* and its subject is *whoever.*

3. **C.** Students from a language minority are more likely to experience an assignment in special education and placement in a program for bilingual students that "tracks" according to school performance. Language minority students may experience difficulties primarily because of their lack of proficiency in English, not due to learning disabilities or other special education needs.

4. **A.** Onomatopoeia is the use of words to imitate natural sounds, such as drip, drop, drip, drop.

5. **B.** This famous first stanza of the poem "The Raven" by Edgar Allan Poe is about a man who is reading in bed and dozing when he is suddenly awakened by what he thinks is a knock on his bedroom door. The speaker then realizes that it is only the wind and continues to think about his lost love, Lenore.

6. **B.** Lines 1 and 3 contain internal rhyme—rhyme that occurs within the line of poetry—of the words *dreary, weary* and *napping, tapping.*

7. **A.** This passage from prologue of *The Giver* provides foreshadowing for the events to come in this science-fiction novel.

8. **C.** Zora Neale Hurston, Langston Hughes, and Countee Cullen are all known for their contributions during the Harlem Renaissance period (1900–1940). John Donne was a metaphysical poet in the 17th century.

9. D. Editing for grammar is not an appropriate activity to complete during the prewriting stage. Prewriting involves planning, gathering information, and reflecting on writing ideas.

10. C. The scarlet letter provides symbolism in the novel. Initially, the scarlet letter symbolizes Hester Prynne's sin, although at the story's conclusion, the letter represents an important part of her past and her identity.

11. C. A semicolon must be used whenever a coordinating conjunction is omitted between independent clauses.

12. A. Holistic scoring of writing takes into consideration the overall piece of writing. In this example, exemplary content, use of conventions, and cohesiveness are assessed as a 5 to provide the writer with feedback on the overall effectiveness of the piece.

Essay Questions

In this chapter, you will learn about the types of essay questions found on the Praxis II: English Language, Literature, and Composition: Essays test (0042)—the only Praxis II English Subject Area Assessment test that includes the essay-format question. Essay questions address two central elements in the study of literature: the ability to analyze texts and the ability to understand and articulate arguments about issues central to the teaching of English. Knowing the format of these questions will get your mind ready to recognize their patterns.

How to Approach the Essay Questions

Let's first look carefully at an essay question and then consider an effective strategy for answering an essay question.

Directions: Read carefully the following excerpt from *Jane Eyre* by Charlotte Bronte. Then, in your own words, identify Bronte's central idea in the passage and discuss how her use of characterization clarifies this central idea.

"Boh! Madam Mope!" cried the voice of John Reed; then he paused: he found the room apparently empty.

"Where the dickens is she!" he continued. "Lizzy! Georgy! (calling to his sisters) Jane is not here: tell mama she is run out into the rain—bad animal!"

"It is well I drew the curtain," thought I; and I wished fervently he might not discover my hiding-place: nor would John Reed have found it out himself; he was not quick either of vision or conception; but Eliza just put her head in at the door, and said at once—

"She is in the window-seat, to be sure, Jack."

And I came out immediately, for I trembled at the idea of being dragged forth by the said Jack.

"What do you want?" I asked, with awkward diffidence.

"Say, 'What do you want, Master Reed?'" was the answer. "I want you to come here"; and seating himself in an armchair, he intimated by a gesture that I was to approach and stand before him.

John Reed was a schoolboy of fourteen years old; four years older than I, for I was but ten: large and stout for his age, with a dingy and unwholesome skin; thick lineaments in a spacious visage, heavy limbs and large extremities. He gorged himself habitually at table, which made him bilious, and gave him a dim and bleared eye and flabby cheeks. He ought now to have been at school; but his mama had taken him home for a month or two, "on account of his delicate health." Mr. Miles, the master, affirmed that he would do very well if he had fewer cakes and sweetmeats sent him from home; but the mother's heart turned from an opinion so harsh, and inclined rather to the more refined idea that John's sallowness was owing to over-application and, perhaps, to pining after home.

John had not much affection for his mother and sisters, and an antipathy to me. He bullied and punished me; not two or three times in the week, nor once or twice in the day, but continually: every nerve I had feared him, and every morsel of flesh in my bones shrank when he came near. There were moments when I was bewildered by the terror he inspired, because I had no appeal whatever against either his menaces or his inflictions; the servants did not like to offend their young master by taking my part against him, and Mrs. Reed was blind and deaf on the subject: she never saw him strike or heard him abuse me, though he did both now and then in her very presence, more frequently, however, behind her back.

You will be presented with four categories of essay questions on test 0042. The Bronte question above is an example of the "Interpreting Literature: Prose" content category, which requires you to read and interpret an excerpt from an authentic literary work of prose. Before we look at the other three categories, let's review a strategic approach that you can apply to all four question types.

1. Understand—5 minutes
2. Plan—5 minutes
3. Write—15 minutes
4. Edit—5 minutes

Understand the Prompt

Spend no more than five minutes reading the excerpt and essay prompt carefully and actively. You can underline or circle key points and make margin notes as you read. Be sure to focus on what the prompt is asking you to do. In the Bronte example, you must identify the author's central idea and then discuss her use of characterization to support the central idea.

Plan

Take approximately five minutes to outline the points you'll make in your response. This may be the most important five minutes of the time you spend on your essay. If you plan carefully, you will write more cohesively and will accurately demonstrate your English content knowledge. Your proctor will provide you with extra paper, or you can use the margins in your test booklet to sketch out an outline for your essay. Here's an example of a plan for the Bronte essay:

Topic sentence: In this excerpt from *Jane Eyre,* the author effectively uses characterization to introduce the novel's main character and to immediately position the reader on Jane's side in this coming-of-age story.

Key point 1: Central idea

Jane is an oppressed child who has been orphaned and lives with a heartless upper-class family.

Key point 2: Characterization

> Overindulged and ungrateful cousin
>
> Unloving and aggressive antagonist
>
> Oppressed and bright young protagonist

Conclusion: Bronte effectively uses her novelistic expertise to communicate her central idea—that Jane Eyre is an oppressed girl with whom the reader will side—through adept characterization.

Write

The format of the essay is similar to the "five-paragraph essay":

- Topic sentence
- Key point 1 and details
- Key point 2 and details
- Possibly additional key points, depending on what the question requires
- Conclusion sentence

Remember these important writing tips:

- Avoid passive construction. For example:

  Passive voice: Our Labrador Retriever was loved by us.

  Active voice: We loved our Labrador Retriever.

- Avoid common errors in spelling, grammar, and conventions—for example, dangling modifiers, run-on sentences, verb tense problems, and errors in pronoun referents.

Edit

Save three to five minutes of your testing time for rereading your essay and editing it as needed. It is important to check for grammar, spelling, and punctuation problems. It's okay to make corrections in your essay; just be sure it's legible. The scorers know that you are writing under timed conditions and do not expect perfectly neat, error-free writing.

Four Formats of Essays

1. **Interpreting Literature: Poetry.** This type of question asks you to interpret a poem from English, American, or world literature from any period.

   Directions: Carefully read the following poem by Emily Dickinson. Then discuss how Dickinson uses metaphors and word choice to convey her message. Be sure to use at least THREE specific examples from the poem to support your points about Dickinson's use of metaphors and word choice.

A Certain Slant of Light

There's a certain slant of light,
On winter afternoons,
That oppresses, like the weight
Of cathedral tunes.

Heavenly hurt it gives us;
We can find no scar,
But internal difference
Where the meanings are.

None may teach it anything
'Tis the seal, despair,—
An imperial affliction
Sent us of the air.

When it comes, the landscape listens,
Shadows hold their breath;
When it goes, 'tis like the distance
On the look of death.

2. **Interpreting Literature: Prose.** These questions require that you interpret a work of literary prose from English, American, or world literature from any period. Review the <u>Jane Eyre</u> example earlier in this chapter.

3. **Issues in English: Understanding Literary Issues.** These questions ask you to evaluate the argument and the rhetorical features of a passage.

   Directions: Read the following excerpt from the essay "On the Duty of Civil Disobedience" by Henry David Thoreau. Then, in your own words, identify Thoreau's central idea in the passage and show how his method of development and prose style (sentence structure, word choice, figurative language) clarify and support his point. Be sure to refer to specific examples from the excerpt in your essay response.

   Some years ago, the State met me in behalf of the Church, and commanded me to pay a certain sum toward the support of a clergyman whose preaching my father attended, but never I myself. "Pay," it said, "or be locked up in the jail." I declined to pay. But, unfortunately, another man saw fit to pay it. I did not see why the schoolmaster should be taxed to support the priest, and not the priest the schoolmaster: for I was not the State's schoolmaster, but I supported myself by voluntary subscription. I did not see why the lyceum should not present its tax-bill, and have the State to back its demand, as well as the Church. However, at the request of the selectmen, I condescended to make some such statement as this in writing:— "Know all men by these presents, that I, Henry Thoreau, do not wish to be regarded as a member of any incorporated society which I have not joined." This I gave to the town clerk; and he has it. The State, having thus learned that I did not wish to be regarded as a member of that church, has never made a like demand on me since; though it said that it must adhere to its original presumption that time. If I had known how to name them, I should then have signed off in detail from all the societies which I never signed on to; but I did not know where to find a complete list.

4. **Issues in English: Literary Issues and Literary Texts.** These questions ask you to take and defend a position on an issue in the study of English, using references to literary works to support your argument.

The writers' primary purpose is to provide social commentary on the effects "progress" has on society.

Choose TWO works from the list below; then write a well-organized essay in which you SUPPORT the statement above. Develop your thesis using specific references to elements of the TWO works you selected (for example, character, theme, setting, plot, language, style, point of view).

- *Fahrenheit 451* by Ray Bradbury
- "On the Duty of Civil Disobedience" by Henry David Thoreau
- *1984* by George Orwell
- *Brave New World* by Aldous Huxley
- *Heart of Darkness* by Joseph Conrad
- *The Sun Also Rises* by Ernest Hemingway
- *Walden* by Henry David Thoreau
- *Utopia* by Sir Thomas More

Scoring Guide

In this section, you will find three scoring guides for the four types of essay questions you will encounter on the Praxis II. As you will see, the same scoring guide applies to both the poetry and the prose Interpreting Literature questions. The Issues in English questions have two different scoring guides: one for Understanding Literary Issues and another for Literary Issues and Literary Texts. All four types of essays are scored on a 0–3 point scale, with 3 being the highest score. Review the scoring guides to help you understand what you need to do in each essay to earn the most points.

Interpreting Literature: Poetry and Prose

3: Exceeds standards

- Analyzes specific literary elements in this selection accurately and in depth
- Shows good understanding of the literary work
- Supports points with accurate examples from the selection and provides explanations to support points
- Writes with coherence and demonstrates control of language, including diction and syntax
- Demonstrates accurate use of conventions of standard written English

2: Meets standards

- Analyzes specific literary elements in this selection with some accuracy, but may misinterpret or overlook some elements
- Shows understanding of the literary work, but may misread some aspects of the literary work
- Supports points with examples from the selection, but may fail to provide explanations to support points
- Writes with coherence and demonstrates control of language, including diction and syntax
- Demonstrates control of conventions of standard written English, but may include some flaws

1: Does not achieve standards

The essay demonstrates some ability to engage with the literary work but is flawed in one or more of the following ways:

- Incorrectly identifies a literary element in the literary work or provides a superficial evaluation of the elements
- Shows an inaccurate interpretation of the literary work
- Points or examples are not supported

- Lacks coherence or has major problems with syntax, diction, or control of language
- Contains serious and multiple errors in conventions of standard written English

0: A score of 0 is given to blank papers, off-topic responses, or responses with severely inaccurate or incoherent points.

Issues in English: Understanding Literary Issues

3: Exceeds standards

- Identifies and summarizes the central idea accurately and thoroughly
- Identifies and analyzes key writing techniques accurately and in depth
- Supports point with strong examples and full explanations
- Writes with coherence and demonstrates control of language, including diction and syntax
- Demonstrates accurate use of conventions of standard written English

2: Meets standards

- Identifies and summarizes the central idea accurately, but may overlook some points
- Identifies and analyzes key writing techniques accurately, but may overlook some points
- Supports point with strong examples, but may not explain fully
- Writes with coherence and demonstrates control of language, including diction and syntax
- Demonstrates control of conventions of standard written English, but may have some errors

1: Does not achieve standards

The essay demonstrates some ability to engage with the literary work but is flawed in one or more of the following ways:

- Incorrectly summarizes the main idea of the passage
- Shows an inaccurate or limited interpretation of the literary work
- Points or examples are not supported
- Lacks coherence or has major problems with syntax, diction, or control of language
- Contains serious and multiple errors in conventions of standard written English

0: A score of 0 is given to blank papers, off-topic responses, or responses with severely inaccurate or incoherent points.

Issues in English: Literary Issues and Literary Texts

3: Exceeds standards

- Analyzes the literary issue in the selection thoughtfully and in depth
- Develops a thesis according to the question and supports the thesis with relevant examples from at least two literary works
- Writes with coherence and demonstrates control of language, including diction and syntax
- Demonstrates accurate use of conventions of standard written English

2: Meets standards

- Analyzes the literary issue in the selection thoughtfully, but may fail to analyze the issue in depth
- Develops a thesis according to the questions and supports the thesis with relevant examples from two literary works, but may include some inaccuracies
- Writes with coherence and demonstrates control of language, including diction and syntax
- Demonstrates accurate use of conventions of standard written English, but may have some flaws

1: Does not achieve standards

The essay demonstrates some ability to engage with the literary work but is flawed in one or more of the following ways:

- Offers a superficial or limited response to the issue, or misunderstands the position stated
- Does not develop a thesis, fails to support thesis with examples, or provides a general characterization of the work

0: A score of 0 is given to blank papers, off-topic responses, or responses with severely inaccurate or incoherent points.

Answers and Explanations

Before you read the sample essay responses, take the time to write your own responses to the four essay questions in this chapter. Spend no more than 30 minutes on each question. As you write, remember the criteria your essays need to meet to earn a score of 3.

Below, you will find sample responses that would earn a score of 3. Of course, these examples were not written under the same testing conditions you will experience when taking the Praxis II. These samples are meant to help you see the structure and content of a strong response. The scorers know that you do not have the luxury of time and word processing when writing your essays.

Interpreting Literature: Poetry

The following is an example of an essay scored as a 3, the highest score you can earn.

Emily Dickinson uses metaphor and word choice to create a heavy, reflective mood in her poem "A Certain Slant of Light." In the first line of the poem, she describes "a certain slant of light" that oppresses. She then describes this particular light as "the seal, despair" and as an "imperial affliction." The poet's use of metaphor invites the reader to vicariously experience her deep sense of oppression, despair that may be too difficult to describe in any other way.

Dickinson's word choice also allows the reader to experience the poem's somber mood. Several images of death and phrases with religious overtones are found in the poem—"Heavenly hurt," "cathedral tunes," and "the look of death." Powerful words such as "oppresses," "despair," and "affliction" all add to the sense of heaviness as the poet recalls these experiences. In the last stanza, Dickinson's use of personification—"Shadows hold their breath" and "the landscape listens"—evokes a sense that she may be feeling a oneness with nature and be awestruck by this "certain slant of light." The poet conjures an image of somber reflection through her choice of words and her use of metaphor.

Interpreting Literature: Prose

The following is an example of an essay scored as a 3, the highest score you can earn.

In this excerpt from <u>Jane Eyre</u>, the author effectively uses characterization to communicate her central idea that Jane Eyre is the novel's oppressed protagonist with whom the reader will immediately side. The passage opens with Jane's cousin John Reed, a terribly overindulged bully who persecutes Jane continually. The author describes his physical characteristics—obsese, unhealthy, and fourteen years old—and then provides an anecdote from John's schoolmaster that lets the reader know that John's mother dotes on him. Next, we learn that Jack treats his sisters and mother unlovingly and treats his orphaned cousin Jane as a social inferior and with "antipathy." The reader almost instantly dislikes John, and just as quickly admires Jane as we witness her subtle defiance and strength against John's bullying and abusive behavior. <u>Jane Eyre</u> is an expertly crafted coming-of-age story in which Charlotte Bronte uses artful characterization to introduce her main characters and her central message—that Jane Eyre is a young woman with inner strength and character, which will transcend her status as a member of the lower social class.

Issues in English: Understanding Literary Issues

The following is an example of an essay scored as a 3, the highest score you can earn.

Thoreau's central idea in this excerpt from his essay "On the Duty of Civil Disobedience" is that the individual should have the right to freedom. In this example, Thoreau argues that the individual should have the freedom to choose which groups or "societies" he belongs to. The author opens the passage with a paradox in which he must pay for the clergyman's preaching at a church that his father attended even though the author has never attended this institution himself. Thoreau chooses not to pay the sum at the risk of being jailed. He then satirically states that, unfortunately, "another man saw fit to pay it." Thoreau then provides a logical argument for his view that he should not have to pay such a tax to an institution he does not belong to; he alone should have the freedom to choose to become a member of a societal institution. The author closes the essay with his thesis: "If I had known how to name them, I should have signed off in detail from all the societies which I never signed on to; but I did not know where to find a complete list." Once again, Thoreau uses the paradoxical nature of his concern to make his point that individuals should have the freedom to choose to be a member of a particular group or society. The author's satirical last line, "but I did not know where to find a complete list," is meant to mock the government and to provoke others to contemplate change in repressive and intrusive governmental laws.

Issues in English: Literary Issues and Literary Texts

The following is an example of an essay scored as a 3, the highest score you can earn.

One of Aldous Huxley's and Ray Bradbury's primary purposes for writing Brave New World and Fahrenheit 451, respectively, is to provide social commentary on the effects "progress" has on society. Both authors criticize the use of technology in society and suggest that governmental control results in a loss of humanity. Each of the futuristic societies in these novels is known as a dystopia, a utopian society gone wrong because of social and technological "advances."

In Huxley's Brave New World, technology is used to control reproduction, to create entertainment machines, and to produce the drug soma that is used to ensure no one feels pain or stress—in short, to maintain the stability and power of the State. The World State controls human reproduction through the use of various technologies at the Central London Hatchery and Conditioning Centre. Through this Centre, the government creates a five-tiered caste system in which social stability is highly valued and individuality is despised. Entertainment machines and the drug soma keep the citizens happy and satisfied so that society is stable. Scientific advances are censored so that the results contribute only to technologies that control individuals. Human thought, religion, and individuality are all controlled or even replaced by technology. For example, religious thought is replaced by technology as citizens of the World State use the word Ford (as in Henry Ford, founder of the Ford Motor Company and pioneer of the factory production of goods) in place of the word Christ or Lord, as in "My Ford" or "A. F." One of Huxley's primary purposes for writing about this futuristic dystopia is to offer social criticism on giving government control over new and powerful technologies.

In Bradbury's Fahrenheit 451, technology is used to dominate society, to limit advancement of knowledge, and to ultimately destroy society. In this dystopia, owning and reading books is against the laws of the society. Technologies, such as oversized television screens, loud music, speedy cars, invasive radio broadcasts, and inventions such as the Mechanical Hound and the Electric-Eyed Snake, dominate human life. Those who have interests outside of these technologies are considered outcasts. Technology is used to limit the advancement of knowledge, to distract individuals from books, learning, and free thinking. Montag, a main character in Fahrenheit 451, is required to burn books, to destroy knowledge, as part of his job as a fireman in this society. Ultimately, the technology of the atomic bomb is used to destroy the society and to offer Montag a chance to escape this society and to rebuild his life to include knowledge, books, and little use of technology.

Huxley and Bradbury warn of the dangers of an all-powerful government that uses technological advances to control and dominate individualism. Both authors present the reader with a dystopian society that in many ways is frighteningly familiar in today's society, reminding us all that humanity is paramount.

PART II

PREPARING FOR THE CONTENT OF THE PRAXIS II

This part of the book reviews the content that is tested on the Praxis II: English Subject Area Assessment tests. As you answer the multiple-choice questions, constructed-response questions, and/or essay questions, you'll be expected to know these key theories, strategies, and concepts. I hope you'll find Part II of this guide, a comprehensive review of the content tested on the Praxis II, to be an invaluable timesaver. Each of the chapters in this part is designed to help you in the following ways:

- To review English language arts content typically found on the Praxis II
- To help you assess your areas of strength and areas you'll need to study further
- To save you time—no need to hunt for information in old English textbooks

I suggest that you carefully study all the chapters in this part as you review for the Praxis II. Then you'll be better prepared to try the full-length practice tests in Part III and pass your English teaching licensure exam.

Reading and Understanding Text

The Reading and Understanding Text content appear on the following Praxis II tests:

- Test 0041: English Language, Literature, and Composition: Content Knowledge
- Test 0042: English Language, Literature, and Composition: Essays
- Test 0043: English Language, Literature, and Composition: Pedagogy
- Test 0048: Teaching Foundations: English
- Test 0049: Middle School English Language Arts

This chapter is organized as a concise outline of the major content assessed on each of these tests. I suggest that you review this outline to refresh your memory of important English content or to note any content that is unfamiliar. If portions of content are unfamiliar, you will want to study further by completing the full-length practice tests in Part III of this book and by using the suggested resources listed in Chapter 13.

Identifying and Interpreting Figurative Language and Other Literary Terminology

This section contains an overview of figurative language and other literary terminology to help you review for the Praxis II. This outline may even prove helpful in your lesson planning for your first classroom!

Allegory. A story in which people (or things or actions) represent an idea or a generalization about life. Allegories usually have a strong lesson or moral.

Alliteration. The repetition of initial consonant sounds in words, such as "Peter Piper picked a peck of pickled peppers."

Allusion. A reference to a familiar person, place, thing, or event—for example, Don Juan, brave new world, Everyman, Machiavellian, utopia.

Analogy. A comparison of objects or ideas that appear to be different but are alike in some important way.

Anapestic meter. Meter that is composed of feet that are short-short-long or unaccented-unaccented-accented, usually used in light or whimsical poetry, such as a limerick.

Anecdote. A brief story that illustrates or makes a point.

Antagonist. A person or thing working against the hero of a literary work (the protagonist).

Aphorism. A wise saying, usually short and written.

Apostrophe. A turn from the general audience to address a specific group of persons (or a personified abstraction) who is present or absent. For example, in a recent performance of Shakespeare's *Hamlet,* Hamlet turned to the audience and spoke directly to one woman about his father's death.

Assonance. A repetition of the same sound in words close to one another—for example, white stripes.

Blank verse. Unrhymed verse, often occurring in iambic pentameter.

Caesura. A break in the rhythm of language, particularly a natural pause in a line of verse, marked in prosody by a double vertical line (´´).

Characterization. A method an author uses to let readers know more about the characters and their personal traits.

Cliché. An expression that has been used so often that it loses its expressive power—for example, "dead as a doornail" or "I'm so hungry I could eat a horse."

Consonance. Repetition of the final consonant sound in words containing different vowels—for example, "stroke of luck."

Couplet. A stanza made up of two rhyming lines.

Diction. An author's choice of words based on their clearness, conciseness, effectiveness, and authenticity.

- **Archaic:** Old-fashioned words that are no longer used in common speech, such as *thee, thy,* and *thou.*
- **Colloquialisms:** Expressions that are usually accepted in informal situations or regions, such as "wicked awesome."
- **Dialect:** A variety of a language used by people from a particular geographic area.
- **Jargon:** Specialized language used in a particular field or content area—for example, educational jargon includes *differentiated instruction, cooperative learning,* and *authentic assessment.*
- **Profanity:** Language that shows disrespect for others or something sacred.
- **Slang:** Informal language used by a particular group of people among themselves.
- **Vulgarity:** Language widely considered crude, disgusting, and oftentimes offensive.

End rhyme. Rhyming of the ends of lines of verse.

Enjambment. Also known as a run-on line in poetry, enjambment occurs when one line ends and continues onto the next line to complete meaning. For example, in Thoreau's poem "My life has been the poem I would have writ," the first line is "My life has been the poem I would have writ," and the second line completes the meaning—"but I could not both live and utter it."

Existentialism. A philosophy that values human freedom and personal responsibility. Jean-Paul Sartre is the foremost existentialist. Other famous existentialist writers include Soren Kierkegaard ("the father of existentialism"), Albert Camus, Freidrich Nietzsche, Franz Kafka, and Simone de Beauvoir.

Flashback. A literary device in which the author jumps back in time in the chronology of a narrative.

Foot. A metrical foot is defined as one stressed syllable and a number of unstressed syllables (from zero to as many as four). Stressed syllables are indicated by the ´ symbol. Unstressed syllables are indicated by the ˘ symbol. There are four possible metrical feet:

- **Iambic:** ˘ ´ (unstressed, stressed)
- **Trochaic:** ´ ˘ (stressed, unstressed)
- **Anapestic:** ˘ ˘ ´ (unstressed, unstressed, stressed)
- **Dactylic:** ´ ˘ ˘ (stressed, unstressed, unstressed)

In addition, there are names for the line lengths; eight feet is the typical maximum.

- **One foot:** Monometer
- **Two feet:** Dimeter
- **Three feet:** Trimeter
- **Four feet:** Tetrameter
- **Five feet:** Pentameter
- **Six feet:** Hexameter
- **Seven feet:** Septameter
- **Eight feet:** Octameter

Foreshadowing. A literary technique in which the author gives hints or clues about what is to come at some point later in the story.

Free verse. Verse that contains an irregular metrical pattern and line length; also known as *vers libre.*

Genre. A category of literature defined by its style, form, and content.

Heroic couplet. A pair of lines of poetic verse written in iambic pentameter.

Hubris. The flaw that leads to the downfall of a tragic hero; this term comes from the Greek word *hybris,* which means "excessive pride."

Hyperbole. An exaggeration for emphasis or rhetorical effect.

Imagery. The use of words to create pictures in the reader's mind.

Internal rhyme. Rhyme that occurs within a line of verse.

Irony. The use of a word or phrase to mean the exact opposite of its literal or expected meaning. There are three kinds of irony:

- **Dramatic:** The reader sees a character's errors, but the character does not.
- **Verbal:** The writer says one thing and means another.
- **Situation:** The purpose of a particular action differs greatly from the result.

Malapropism. A type of pun, or play on words, that results when two words become mixed up in the speaker's mind—for example, "Don't put the horse before the cart."

Metaphor. A figure of speech in which a comparison is implied but not stated, such as "This winter is a bear."

Meter. A rhythmical pattern in verse that is made up of stressed and unstressed syllables.

Mood. The feeling a text evokes in the reader, such as sadness, tranquility, or elation.

Moral. A lesson a work of literature is teaching.

Narration. The telling of a story.

Onomatopoela. The use of sound words to suggest meaning, as in *buzz, click,* or *vroom.*

Oxymoron. A phrase that consists of two contradictory terms—for example, "deafening silence."

Paradox. A contradictory statement that makes sense—for example, Hegel's paradox "Man learns from history that man learns nothing from history."

Personification. A literary device in which animals, ideas, and things are represented as having human traits.

Point of view. The perspective from which a story is told.

- **First person:** The story is told from the point of view of one character.
- **Third person:** The story is told by someone outside the story.
- **Omniscient:** The narrator of the story shares the thoughts and feelings of all the characters.
- **Limited omniscient:** The narrator shares the thoughts and feelings of one character.
- **Camera view:** The narrator records the action from his or her point of view, unaware of any of the other characters' thoughts or feelings. This perspective is also known as the objective view.

Refrain. The repetition of a line or phrase of a poem at regular intervals, particularly at the end of each stanza.

Repetition. The multiple use of a word, phrase, or idea for emphasis or rhythmic effect.

Rhetoric. Persuasive writing.

Rhythm. The regular or random occurrence of sound in poetry.

Setting. The time and place in which the action of a story takes place.

Simile. A comparison of two unlike things, usually including the word *like* or *as*.

Style. How the author uses words, phrases, and sentences to form ideas.

Symbol. A person, place, thing, or event used to represent something else, such as the white flag that represents surrender.

Tone. The overall feeling created by an author's use of words.

Transcendentalism. During the mid-19th century in New England, several writers and intellectuals worked together to write, translate works, and publish and became known as transcendentalists. Their philosophy focused on protesting the Puritan ethic and materialism. They valued individualism, freedom, experimentation, and spirituality. Noted transcendentalists included Ralph Waldo Emerson, Nathaniel Hawthorne, Henry David Thoreau, Henry Wadsworth Longfellow, and Oliver Wendell Holmes.

Verse. A metric line of poetry. A verse is named based on the kind and number of feet composing it (see "Foot").

Voice. Distinctive features of a person's speech and speech patterns.

Identifying Patterns, Structures, and Characteristics of Literary Genres

This section is designed to help you review the patterns, structures, and characteristics of literary genres. The outline format is meant to provide a concise review. If some of this information is completely new to you, you may want to refer to the resources in Chapter 14 to gain a more in-depth understanding of this important content.

Elements of Poetry

Ballad. A short poem, often written by an anonymous author, comprised of short verses intended to be sung or recited.

Canto. The main section of a long poem.

Elegy. A poem that is a mournful lament for the dead. Examples include William Shakespeare's "Elegy" from *Cymbeline*, Robert Louis Stevenson's "Requiem," and Alfred Lord Tennyson's "In Memoriam."

Epic. A long narrative poem detailing a hero's deeds. Examples include *The Aeneid* by Virgil, *The Iliad* and *The Odyssey* by Homer, *Beowulf*, *Don Quixote* by Miguel Cervantes, *War and Peace* by Leo Tolstoy, *Faust* by Johann Wolfgang von Goethe, and *Hiawatha* by Henry Wadsworth Longfellow.

Haiku. A type of Japanese poem that is written in 17 syllables with three lines of five, seven, and five syllables, respectively. Haiku expresses a single thought.

Limerick. A humorous verse form of five anapestic (composed of feet that are short-short-long or unaccented-unaccented-accented) lines with a rhyme scheme of aabba.

Lyric. A short poem about personal feelings and emotions.

Sonnet. A fourteen-line poem, usually written in iambic pentameter, with a varied rhyme scheme. The two main types of sonnet are the Petrarchan (or Italian) and the Shakespearean (or English). A Petrarchan sonnet opens with an octave that states a proposition and ends with a sestet that states the solution. A Shakespearean sonnet include three quatrains and a couplet.

Stanza. A division of poetry named for the number of lines it contains.

- **Couplet:** Two-line stanza
- **Triplet:** Three-line stanza
- **Quatrain:** Four-line stanza
- **Quintet:** Five-line stanza
- **Sestet:** Six-line stanza
- **Septet:** Seven-line stanza
- **Octave:** Eight-line stanza

Elements of Prose

Fiction (or Narrative)

Fable. A short story or folktale that contains a moral, which may be expressed explicitly at the end as a maxim. Examples of Aesop's fables include *The Country Mouse and the Town Mouse, The Tortoise and the Hare,* and *The Wolf in Sheep's Clothing.*

Fairy tale. A narrative that is made up of fantastic characters and creatures, such as witches, goblins, and fairies, and usually begins with the phrase "Once upon a time . . . ." Examples include *Rapunzel, Cinderella, Sleeping Beauty,* and *Little Red Riding Hood.*

Fantasy. A genre that uses magic and other supernatural forms as a primary element of plot, theme, and/or setting. Examples include J. R. R. Tolkien's *The Lord of the Rings,* C. S. Lewis' *The Chronicles of Narnia,* and William Morris' *The Well at the World's End.*

Folktale. A narrative form, such as an epic, legend, myth, song, poem, or fable, that has been retold within a culture for generations. Examples include *The People Could Fly* retold by Virginia Hamilton and *And the Green Grass Grew All Around: Folk Poetry from Everyone* by Alvin Schwartz.

Frame tale. A narrative technique in which the main story is composed primarily for the purpose of organizing a set of shorter stories, each of which is a story within a story. Examples include Geoffrey Chaucer's *Canterbury Tales,* Ovid's *Metamorphoses,* and Emily Bronte's *Wuthering Heights.*

Historical fiction. Narrative fiction that is set in some earlier time and often contains historically authentic people, places, or events—for example, *Lincoln* by Gore Vidal.

Horror. Fiction that is intended to frighten, unsettle, or scare the reader. Horror fiction often overlaps with fantasy and science fiction. Examples include Stephen King's *The Shining,* Mary Shelley's *Frankenstein*, and Ray Bradbury's *Something Wicked This Way Comes.*

Legend. A narrative about human actions that is perceived by both the teller and the listeners to have taken place within human history and that possesses certain qualities that give the tale the appearance of truth or reality. Washington Irving's *The Legend of Sleepy Hollow* is a well-known legend; others include *King Arthur* and *The Holy Grail.*

Mystery. A suspenseful story that deals with a puzzling crime. Examples include Edgar Allan Poe's "The Murder in Rue Morgue" and Charles Dickens' *The Mystery of Edwin Drood.*

Myth. Narrative fiction that involves gods and heroes or has a theme that expresses a culture's ideology. There are myths from around the world. Examples of Greek myths include *Zeus and the Olympians* and *Achilles and the Trojan War.* Roman myths include *Hercules, Apollo,* and *Venus.*

Novel. An extended fictional prose narrative.

Novella. A short narrative, usually between 50 and 100 pages long. Examples include George Orwell's *Animal Farm* and Franz Kafka's *The Metamorphosis*.

Parody. A text or performance that imitates and mocks an author or work.

Romance. A novel comprised of idealized events far removed from everyday life. This genre includes the subgenres gothic romance and medieval romance. Examples include Mary Shelley's *Frankenstein,* William Shakespeare's *Troilus and Cressida,* and *King Horn* (anonymous).

Satire. Literature that makes fun of social conventions or conditions, usually to evoke change.

Science fiction. Fiction that deals with the current or future development of technological advances. Examples include Kurt Vonnegut's *Slaughterhouse-Five,* George Orwell's *1984,* Aldous Huxley's *Brave New World,* and Ray Bradbury's *Fahrenheit 451.*

Short story. A brief fictional prose narrative. Examples include Shirley Jackson's "The Lottery," Washington Irving's "Rip van Winkle," D. H. Lawrence's "The Horse Dealer's Daughter," Arthur Conan Doyle's "Hound of the Baskervilles," and Dorothy Parker's "Big Blond."

Tragedy. Literature, often drama, ending in a catastrophic event for the protagonist(s) after he or she faces several problems or conflicts.

Western. A novel set in the western United States featuring the experiences of cowboys and frontiersmen. Examples include Zane Grey's *Riders of the Purple Sage, Trail Driver;* Larry McMurtry's *Lonesome Dove;* Conrad Richter's *The Sea of Grass;* Fran Striker's *The Lone Ranger;* and Owen Wister's *The Virginian.*

Nonfiction (or Expository)

Autobiography. A person's account of his or her own life.

Biography. A story about a person's life written by another person.

Document (letter, diary, journal). An expository piece written with eloquence that becomes part of the recognized literature of an era. Documents often reveal historical facts, the social mores of the times, and the thoughts and personality of the author. Some documents have recorded and influenced the history of the world. Examples include the Bible, the Koran, the Constitution of the United States, and Adolf Hitler's *Mein Kampf.*

Essay. A document organized in paragraph form that can be long or short and can be in the form of a letter, dialogue, or discussion. Examples include *Politics and the English Language* by George Orwell, *The American Scholar* by Ralph Waldo Emerson, and *Moral Essays* by Alexander Pope.

Historical and Cultural Contexts of Texts

It is important to know the historical and cultural contexts of texts in order to be able to apply your knowledge of the various schools of writers, to associate works with certain authors, to identify the period within which an author wrote or a piece was written, and to identify representative works from a period. In this section, I have organized a comprehensive outline by schools of writers, the periods within each school, and representative authors and works.

Classicism

Greek Classical and Hellenistic periods (8th to 2nd centuries BC). Examples: Homer's *The Iliad,* Sophocles' *Oedipus Rex,* Aristophanes' *Lysistrata*, Aristotle's *Organum*, and Plato's *The Republic.*

Roman Classical period (1st century BC to 2nd century AD–5th century AD). Examples: Cicero's letters to Atticus, Brutus, Quintus, and others; Virgil's *The Aeneid;* Ovid's *Metamorphoses;* Polybius' universal history of Rome; Plutarch's "Life of Pericles"; and Lucian's *Dialogues of the Gods.*

Renaissance

Renaissance (13th–15th centuries). A period during which learning and the arts flourished in Europe. Examples: Dante's *The Divine Comedy*, Chaucer's *Canterbury Tales*, and Malory's *Le Morte d'Arthur*.

Neoclassicism

French Neoclassical period (17th century). Examples: Racine's *Andromaque* and de la Fontaine's *Fables choisies, mises en vers* (selected fables versified).

English Neoclassical period (17th and 18th centuries). Examples: Dryden's *The Conquest of Granada* and "Alexander's Feast," Swift's *The Battle of the Books* and *Gulliver's Travels*, and Pope's *The Rape of the Lock*.

German Neoclassical period (18th and 19th centuries). Examples: Lessing's *Zur Geschichte und Literatur* (On History and Literature), von Schiller's *Don Carlos*, and Goethe's *Faust*.

British Literature

Old English period (450–1066 AD). Example: *Beowulf.*

Middle English period (1066–1550). Examples: Chaucer's *Canterbury Tales*, More's *Utopia*, Malory's *Le Morte d'Arthur*, and the morality play *Everyman.*

Elizabethan period (1550–1625). Examples: Shakespeare's *Macbeth* and *Hamlet;* Marlowe's *Tamburlaine the Great, Dr. Faustus, The Jew of Malta*, and *Edward II;* Bacon's *Reports;* and Spenser's *The Faerie Queene.*

Puritan period (1625–1660). Examples: Walton's *The Compleat Angler,* Milton's "Lycidas," and Bunyan's *The Pilgrim's Progress.*

Neoclassical period (1660–1780). Examples: Dryden's *The Conquest of Granada* and Pepys' *Memoirs of the Royal Navy.*

Romantic period (1780–1840). Examples: Keats' *Lamia, Isabella, The Eve of St. Agnes, and Other Poems;* Burns' "Auld Lang Syne" and "Tam o' Shanter"; Shelley's *Prometheus Unbound;* Byron's *Don Juan;* and Austen's *Pride and Prejudice* and *Northanger Abbey.*

Victorian period (1840–1900). Examples: Dickens' *Great Expectations*, Tennyson's *Poems*, Hardy's *Tess of the D'Urbervilles* and *Jude the Obscure*, and Browning's *Sonnets from the Portuguese.*

Modernism (1900–1945). Examples: Yeats' *In the Seven Woods*, Remarques' *All Quiet on the Western Front*, and Woolf's *Mrs. Dalloway.*

Postmodernism (1945–present). Examples: Nietzsche's *The Antichrist*, Orwell's *1984*, and Eliot's "The Waste Land."

American Literature

Colonial period (1630–1760). Examples: Williams and Hooker's *Bay Psalm Book*, Franklin's *Poor Richard's Almanack*, Bradstreet's *The Tenth Muse Lately Sprung Up in America*, and Edwards' *The Freedom of the Will.*

Revolutionary period (1760–1787). Examples: The Declaration of Independence; Jefferson's *Summary View of the Rights of British America;* Freneau's *The British Prison Ship,* "The Wild Honeysuckle," and "The Indian Burying Ground"; Tyler's *The Contrast* (the first comedy performed in early American theater); and Brown's *The Power of Sympathy* (the first American novel).

Nationalist period (1828–1836). Examples: Cooper's *Leatherstocking Tales,* which included *The Deerslayer, The Last of the Mohicans, The Pathfinder, The Pioneers,* and *The Prairie;* Emerson's *Nature,* "The Over-Soul," "Compensation," and "Self-Reliance"; Irving's "Rip van Winkle" and "The Legend of Sleepy Hollow" in *The Sketch Book of Geoffrey*

Crayon, Gent; Poe's *The Raven and Other Poems, Tales of the Grotesque and Arabesque;* and Longfellow's *Evangeline, The Song of Hiawatha, The Courtship of Miles Standish,* and *Tales of a Wayside Inn,* which included "Paul Revere's Ride."

American Renaissance period (1830–1860). Examples: Dickinson's poems "Life," "Love," and "Time and Eternity"; Melville's *Moby-Dick;* Whitman's "Oh, Captain, My Captain!" and *Leaves of Grass;* and Thoreau's *Walden.*

Modern period (1900–1945). Examples: Twain's *The Adventures of Huckleberry Finn* and *A Connecticut Yankee in King Arthur's Court;* London's *White Fang* and *The Call of the Wild;* Frost's "Nothing Gold Can Stay," "The Road Not Taken," and "Stopping by Woods on a Snowy Evening"; Eliot's "The Love Song of J. Alfred Prufrock," "The Waste Land," and "Hamlet and His Problems"; James' "Daisy Miller" and *Washington Square;* and Parker's *Enough Rope* and *Death and Taxes.*

Contemporary (1945–present). Examples: Miller's *The Crucible* and *Death of a Salesman;* Morrison's *Beloved;* Salinger's *The Catcher in the Rye;* Updike's *Rabbit, Run;* Plath's *The Bell Jar;* and Vidal's *Lincoln.*

Teaching Reading and Text Interpretation

Teaching reading across all content areas, including English, is a hot-button issue in schools today. Students not only need to learn how to read, but they also must read to learn. Secondary English teachers must be well versed in teaching strategies to help students read and interpret texts. In this section, you will find an outline of the key components and research-based teaching strategies for teaching reading in the secondary English classroom.

Fostering Reading Appreciation and Motivation to Learn

- Using trade books, electronic texts, and the Internet
- Using nonprint materials such as film, music, art, and advertisements
- Creating authentic literacy experiences
- Connecting students' prior knowledge and interests with texts
- Reading aloud excerpts to students
- Selecting quality texts and other lesson materials

Teaching Vocabulary

- Linking vocabulary with text themes or concepts
- Providing time to read and discuss quality texts
- Teaching students the role of "Word Finder" in a literature circle
- Teaching students structural cues such as common prefixes, suffixes, and roots
- Teaching students how to effectively use context cues to identify the meanings of words and phrases
- Using graphic organizers to help students see relationships among vocabulary words

Teaching Comprehension

Modeling

- Teachers and capable peers should model their comprehension processes in either oral or written form.
- The teacher thinks or talks aloud to share his or her thought process while reading.

Questioning

Teachers should use questions and teach students to ask questions at a variety of levels. Bloom's taxonomy is a helpful construct to guide the formulation of questions:

- **Knowledge:** Remember; recognize; recall who, what, where . . . .
- **Comprehension:** Interpret, retell, organize, and select facts.
- **Application:** Subdivide information and show how it can be put back together; how is this an example of that?
- **Analysis:** What are the features of . . . ? How does this compare with . . . ?
- **Synthesis:** Create a unique product that combines ideas from the lesson; what would you infer from . . . ?
- **Evaluation:** Make a value decision about an issue in the lesson; what criteria would you use to assess . . . ?

Scaffolding

Scaffolding involves an adult or a more capable peer providing structural supports to a student in a learning situation. The more capable the student becomes with a certain skill or concept, the less instructional scaffolding the adult or peer needs to provide. Scaffolding might take the form of a teacher reading aloud a portion of the text and then asking the student to repeat the same sentence, for example.

Activating Prior Knowledge

Also known as set induction, creating an anticipatory set is an activity at the start of a lesson that is used to set the stage for learning in order to motivate students and activate prior knowledge. For example, a lesson on *To Kill a Mockingbird* might begin with primary source documents of trials set during the Civil Rights Movement. Other methods for activating prior knowledge in a lesson include

- Use of a concrete experience or object
- Pretesting
- Discussions
- Anticipation guides

Identifying Text Structures

- Problem/solution
- Compare/contrast
- Argument
- Analysis of an issue

Strategies

- Identifying important information
- Predicting and verifying
- Summarizing and note-taking
- Identifying cause and effect
- Synthesizing
- Visualizing and thinking aloud

Metacognition

Metacognition is a person's ability to think about his or her own thinking and regulate his or her own thinking.

- Ask students what they do before, during, and after reading.
- Teach students effective strategies to use before, during, and after reading in your content area.
- Ask students to support their statements or responses with examples and text citations—ask why.
- Encourage students to ask and create questions rather than just respond to the teacher's questions.
- Allow time in class to discuss not only the content of your course, but also the thinking processes people are using.

Story Elements

Antagonist. A person who opposes or competes with the main character; often the villain in the story.

Character. A person or being in a narrative.

Conflict. Opposing elements or characters in a plot.

- **Person versus person:** A character has a problem with one or more of the other characters.
- **Person versus society:** A character has a problem with an element of society: the school, an accepted way of doing things, the law, etc.
- **Person versus self:** A character has a problem determining what to do in a situation.
- **Person versus nature:** A character has a problem with nature: natural disasters, extreme heat, or freezing temperatures, for example.
- **Person versus fate (God):** A character has to battle what appears to be an uncontrollable problem that is attributed to fate or God.

Denouement. The outcome or resolution of plot in a story.

Plot. The structure of a work of literature; the sequence of events.

Protagonist. The main character or hero of a written work.

Setting. The time and place in which a story occurs.

Study Strategies and Reading to Learn

Skimming

Skimming is a way to read a text to get a general sense of it.

Note-Taking

Common approaches to note-taking include the **double-entry page** and **SQ3R** (survey, question, read, recite, review).

On a double-entry notebook page, the student draws a line down the middle of the page. On the left side, he or she takes notes from the reading or lecture. After the reading or lecture, the student rereads the notes and writes his or her reactions, reflections, and connections in the right-hand column next to the corresponding information on the left.

The SQ3R method for note-taking while reading a text is widely used in schools today. The steps are as follows:

1. **Survey:** The student previews the chapter to assess the organization of the information.
2. **Question:** The student examines the chapter's headings and subheadings and rephrases them into questions.

3. **Read:** The student reads one section of the chapter at a time selectively, primarily to answer the questions.

4. **Recite:** The student answers each question in his or her own words and writes the answers in his or her notes. The student repeats this note-taking sequence for each section of the chapter.

5. **Review:** The student immediately reviews what has been learned.

Graphic Organizers

A graphic organizer is a note-taking guide used before, during, or after reading a text. If you haven't used each of the graphic organizers listed below, you may want to refer to the graphic organizer resources listed in Chapter 14 to examine examples and consider ways to use graphic organizers in your English lessons.

- Concept map
- Semantic feature analysis
- Matrix
- Venn diagram
- Cause-effect
- Cycle map
- Sequence
- Problem-solution
- Continuum

Anticipation Guides

An anticipation guide is a lot like a pretest, although there is no right or wrong answer. An anticipation guide provides students with an opportunity to respond to and discuss a series of open-ended questions or opinion questions that address various themes, vocabulary words, and concepts that will appear in an upcoming text.

Language and Linguistics

The Language and Linguistics content appears on the following Praxis II tests:

- Test 0041: English Language, Literature, and Composition: Content Knowledge
- Test 0049: Middle School English Language Arts

This chapter is organized as a concise outline of the major content assessed on each of these tests. I suggest that you review this outline to refresh your memory of important English content. If portions of content are unfamiliar to you, study further by completing the full-length practice tests in Part III of this book and by using the suggested resources in Chapter 13.

Principles of Language Acquisition and Development

Social, Cultural, and Historical Influences

Linguistics is the formal study of the structures and processes of a language. Linguists strive to describe language acquisition and language in general. There are several key areas of study in this field:

- **Phonetics:** The study of the sounds of language and their physical properties
- **Phonology:** The analysis of how sounds function in a language or dialect
- **Morphology:** The study of the structure of words
- **Semantics:** The study of the meaning in language
- **Syntax:** The study of the structure of sentences
- **Pragmatics:** The role of context in the interpretation of meaning

We understand language acquisition and development through several frameworks, including

- **Sociolinguistics:** The study of language as it relates to society, including race, class, gender, and age.
- **Ethnolinguistics:** The study of language as it relates to culture, frequently associated with minority linguistic groups within the larger culture.
- **Psycholinguistics:** The study of language as it relates to the psychological and neurobiological factors that enable humans to learn language.
- **Historical and political influences on language acquisition:** Some experts view every language as a dialect of an older communication form. For example, the Romance languages (French, Spanish, Portuguese, etc.) are dialects of Latin. Political relationships also influence views of language as either a new entity or a dialect. For example, English is thought to have two primary dialects—American English and British English. The United States and Great Britain are close political allies.

The Role and Nature of Dialects

A **dialect** is a variation of a language used by people who live in a particular geographical area. It is a complete system of verbal (and sometimes written) communication with its own vocabulary and grammar. Dialects, particularly those spoken by a large number of people, can have subdialects.

Standard dialects are supported by institutions, such as governments and schools. In English, for example, standard dialects include Standard American English, Standard Indian English, and Standard British English. Subdialects of Standard American English include African American English Vernacular (also known as Black English Vernacular or Ebonics), Southern American English, Hawaiian English, Spanglish, and Appalachian English.

Language and dialect can be difficult to distinguish and often are differentiated with respect to status or power. Often, the standard language is spoken as a "sociolect," in which a variety of a language is spoken by the elite class. Where power and status are not as important, dialects refer to the regional variations of a language.

In the English classroom, dialects play an important role in understanding literature, composition, and rhetoric. Students learn to read dialects, such as Southern American English, in *The Adventures of Huckleberry Finn;* they learn to write in Standard American English and in other dialects they may speak or try to imitate; and they learn to speak in Standard American English for certain audiences and in other dialects for other audiences, such as peers, dramatic performances, and debates.

History and Development of the English Language

Linguistic Change

English is derived from Anglo-Saxon, which is a dialect of West Germanic, although English today contains vocabulary words with roots from many languages, including Chinese, Hebrew, and Russian. The most common root words are of Anglo-Saxon descent, although more than half of the words in English either come from the French or have a French cognate (a word with a common origin). Scientific words in English often have Greek or Latin roots. The Spanish language is found in many English words, especially in terms originating in the southwestern United States.

Etymology and the Process of Word Formation

Etymology is the study of the history and origin of words. Some words are derived from other words and other languages. Key parts of words and origins of words include

- Language origin of the word (for example, *elaborate* is derived from the Latin *elaborare,* which means "to work out")
- Affixes, prefixes, and suffixes
- Compound words
- Slang words that become common language
- Common words that become slang (for example, *copper* is slang for *police officer*)
- Portmanteau words, which are words that have been melded together, such as Ebonics—*ebony + phonics*
- Taboo words that become euphemisms

Traditional Grammar

Syntax and Sentence Structure

Kinds of Sentences

A **declarative** sentence makes a statement and tells about a person, place, thing, or idea.

> *Example:* Tory is my daughter.

An **interrogative** sentence asks a question.

> *Example:* Is that my son Jimmy?

An **imperative** sentence issues a command.

> *Example:* Please clear the dinner table.

An **exclamatory** sentence communicates strong ideas or feelings.

> *Example:* That was a great shot!

A **conditional** sentence expresses wishes or conditions contrary to fact.

> *Example:* If you were to hang onto the basketball rim, then you could experience the glory of every NBA player.

Sentence Types

A **simple** sentence can have a single subject or a compound subject and a single predicate or a compound predicate. The distinguishing factor is that a simple sentence has only *one* independent clause, and it has *no* dependent clauses. A simple sentence can contain one or more phrases.

- **Single subject, single predicate:** My dog growls.
- **Compound subject, single predicate:** My dog and my cat growl.
- **Compound subject, compound predicate:** My dog and my cat growl and appear agitated.
- **Independent clause with two phrases:** I must have vicious pets from the pound in my town.

A **compound** sentence is made up of two independent clauses. The clauses must be joined by a semicolon or by a comma and a coordinating conjunction.

> My dog growls at the mailman, but my cat growls at her littermate.
>
> My dog growls at the mailman; my cat growls at her littermate.

A **complex** sentence has one independent clause and one or more dependent clauses.

> When you pass the Praxis II test [dependent clause], you'll enjoy a career in teaching [independent clause].
>
> You will get a teaching job [independent clause], even though it will be challenging [dependent clause].

A **compound/complex** sentence has two or more independent clauses and one or more dependent clauses.

> I just earned my teaching degree [independent clause], and I plan to get a teaching job [independent clause] because I need a career [dependent clause].

Effective Sentences

Effective sentences are clear and concise. In addition, effective sentences employ imagery, precise language, and rhythm. Ineffective sentences often contain one or more of the following problems:

- Unnatural language, such as clichés or jargon
- Nonstandard language or unparallel construction
- Errors such as pronoun referent problems
- Short, stilted sentences; run-on sentences; or sentence fragments

Parts of Speech

Nouns

Types of nouns:

- **Common nouns** do not name specific people, places, or things. Common nouns are not capitalized.
  Examples: person, animal, car
- **Proper nouns** name particular people, places, or things. Proper nouns are capitalized.
  Examples: President Clinton, Chicago, Judaism

- **Concrete nouns** name a thing that is tangible (it can be seen, heard, touched, smelled, or tasted). They are either proper or common.

  Examples: dog, Campus Cinema, football

- **Abstract nouns** name an idea, condition, or feeling (in other words, something that is not concrete).

  Examples: ideals, justice, Americana

- **Collective nouns** name a group or unit.

  Examples: gaggle, herd, community

Number of nouns:

- **Singular:** book, library, child, bacterium, man
- **Plural:** books, libraries, children, bacteria, men

Gender of nouns:

- **Masculine:** father, brother, uncle, men, bull
- **Feminine:** mother, sister, aunt, women, cow
- **Neuter:** window, shrub, door, college, car
- **Indefinite:** chairperson, politician, president, professor, flight attendant

Case of nouns:

- A **nominative case noun** can be the subject of a clause or the predicate noun when it follows the verb *be*.
- A **possessive case noun** shows possession or ownership.
- An **objective case noun** can be a direct object, an indirect object, or an object of a preposition.

Verbs

Types of verbs:

- **Transitive verbs** take *direct objects*—words or word groups that complete the meaning of a verb by naming a receiver of the action.

                 Subject   Verb   Direct object

  Example: The secondary English student <u>learns</u> the methods of the master teacher.

- **Intransitive verbs** take no objects or complements.

  Example: An airplane <u>flew</u> overhead.

- **Linking or connecting verbs** connect the subject and the subject complement (an adjective, noun, or noun equivalent)

  Example: It <u>was</u> rainy.

- An **auxiliary or helping verb** comes before another verb.

  Example: She <u>must have</u> passed the Praxis II exam.

Verb tenses:

- **Present tense** is used to describe situations that exist in the present time.

  Example: Celia and Tory <u>attend</u> Curtis Corner Middle School.

- **Past tense** is used to tell about what happened in the past.

  Example: They <u>attended</u> Wakefield Elementary School.

- **Future tense** is used to express action that will take place in the future.

  Example: Next year, they <u>will attend</u> Broad Rock High School.

- **Present perfect tense** is used when action began in the past but continues into the present.
  Example: Annie <u>has attended</u> a charter school for two years.
- **Past perfect tense** is used to express action that began in the past and happened prior to another past action.
  Example: Dr. Hicks reported that redistricting <u>had alleviated</u> the crowding problem in schools.
- **Future perfect tense** is used to express action that will begin in the future and will be completed in the future.
  Example: By this time next year, Tory and Celia <u>will have graduated</u> eighth grade.

Verbals versus verbs:

- An **infinitive phrase** is usually made up of *to* and the base form of a verb, such as *to order* or *to abandon*. It can function as an adjective, adverb, or noun.
- A **participle** is a verb form that usually ends in *–ing* or *–ed*. Participles operate as adjectives but also maintain some characteristics of verbs. You might think of a participle as a verbal adjective. Examples include *barking* dog and *painted* fence.
- A **gerund phrase** is made up of a present participle (a verb ending in *–ing*) and always functions as a noun.
  Example: <u>Gardening</u> is my favorite leisure activity.

Pronouns

There are three types of pronouns:

- **Simple:** I, you, he, she, it, we, they, who, what
- **Compound:** Itself, myself, anybody, someone, everything
- **Phrasal:** Each other, one another

Pronoun antecedents:

An **antecedent** is the noun to which a pronoun refers. Each pronoun must agree with its antecedent.

> *Example:* <u>Jimmy</u> is playing in a basketball tournament tomorrow. <u>He</u> hopes to play well.

Classes of pronouns:

- **Personal pronouns** take the place of nouns.
  Example: Coach Spence changed <u>his</u> starting line-up and won the game.
- **Relative pronouns** relate adjective clauses to the nouns or pronouns they modify.
  Example: A basketball player <u>who</u> plays with intensity and skill gets a place in the starting line-up.
- **Indefinite pronouns** usually refer to unnamed or unknown people or things.
  Example: Perhaps you know <u>somebody who</u> can slam-dunk a basketball.
- **Interrogative pronouns** ask questions.
  Example: <u>Who</u> are you and <u>why</u> do you play basketball?
- **Demonstrative pronouns** point out people, places, or things without naming them.
  Example: <u>This</u> should be an easy win. <u>They</u> are undefeated.

Modifiers

Modifiers are words, clauses, or phrases that limit or describe other words or groups of words.

Adjectives describe or modify nouns or pronouns.

> *Examples:* big, blue, old, tacky, shiny, an

Adverbs describe four different things:

- **Time:** tomorrow, monthly, momentarily, presently
- **Place:** there, yonder, here, backward
- **Manner:** exactly, efficiently, clearly, steadfastly
- **Degree:** greatly, partly, too, incrementally

Phrases and Clauses

Phrases are groups of related words that operate as a single part of speech, such as a verb, verbal, prepositional, appositive, or absolute. For example, "in the doghouse" is a prepositional phrase.

Clauses are groups of related words that have both a subject and a predicate. For example, "I have a tendency to procrastinate when I have a high-stakes assignment" contains the clause "I have a tendency to procrastinate."

Punctuation

There are various forms of punctuation and guidelines for using punctuation correctly. Below, you will find a brief overview of the rules that guide editing for proper punctuation.

- A **comma** is used between two independent clauses, to separate adjectives, to separate contrasted elements, to set off appositives, to separate items in a list, to enclose explanatory words, after an introductory phrase, after an introductory clause, to set off a nonrestrictive phrase, to ensure clarity, in numbers, to enclose titles, in a direct address, to set off dialogue, to set off items in an address, and to set off dates. Clearly, commas have several uses and rules that make their use a challenge for writers!
- A **period** is used at the end of a sentence, after an initial or abbreviation, or as a decimal point.
- A **question mark** is used at the end of a direct or indirect question and to show uncertainty.
- A **semicolon** is used to separate groups that include commas and to set off independent clauses.
- An **exclamation point** is used to express strong feeling.
- An **apostrophe** is used in contractions, to form plurals, to form singular possessives, to form plural possessives, in compound nouns, to show shared possession, and to express time or amount.
- A **dash** is used for emphasis, to set off interrupted speech, to set off an introductory series, and to indicate a sudden break.
- **Parentheses** are used to set off explanatory information and to set off full sentences.
- **Brackets** are used to set off added words, editorial corrections, and clarifying information.
- A **hyphen** is used between numbers, between fractions, in a special series, to create new words, and to join numbers.

Semantics

As mentioned earlier in this chapter, semantics is the study of the meaning in language.

Ambiguity occurs when there are two or more possible meanings to a word or phrase.

A **euphemism** is a socially accepted word or phrase used to replace unacceptable language, such as expressions for bodily functions or body parts. Euphemisms also are used as substitutes for straightforward words to tactfully conceal or falsify meaning.

Example: My grandmother <u>passed away</u> last April.

Doublespeak is language that is intended to be evasive or to conceal. The term began to be used in the 1950s and is similar to *newspeak,* a term coined by George Orwell in the novel *1984.* Doublespeak is related to euphemism but is distinguished by its use by government, military, and business organizations.

> *Example:* "downsized" actually means fired or loss of a job.

Jargon is the specialized language of a particular group or culture. Education-related jargon includes words such as *rubric, tuning protocol,* and *deskilling.*

Composition and Rhetoric

The Composition and Rhetoric content appears on the following Praxis II tests:

- Test 0041: English Language, Literature, and Composition: Content Knowledge
- Test 0042: English Language, Literature, and Composition: Essays
- Test 0043: English Language, Literature, and Composition: Pedagogy
- Test 0048: Teaching Foundations: English
- Test 0049: Middle School English Language Arts

This chapter is organized as a concise outline of the major content assessed on each of these tests. I suggest that you review this outline to refresh your memory of important English content. If portions of content are unfamiliar to you, study further by completing the full-length practice tests in Part III and by using the suggested resources in Chapter 13.

Elements of Teaching Writing

Stages of the Writing Process

1. **Prewriting (also called *planning* or *rehearsal*):** This stage of the writing process involves gathering and selecting ideas. English teachers can help students prewrite in several ways: by creating lists, researching, brainstorming, reading to discover more about the author's style, talking, collecting memorabilia or clips from other texts, and free-writing.

2. **Drafting:** In this stage, students begin writing, connecting, and developing ideas. Depending on the purpose for writing and the audience of the piece, there may be few drafts or many.

3. **Revising:** This stage of the writing process involves rewriting, or "re-seeing." At this point, the writer looks at the piece again, either alone or with the help of a teacher or capable peer. The writer strives to ensure that the reader is able to make meaning of the piece of writing. In the revising stage, emphasis is placed on examining sentence structure, word choice, voice, and organization of the piece.

4. **Editing:** This stage involves checking for style and conventions—spelling, grammar, usage, and punctuation. At this point in the writing process, the writer ensures that errors in conventions will not be intrusive when others read the piece of writing.

5. **Publishing:** The "going public" stage. A writer can share his or her writing with a larger audience in many ways. Teachers can encourage students to publish their writing in newsletters, online publications, performance, brochures, and magazines.

6. **Evaluating:** In this stage, the writer looks back at his or her work and self-evaluates, and the audience evaluates the effectiveness of the writing.

Writing Activities

- **Personal writing:** Students can express their innermost thoughts, feelings, and responses through a variety of personal writing, including journal writing, diaries, logs, personal narratives, and personal essays.

- **Workplace writing:** Middle- and secondary-level students must learn how to prepare resumes, cover letters, job applications, and business letters.

- **Subject writing:** In subject writing activities, middle- and secondary-level students write interviews, accounts, profiles, or descriptions to capture the meaning of the subject being written about.

- **Creative writing:** Creative writing provides students with the opportunity to play with language, to express emotions, to articulate stories, or to develop a drama for others to enjoy.

- **Persuasive writing:** In this genre of writing, students learn rhetorical strategies to persuade others, such as by writing editorials, arguments, commentaries, and advertisements.
- **Scholarly writing:** Essays, research papers, bibliographies—these types of scholarly writing are the most prevalent in middle- and secondary-level classrooms.

Types of Source Materials for Writing

- **Reference works:** Dictionaries, encyclopedias, writers' reference handbooks, books of lists, almanacs, thesauruses, books of quotations, and so on.
- **Internet:** Each of the types of reference works above is available online. In addition, writers can use search engines or portals (sites that list many resources and websites) to gather ideas and information.
- **Student-created sources:** For example, a student's personal dictionary of words to know or spell, note cards, graphic organizers, oral histories, and journals.
- **Other sources:** Film, art, media, and so on.

Evaluating Source Materials

Writers and readers must evaluate sources carefully to ensure that each source is reliable, worthwhile, and accurate. The following general guidelines will help student writers and readers to determine whether print (such as journal articles) and nonprint sources (such as Internet sources) are reliable:

1. **Check the basic information about the source, such as author, year published, and publisher.** Review this initial information to check for credibility, evidence of bias, conflict of interest or other agendas, and accuracy. Is your source peer-reviewed or edited by others? Have other works by this author proven to be credible and accurate?

2. **If your source initially appears reliable, take time to read a portion of the material.** Use the following questions to guide your next level of review: Is the writing style factual, credible, and free of errors in conventions? Are you the intended audience, or is this piece written for a different purpose other than yours? Is the coverage of the content thorough and accurate for your purposes? Have other people read the source and found it credible, accurate, and helpful?

MLA and APA Citations

Take a look at the following citation for a book in both MLA and APA formats:

MLA: Salinger, J. D. <u>The Catcher in the Rye</u>. New York: Little, Brown, and Company, 1945.

APA: Salinger, J. D. (1945). *The Catcher in the Rye.* New York: Little, Brown and Company.

As you can see, MLA and APA formats are slightly different ways to document a source. Each format has unique rules for citing books, journals, and periodicals; in-text citations; and more. Middle- and secondary-school students must be taught how to use appropriate formats and the proper way to cite the words or ideas of others. I suggest that you use the following websites for more in-depth information about MLA and APA formats, the most common formats used for secondary-level writing:

- www.mla.org
- www.apa.org

Avoiding plagiarism is an important topic in American schools; teaching students to cite sources responsibly is often the role of the English teacher. Students should be taught how to paraphrase a source, cite a source, and quote a source directly.

Understanding and Evaluating Rhetorical Features in Writing

Audience and Purpose

Successful writers know the importance of writing for a specific audience and a specific purpose. Imagine you're writing a personal letter to a former teacher or mentor. Then imagine the differences between that letter and a letter that you write to your prospective employer or to your best friend. The words you choose, the style of writing you employ, and the formality of your letter format all depend on knowing your audience. In middle and high school English classrooms, teachers provide students with a variety of opportunities to practice writing for different purposes and for specific audiences. Here are just a few prompts to get your future students thinking about audience and purpose in your writing classroom:

- Besides you (the English teacher), who is the intended or imaginary audience of the piece?
- What is the background knowledge of the audience? What kinds of information will you need to provide to communicate your message clearly?
- How might this piece of writing be used beyond the classroom? Will it be helpful in some other real-life context, such as for a local nonprofit agency or to persuade readers of a local newspaper?
- What is the purpose of this writing assignment? Be sure to consider your (the teacher's) reason for assigning the task and your students' purpose for writing. For example, is the purpose to persuade, to entertain, to mesmerize?
- What voice is the writer to use to communicate most effectively? For example, is the purpose a formal piece, or would the local dialect or informal language be more effective?

Organization of the Passage

Writing requires organization. There are several general ways to organize passages that will help your students communicate effectively:

- **Chronological order:** The writer shows order of time or the steps in a process.
- **Classification:** The writer explains the relationships between terms or concepts.
- **Illustration:** The topic sentence is stated and then followed by the details.
- **Climax:** The details are stated first, followed by the topic sentence.
- **Location:** In this structure, the writer describes a person, place, or thing and organizes the description in a logical manner.
- **Comparison:** The writer demonstrates similarities and differences between two or more subjects.
- **Cause and effect:** The writer shows the relationship between events and their results.

Types of Discourse

- **Creative:** Speech or written form in which one expresses thoughts and feelings with imagination and creativity.
- **Expository:** Speech or written form in which one explains or describes.
- **Persuasive:** Speech or written form in which one sets forth to convince.
- **Argument:** Speech or written form that debates or argues a topic in a logical way.

Rhetorical Strategies

- **Analogies** are comparisons of two pairs that have the same relationship.
- **Extended metaphor** is a metaphor (a comparison of two unlike things) used throughout a work or over a series of lines in prose or poetry.

- **Appeal to authority** is a type of argument in logic in which an expert or knowledgeable other is cited for the purpose of strengthening the argument.
- **Appeal to emotion** is a type of argument in which the author appeals to the reader's emotion (fear, security, pity, flattery) to prove the argument.

Rhetorical Features

- **Style** is the way an author uses words, phrases, and sentences to formulate ideas. In addition, style is thought of as the ways one writer's work is distinguished from the work of others.
- **Tone** is the overall feeling created in a piece of writing. The tone of a piece can be humorous, satiric, serious, morose, etc.
- **Point of view** is the perspective from which a piece is written. First-person point of view is told from the view of one of the characters. Third-person point of view is told by someone outside the story. Third-person point of view can be told from three different views: 1) omniscient—in which the narrator shares the thoughts and feelings of all the characters; 2) limited omniscient—in which the narrator shares the thoughts and feelings of only one character; and 3) camera view—in which the storyteller records the action from his or her point of view, unaware of any of the other characters' thoughts or feelings, as if taking a film of the event.
- **Sarcasm** is the use of positive feedback or cutting wit to mock someone.
- **Counterpoints** is the use of contrasting ideas to communicate a message.
- **Praise** is the use of positive messages to recognize or influence others.

Presentation Strategies

As the final step of the composition and rhetoric processes, students go public with their ideas. There are many ways for students to present their writing and ideas. Below, you'll find a few common ways to help your students make effective presentations in your English classroom:

- Performing speeches, plays, videos, or readers' theater productions
- Making a speech, participating in a debate, or giving a PowerPoint presentation
- Creating booklets, brochures, family scrapbooks, or personal websites
- Publishing a school newspaper, student magazine, or portfolio of work
- Submitting work for publication beyond the classroom in a literary magazine for young adults, in the local newspaper, in a professional publication for writers, in a contest, or for an online publication

Teaching English

The Teaching English content category on the Praxis II requires that you know the key theories, theorists, terms, and methods related to teaching English in middle and secondary school classrooms today. You will be expected to apply your knowledge in this category to the following two English Subject Area Assessment tests:

- Test 0043: English Language, Literature, and Composition: Pedagogy
- Test 0048: Teaching Foundations: English

This chapter is organized into seven sections that correspond to the specific content categories you'll find on these two tests. If you're like my students (and like I was when I was in your shoes), you'll find the outline format of this content helpful as you prepare to answer questions on the Praxis II. There is a lot of important information to remember here, so you may want to use this outline to ascertain how much you remember and how much you need to study this content. If you are completely unfamiliar with a term, method, theory, or theorist, I suggest that, in addition to studying this outline, you review the current edition of an education psychology textbook or search the Internet for reliable sources on the topic.

Human Development

Students learn and develop in a variety of ways. You will recognize many of the names of these theorists and theories from your education psychology or psychology of learning coursework—Piaget, Erikson, Maslow, and so on.

Bandura, Albert

Theory: Social (or Observational) Learning

Bandura found that people learn by observing others. In a classroom setting, students learn through modeling or vicariously through others' experiences.

Bandura suggests that learning by observation, or by teacher modeling, requires several steps:

1. **Attention:** Attending to the lesson
2. **Retention:** Remembering what was learned
3. **Reproduction:** Trying out the skill or concept
4. **Motivation:** Being willing to learn and having the ability to self-regulate behavior

Dewey, John

Theory: Learning through Experience

Dewey is considered the father of progressive education practice, which promotes individuality, free activity, and learning through experience, such as project-based learning, cooperative learning, and arts integration activities. He theorized that school is primarily a social institution and a process of living, not an institution in which to prepare for future living. He believed that schools should teach students to be problem-solvers by helping them learn to think as opposed to helping them learn only the content of a lesson. He also believed that students should be active decision-makers in their own education.

Erikson, Erik

Theory: Eight Stages of Human Development

Erik Erikson was a psychologist who suggested the following eight stages of human development, which are based on a crisis or conflict that a person resolves. Be sure to focus on those that typically occur in adolescence and young adulthood.

Stage	Age Range	Crisis or Conflict	Key Event
Stage 1: Infancy	Birth–1	Trust vs. mistrust	Feeding
Stage 2: Toddlerhood	1–2	Autonomy vs. doubt	Toilet training
Stage 3: Early childhood	2–6	Initiative vs. guilt	Independence
Stage 4: Elementary and middle school	6–12	Competence vs. inferiority	School
Stage 5: Adolescence	12–18	Identity vs. role confusion	Sense of identity
Stage 6: Young adulthood	18–40	Intimacy vs. isolation	Intimate relationships
Stage 7: Middle adulthood	40–65	Generativity vs. stagnation	Supporting the next generation
Stage 8: Late adulthood	65–death	Integrity vs. despair	Reflection and acceptance

Kohlberg, Lawrence

Theory: Moral Development

According to Kohlberg, elementary school–aged children are generally at the first level of moral development, known as Preconventional. At this level, an authority figure's threat or application of punishment inspires obedience.

The second level, Conventional, is found in society. Stage 3 is characterized by seeking to do what will gain the approval of peers or others. Stage 4 is characterized by abiding by the law and responding to obligations. These stages are typically achieved in middle or secondary school.

The third level of moral development, Postconventional, is rarely achieved by the majority of adults, according to Kohlberg. Stage 5 shows an understanding of social mutuality and genuine interest in the welfare of others. Stage 6 is based on respect for universal principles and the requirements of individual conscience.

Level	Stage	Social Orientation
Preconventional	1	Obedience and punishment
Preconventional	2	Individualism, instrumentalism, and exchange
Conventional	3	"Good boy/good girl"
Conventional	4	Law and order
Postconventional	5	Social contract
Postconventional	6	Principled conscience

Maslow, Abraham

Theory: Hierarchy of Needs

Maslow is known for establishing a theory of a hierarchy of needs in which certain lower needs must be satisfied before higher needs can be met.

1. **Physiological needs:** These very basic needs include air, water, food, sleep, and sex.

2. **Safety needs:** These needs, such as a secure home and family, help us establish stability and consistency in a chaotic world. Safety needs sometimes motivate people to be religious, ensuring the promise of safety after we die.

3. **Love and belongingness needs:** This next level of the hierarchy occurs when people need to belong to groups: churches, schools, clubs, gangs, families, and so on. People need to be needed at this level.

4. **Esteem needs:** At this level, self-esteem results from competence or the mastery of a task and the ensuing attention and recognition received from others.

5. **Self-actualization:** People who have achieved the first four levels can maximize their potential. They seek knowledge, peace, oneness with a higher power, self-fulfillment, etc.

Piaget, Jean

Theory: Stages of Cognitive Development

Piaget, a cognitive theorist, suggested four stages of cognitive development. Be sure to focus on those that typically occur during the middle and secondary school years.

Stage	Age Range	Behavior
Sensorimotor	Birth–2	Explore the world through senses and motor skills
Preoperational	2–7	Believe that others view the world as they do; can use symbols to represent objects
Concrete operational	7–11	Reason logically in familiar situations; can conserve and reverse operations
Formal operational	11–up	Can reason in hypothetical situations and use abstract thought

Skinner, B. F.

Theory: Operant Conditioning

Skinner is thought of as the grandfather of behaviorism, as he conducted much of the experimental research that forms the basis of behavioral learning theory. His theory of operant conditioning is based on the idea that learning is a function of change in observable behavior. Changes in behavior are the result of a person's response to events (stimuli). When a stimulus-response is reinforced (rewarded), the individual becomes conditioned to respond.

Vygotsky, Lev

Theory: Zone of Proximal Development

Vygotsky, credited with the social development theory of learning, suggested that social interaction influences cognitive development. His learning theory, called the zone of proximal development, suggests that students learn best in a social context in which a more able adult or peer teaches the student something he or she could not have learned on his or her own. In other words, teachers must determine what a student can do independently and then provide the student with opportunities to learn with the support of an adult or a more capable peer. I think of this as finding the "just right" next lesson to teach a student and providing just the right amount of educational support.

Addressing Learning Differences and Special Needs

This section reviews the key theorists and theories related to teaching all students as well as meeting students' individual learning needs.

Gardner, Howard

Theory: Multiple Intelligences

Gardner developed his theory of the following eight multiple intelligences in the early 1980s:

- **Verbal/linguistic intelligence:** These students learn best by saying, hearing, and seeing words.
- **Logical/mathematical intelligence:** These students are conceptual thinkers, compute arithmetic in their heads, and reason problems easily.
- **Visual/spatial intelligence:** These students think in mental pictures and visual images.
- **Bodily/kinesthetic intelligence:** These students are athletically gifted and acquire knowledge through bodily sensations.
- **Musical intelligence:** These students are sensitive to pitch, sound, melody, rhythm, and tone.
- **Interpersonal intelligence:** These students have the ability to engage and interact with people socially and make sense of their world through relationships.
- **Intrapersonal intelligence:** These students have the ability to make sense of their own emotional life as a way to interact with others.
- **Naturalist intelligence:** These students have the ability to observe nature and see patterns.

Hidalgo, Nitza

Theory: Three Levels of Culture

Teachers must understand that culture is complex and multidimensional. In her work starting in the early 1990s, Nitza Hidalgo offers three levels of culture to help us more deeply understand the cultural backgrounds of our students and their families.

- **Concrete:** This level of culture is the most visible and tangible. It includes surface-level aspects such as clothes, music, games, and food.
- **Behavioral:** This level of culture is defined by our social roles, language, and approaches to nonverbal communication that help us situate ourselves organizationally in society (for example, gender roles, family structure, and political affiliation).
- **Symbolic:** This level of culture involves our values and beliefs. It is often abstract, yet is key to how one defines oneself (for example, customs, religion, and mores).

Moll, Luis

Theory: Funds of Knowledge

Moll's research into the lives of working-class Mexican-American students and their families revealed that many families have abundant knowledge that schools do not know about. His view that multicultural families have "funds of knowledge" contends that these families can become social and intellectual resources for schools. Moll urges teachers to seek out and use these funds of knowledge and gain a more positive view of these capable, but misjudged, students and their families.

Specific Learning Differences

ADD: Attention deficit disorder may be found to impact student learning. Students with ADD may have difficulty focusing, following directions, organizing, making transitions, completing tasks, and so on. The diagnosis is made by a medical professional, not by school personnel.

ADHD: Attention deficit hyperactivity disorder may be found to impact student learning. Students with ADHD may have many of the same difficulties as students with ADD (difficulty focusing, organizing, etc.) but also may have difficulty controlling impulsivity, sitting still, and taking turns. The diagnosis is made by a medical professional, not by school personnel.

Auditory (or aural) learner: Auditory learners process information through listening. They learn through lectures, discussions, listening to tapes or CDs, repeating information orally, and reading aloud.

Autism spectrum disorders: Autism spectrum disorders include autism, Asperger syndrome, and other pervasive developmental delays (PDD). Students with these disorders have difficulty socializing and communicating.

Behavior disorder (BD): Behavior disorder (also known as conduct disorder) is a type of disruptive behavior disorder found in children and adolescents. Students with behavior disorder may violate rules, show aggression toward people or animals, destroy property, or practice deceitfulness.

Concrete operational thinker: Children approximately ages 7–11 are known as concrete operational thinkers; they think in logical terms, not in abstract terms. Students in this age range require hands-on experiences to learn concepts and manipulate symbols logically.

Developmental delays: Developmental delays are identified by a medical professional in a child before the age of 22. The student may have difficulties in one or more of the following areas: self-care, expressive or receptive language, learning, mobility, self-direction, independent living, and economic self-sufficiency.

Formal operational thinker: Children approximately ages 11–15 develop hypothetical and abstract thinking. Students at this stage are known as formal operational thinkers and can use logical operations to work abstract problems. For example, these students are better able to complete algorithms when working math problems as opposed to needing to use math manipulatives to understand the problems.

Functional mental retardation (MR): A child with functional MR, which is diagnosed by a medical professional, exhibits difficulties with age-specific activities (for example, playing), communication, daily living, and getting along with others.

Kinesthetic learner: Kinesthetic learners process information through moving and doing. They learn through acting out scenes, putting on plays, moving to the beat, pacing out measurements on the sidewalk, and so on.

Learning disabilities (LD): Learning disabilities are determined by a multidisciplinary team or a physician. Students with learning disabilities are not learning to their potential in one or more areas, such as reading, writing, oral language, or mathematics. There are three main types of learning disabilities: reading, mathematics, and written. Common characteristics of students with learning disabilities include

- Poor coordination
- Poor depth perception
- Short attention span
- Impulsivity
- Difficulty following simple directions
- Hyperactivity
- Perseveration (getting stuck on one thought or idea and/or repeating a behavior)
- Distractibility
- Delayed speech
- Limited vocabulary
- Inappropriate use of words
- Difficulty recalling what is heard
- Dislike of being touched or cuddled
- Low or high pain threshold
- Overreaction to noise

Tactile learner: Tactile learners process information through touching. They learn through active involvement with the physical world—hands-on experiences.

Visual learner: Visual learners process information through seeing. They learn through visual displays, films, illustrated books, handouts, graphic organizers, bulletin boards, and so on.

Legislation Related to Teaching Students with Learning Differences

Americans with Disabilities Act (ADA): The Americans with Disabilities Act is a federal law that prohibits discrimination on the basis of a person's disability for all services, programs, and activities provided or made available by state and local governments. The ADA is not dependent on the receipt of federal funds.

Due process: Due process is a set of procedures or safeguards that give students with disabilities and their parents/guardians extensive rights. Those rights include notice of meetings, opportunities to examine relevant records, impartial hearings, and a review procedure.

Individuals with Disabilities Education Act (IDEA): The Individuals with Disabilities Education Act is a federal statute made up of several grant programs to states in educating students with disabilities. The IDEA lists specific types of disabilities and conditions that entitle a student to special education.

Individualized Education Plan (IEP): An Individualized Education Plan is a written plan for a student with disabilities developed by a team of professionals (teachers, special educators, school psychologists, and so on) and the student's parents or caregivers. An IEP is based on a multidisciplinary team's (MDT) evaluation of the student and describes how the student is doing, what the student's learning needs are, and what services the student will need. IEPs are reviewed and updated yearly. They are required under Public Law 94-142, the Individuals with Disabilities Education Act (IDEA).

Least restrictive environment (LRE): The least restrictive environment is the educational setting in which, to the maximum extent appropriate, students with disabilities are educated with nondisabled peers.

Section 504 of the Rehabilitation Act: Section 504 of the Rehabilitation Act of 1973 is a civil rights law prohibiting discrimination against individuals with disabilities by federally assisted programs or activities. Eligibility for protection under Section 504 is not restricted to school-age children; it covers individuals from birth to death.

Differentiated instruction: According to Tomlinson (1995), differentiated instruction involves a flexible approach to teaching. A teacher plans and implements varied approaches to teaching content, process, and product in an effort to respond to student differences in readiness, interests, and learning needs.

Testing accommodations: Common testing accommodations provided to students include longer testing times, untimed tests, having a scribe write or type for the student, Braille or large-print fonts, short breaks during testing, and sign-language interpretation for directions. Offering approved testing accommodations for students who qualify is a desirable differentiation of assessment and is especially important on higher-stakes tests and standardized assessments.

Age-appropriate knowledge and behavior: Teachers must understand their students' physical, social, emotional, and cognitive development. Student progress is seen on a developmental continuum, and growth, or lack of progress toward age-appropriate growth, must be recorded and reported to parents. Students whose knowledge or behavior falls outside the norm for the age group may need differentiated instruction or other supports. For example, a teacher can break down an assignment into smaller chunks and check in with the student to ensure that he or she is completing the work correctly.

Cognitive patterns: Students make meaning in a variety of ways. According to Piaget's theory, children move from the preoperational to the concrete operational and then to the formal operational stage during their school years. One student can make sense more easily through listening, while another may prefer visual information. Successful teachers understand their students' thinking styles—especially for those with learning disabilities and those who are accelerated—and plan lessons to accommodate a wide variety of ways to make meaning.

Physical issues: Successful teachers communicate with the school nurse, families, school mental health professionals, teacher assistants, and students to understand how students' physical issues can be supported so that the students can learn at an optimal level. Physical issues common among students include vision, hearing, and mobility problems. Some students suffer from asthma, seizures, and allergies. A teacher should be aware of any physical issues and procedures to ensure the students' safety, especially during field trips, fire drills, and other emergencies.

Social and emotional issues: As Maslow's theory reminds us, students whose most fundamental needs (nutrition, emotional support, and so on) are not met may experience social or emotional issues in school until those needs are met. Teachers can report observations to families, the principal, school social workers, nurses, or mental health professionals to advocate for a student's basic needs. Differences in socioeconomic status (SES) among students and between the teacher and the students can lead to misunderstandings about students' social and emotional needs. For example, a student from a low or high SES may act out or demand excessive amounts of attention. A teacher must consciously set high expectations for all students regardless of SES and modify instructional methods to help each student achieve a sense of success in the classroom. Some students have physical or mental health issues that lead to social or emotional issues in the classroom. Collaborating with families and colleagues who know the student's needs can help a teacher create a successful learning environment for a particular student. Students who have low self-esteem, experience anxiety, or are easily distractible may also present social or emotional behavioral issues in school.

Students and school culture: Students are affected by the school's student culture. Issues that impact student culture include bullying, teasing, cliques, threats to personal safety, freedom to take risks or make mistakes, collaborative groups, gender relationships, and the structure of the classroom environment. Students also are affected by the larger school culture. School policies, procedures, norms for dress, communication expectations, and teacher responsiveness all affect a student's experience in school.

Working with English Learners

English language learner (ELL), English as a second language (ESL), and primary language not English (PLNE): These terms are used to describe students who are learning English as a second (or third or fourth) language. Teachers of bilingual and multilingual students can support English language acquisition and learning in several important ways, including building on students' culture, supporting students' proficiency in their native language, giving students time to learn English (two years for conversational English, seven years for academic English), and offering opportunities for students to work and talk in small groups.

Family culture: Families can provide valuable funds of knowledge (Moll) for teachers to tap into and utilize for successful lessons. Communicating with families, knowing the school community, and appreciating the differences and similarities among family cultures will help teachers offer instruction that meets the needs of all students.

Linguistic patterns: Many students' first language is not English; furthermore, students within the same school district may speak in various dialects. Students whose first language is not English or who use a dialect that is not standard American English (SAE) benefit when a teacher views these differences as sources of enrichment in the classroom. Students who are new to speaking English may experience a period of silence and may prefer listening in the classroom, which is to be expected and respected. Language is always used in a social context; therefore, students who have linguistically diverse language patterns may "code switch." In other words, a student may use a certain dialect on the playground and another in the classroom. One dialect, African American English Vernacular (AAEV), or Ebonics, is spoken by many African Americans. Which is the best teaching method for students who speak AAEV became a political controversy in the 1990s. Teaching techniques similar to those used with students whose primary language is not English appear to be most successful for students who speak in dialects of standard American English.

Multiculturalism: Students come from a wide variety of cultures, and successful teachers help students define and understand their own cultures to deal with mutual misconceptions and inform future lesson planning. Hidalgo's three levels of culture—concrete, behavioral, and spiritual—can be discussed to build a sense of relatedness and respect in the classroom. Sometimes a family's expectations may differ from a teacher's expectations for a student. Making positive connections between schoolwork and home life can support students' success.

Reading Instruction

Fluency methods: Fluency is the ability to read with expression and ease without halting to sound out words or figure out the text's meaning. English teachers can promote fluency by using methods such as echo-reading (repeat-reading after another capable reader), choral reading (performing a text simultaneously with other readers), and readers' theater (performing parts of a text, much like a play, with emphasis on reading with expression rather than on props, scenery, or movement).

Vocabulary instruction: Middle- and secondary-school students benefit from direct vocabulary instruction in addition to reading quality books. Effective vocabulary instruction methods include concept mapping (defining a vocabulary word and its related words), teaching word origins (prefixes, suffixes, and root words), and using vocabulary words in context.

Comprehension strategy instruction: In most teaching circumstances, the majority of students will know how to read at grade level but may need to learn strategies to help them read to learn, particularly when reading nonfiction texts. English teachers can facilitate student comprehension by explicitly teaching comprehension strategies using a variety of texts. Key comprehension strategies include identifying important information, summarizing, sequencing, comparing and contrasting, envisioning character change, and predicting/verifying.

Writing instruction: English teachers provide students with the opportunity to express their thoughts through writing in a variety of forms, such as argument, persuasive, creative, and research.

Speaking and listening methods: Middle- and secondary-school students have multiple opportunities to practice speaking and listening in the English classroom. For example, students engage in discussions, participate in literature circles or debates, analyze famous speeches online, and make presentations to the class.

Teaching literary response and analysis: Students have multiple opportunities to respond to quality literature and analyze the meaning of what they are reading. English teachers often ask students to provide both an efferent (factual) response and an aesthetic (emotive) response to what they have read.

Metacognition: A person's ability to think about his or her own thinking. Metacognition (*meta* = between; *cognition* = thinking) requires self-awareness and self-regulation of thinking. A student who demonstrates a high level of metacognition is able to explain his or her own thinking and describe which strategies he or she uses to read or solve a problem.

Scaffolding: Instructional supports provided to a student by an adult or a more capable peer in a learning situation. The more capable a student becomes with a certain skill or concept, the less instructional scaffolding the adult or peer needs to provide. Scaffolding might take the form of a teacher reading aloud a portion of the text and then asking the student to repeat the same sentence, for example.

Schema: A concept in the mind about events, scenarios, actions, or objects that have been acquired from past experience. The mind loves organization and must find previous events or experiences with which to associate information, or the information may not be learned.

Transfer: The ability to apply a lesson learned in one situation to a new situation—for example, a student who has learned to read the word *the* in a book about cows and then goes home and reads the word *the* successfully in a note that a parent left on the counter.

Planning for Reading Instruction

Objectives are written to answer the question "What are students supposed to know or be able to do at the conclusion of the lesson or unit?" Be sure to write lesson objectives that include all levels of Bloom's taxonomy, not just the knowledge level.

You should be familiar with the state and national **standards** for content and student performance and know how to use them in lesson planning. In addition, you should be familiar with local curriculum guidelines and how a scope and sequence informs your lesson planning.

Learner factors inform your lesson planning. Be familiar with ways to differentiate instruction for a variety of learners, such as English language learners, students with learning disabilities, and students with attention difficulties. Also consider students' different learning styles and multiple intelligences when planning lessons.

Environmental factors also must be considered in lesson planning. Will students work in small groups, as a whole group, or individually? Will they have access to learning centers, technology resources, and multimedia as part of the instruction? Is the room temperature too warm or cold for all students to concentrate? Is there too much print material on the wall that might distract or overstimulate a learner?

You should know a variety of ways to effectively **open, develop, and close a lesson.** Know how to incorporate a variety of teaching strategies into your lesson plans across the content areas, such as mathematics, science, language arts, and history.

Finally, **assessing a lesson's objectives** is an important part of lesson planning. Know how to set criteria for student performance of a lesson's objectives and show how you can measure and evaluate student success. Key assessments include criterion-referenced tests, norm-referenced tests, performance assessments, and rubrics.

David Ausubel suggested a teaching technique called the **advance organizer.** Introduced before learning begins, the advance organizer is designed to help students link their prior knowledge to the current lesson's content—for example, semantic webs, KWL charts, and concept maps.

Classroom Management Techniques

Know Your Students

- **Age:** Remember that middle-school students need more active experiences, shorter lessons, less lecture, and more small-group and individual instruction. Older students need less teacher-directed structure, longer lessons, more detailed information, many opportunities to share ideas, time to talk with peers, and more time working with the whole class.
- **Strengths:** Get to know your students' interests, talents, favorite subjects, learning styles, family backgrounds, and cultural and linguistic backgrounds in order to highlight these strengths in your classroom.
- **Areas to support:** Get to know the areas in which your students may need support, such as reading (and other content knowledge) levels, learning differences, physical impairments, and English language background in order to make instructional decisions and support all students' learning needs.

Know Your Role as a Teacher

- Set clear expectations.
- Enforce rules fairly and consistently.
- Possess positive and realistically high expectations that all students can learn.
- Highlight students' strengths and support their achievement of goals.
- Model appropriate behavior.
- Accept and understand students within the student-teacher relationship.

Set Up the Classroom for Learning

- Place materials for student use in easy-to-access places.
- Use wait time when questioning students.
- Create a safe and comfortable learning environment that promotes students' risk-taking and deters bullying, harassment, and disrespectful behavior.

- Have student materials simultaneously available whenever possible. For example, set up four crates of student notebooks and place one crate next to each of the four worktables in your classroom. Each group of students will be able to get materials rather than wait for notebooks to be handed out individually.

Punishment versus Discipline

Understand the fine line between punishment and discipline and set clear expectations for student behavior in the classroom.

Punishment	Discipline
Is teacher-centered and authoritative	Is student-centered and based on logical consequences
Communicates anger or disappointment	Communicates concern
Closes choices for students	Keeps choices open for modifications
Is concerned with retribution or revenge	Is concerned with changing behavior
Is negative and short-term	Is positive and long-term

Other Education Theorists' Ideas on Classroom Management

Canter and Canter: In the 1980s, Lee Canter and Marlene Canter suggested a model of classroom management that is known as assertive discipline. The approach, still used today, includes teachers setting clear expectations for behavior and following through consistently and fairly with consequences. Students have a choice to follow the rules or face the natural consequences.

Kounin: Jacob Kounin's research from the 1970s shows that teacher "with-it-ness" (constant monitoring and awareness of student behavior), grouping decisions, and lesson planning are hallmarks of effective classroom management. Smooth transitions between lessons and lessons that maximize learning time are more effective.

Ginott: Haim Ginott's research from the late 1960s and 1970s promotes supportive and preventive discipline by recognizing the importance of the classroom atmosphere—socially and emotionally. He suggested that teachers use "sane messages" in which they simply describe the issue or event of concern. This approach attempts to leave students' self-esteem intact and enables students to consider the situation and develop their own solutions with respectful support from their teacher.

Glasser: William Glasser's choice theory guides teachers who use this approach to conduct class meetings with students to codetermine class rules, guidelines, and consequences. Teachers use these class meetings to change students' behavior, focusing on general student behavior, not an individual student's behavior problems.

Hunter: Madeline Hunter's approach to classroom management centers on the strength of effective lesson planning. The teacher opens a lesson with an "anticipatory set" to help students connect the new content to prior knowledge or experiences. Next, the teacher models and provides guided practice for the new content to be learned. Then the teacher provides an opportunity for individual and extended practice.

Jones: Fredric Jones studied time on task and found that 50 percent of instructional time is lost because students are off task. He noted two common types of misbehavior: talking (80 percent) and goofing off (20 percent). Jones found that most misbehavior occurs during independent practice. He suggests three strategies to improve student time on task:

- Teacher body language (a.k.a. "the look")
- Incentive systems
- Efficient individual help for students

Assessment of Student Progress

Informal assessments: Informal assessment techniques include observation, checklists, homework checks, and class and group participation.

Formal assessments: Formal assessment techniques include quizzes, tests, projects, and norm-referenced testing.

Alternative assessments: Alternative or authentic assessments include anecdotal records of student behavior, portfolios, checklists of student progress, performance-based assessments, and student/teacher conferences. Alternative assessments can be contrasted with traditional assessments. Alternative assessments provide a view of a student's process and product, which is closely related to the instructional activity. Traditional assessments usually provide only a view of the product of the learning, such as the score on a test, and may not be as closely related to classroom instruction.

Criteria and rubrics: English teachers provide clear criteria for assignments to ensure that students understand the requirements of the task. A rubric is aligned with the criteria for the assignment to clearly delineate how the assignment will be scored.

Teaching Methods in the Middle and High School English Classroom

Many English teachers use the teaching methods described in this section. It's important to know that teachers also combine several methods during a lesson, particularly if they are teaching in a block schedule.

Hunter's method of direct instruction emphasizes the following parts of an effective lesson:

- Objectives
- Standards of performance
- Anticipatory set or advance organizer
- Teaching (which includes modeling, student input, directions, and checking for understanding)
- Guided practice and monitoring
- Lesson closure
- Extended practice

Lecture: In this method, the teacher or a guest "expert" shares information with students orally and perhaps visually. Lecturers often use a chalkboard, an overhead projector, poster displays, charts, or PowerPoint presentations to enhance the lecture.

Whole-class discussion: The teacher facilitates discussion with students about the content of a lesson. In this method, the teacher frequently is the questioner, although in some classrooms the students also pose questions and help facilitate the discussion.

Cooperative learning: The teacher selectively places students in groups. In most cooperative learning structures, the students are grouped heterogeneously. In a few cooperative learning structures, such as Student Teams Achievement Divisions (STAD), students are placed in homogeneous groups to compete, but earn group rewards for a heterogeneously grouped team. In essence, cooperative learning is designed to foster collaboration among peers so that all students achieve academic excellence. Successful cooperative learning structures contain the following essential elements:

- Positive interdependence, in which students encourage teammates to complete tasks well
- Individual accountability, in which each group member is individually assessed by the teacher
- Simultaneous management, in which materials and tasks are provided to the groups in an efficient way so that little or no class time is wasted and all students can be actively engaged in the task

Ad hoc group work: In this teaching method, the teacher allows students to form their own small groups to complete a short-term task.

Literature circle: A literature circle is a structure to support student-directed discussion about literature. The literature circle may be heterogeneously or homogeneously grouped. The students all read the same selection independently and then get together to discuss the piece. Students prepare for the discussion by actively reading with a role in mind, such as Discussion Director, Connector, Word Finder, Character Sketcher, or Summarizer. During the discussion, each student offers contributions to the discourse based on their various roles and their ideas about the literature.

Socratic seminar: In this method, teachers help students understand information through a logical examination of opinions and ideas. Texts for discussion are carefully chosen for their quality, richness of ideas, and ability to stimulate extended and thoughtful discourse. A Socratic seminar opens with an open-ended question without a right or wrong answer. Students and teacher refer to the text to make points and listen carefully to ideas.

Reading workshop: In the reading workshop method, an English teacher plans for reading instruction by using the following structure:

- Mini-lesson on reading skills or strategies led by the teacher or a capable student based on individual and group instructional needs.

- Status of the class, in which the teacher asks each student to provide a brief update on what he or she will be working on during the workshop.

- Time for reading, in which students work alone or with the teacher in a small group to advance skills, knowledge, and appreciation. The teacher often confers with students during this time. Students also might participate in a peer-group conversation about their reading.

- Sharing, in which the teacher selects one or a few students to share aspects of their reading.

Writing workshop: When an English teacher uses the writing workshop method, he or she structures the instructional time in the following way:

- Mini-lesson led by the teacher or a capable student based on individual and group instructional needs.

- Status of the class, in which the teacher asks each student to provide a brief update on what he or she will be working on during the workshop.

- Time for writing, in which students work alone, with a partner, or with the teacher to advance through the stages of the writing process. The teacher often confers with students during this time. Students also might participate in a peer revising or editing conference.

- Sharing, in which the teacher selects one or a few students to share aspects of their writing.

PART III

FULL-LENGTH PRACTICE TESTS

This part offers you the chance to simulate taking the Praxis II test that you are required to pass in order to get your teaching license. Five different practice tests are covered in this part:

- 0041: English Language, Literature, and Composition: Content Knowledge
- 0042: English Language, Literature, and Composition: Essays
- 0043: English Language, Literature, and Composition: Pedagogy
- 0048: Teaching Foundations: English
- 0049: Middle School English Language Arts

Of course, you will find it most helpful to take the practice test that corresponds to the Praxis II test your state requires, but you also may find it helpful to review the other practice tests in this part to study for the *content* of your exam.

English Language, Literature, and Composition: Content Knowledge (0041)

This chapter includes one full-length practice test for the Praxis II: English Language, Literature, and Composition: Content Knowledge (0041) test. The practice test will give you a sense of the format of the test and help you determine which content areas you need to study. You also may want to practice your pacing while taking this full-length practice test. Remember, you will have a total of two hours to complete it.

After you complete the practice test, score your answers and use the explanations to assess content areas to study in Part II of this book. You may want to complete, or at least review, the full-length practice tests in Chapters 9, 10, 11, and 12 to help you determine further content areas to study. Even though these additional practice tests are written for other English Content Knowledge tests, the broad content categories of the questions—Reading and Understanding Text, Language and Linguistics, and Composition and Rhetoric—remain virtually the same. Note that the Teaching English content is not assessed on this test.

It's time to set yourself up in a quiet place with no interruptions, get your pencils ready, take a look at the clock, and begin your practice test.

(Remove this sheet and use it to mark your answers to the multiple-choice questions.)

Answer Sheet

1 Ⓐ Ⓑ Ⓒ Ⓓ	41 Ⓐ Ⓑ Ⓒ Ⓓ	81 Ⓐ Ⓑ Ⓒ Ⓓ
2 Ⓐ Ⓑ Ⓒ Ⓓ	42 Ⓐ Ⓑ Ⓒ Ⓓ	82 Ⓐ Ⓑ Ⓒ Ⓓ
3 Ⓐ Ⓑ Ⓒ Ⓓ	43 Ⓐ Ⓑ Ⓒ Ⓓ	83 Ⓐ Ⓑ Ⓒ Ⓓ
4 Ⓐ Ⓑ Ⓒ Ⓓ	44 Ⓐ Ⓑ Ⓒ Ⓓ	84 Ⓐ Ⓑ Ⓒ Ⓓ
5 Ⓐ Ⓑ Ⓒ Ⓓ	45 Ⓐ Ⓑ Ⓒ Ⓓ	85 Ⓐ Ⓑ Ⓒ Ⓓ
6 Ⓐ Ⓑ Ⓒ Ⓓ	46 Ⓐ Ⓑ Ⓒ Ⓓ	86 Ⓐ Ⓑ Ⓒ Ⓓ
7 Ⓐ Ⓑ Ⓒ Ⓓ	47 Ⓐ Ⓑ Ⓒ Ⓓ	87 Ⓐ Ⓑ Ⓒ Ⓓ
8 Ⓐ Ⓑ Ⓒ Ⓓ	48 Ⓐ Ⓑ Ⓒ Ⓓ	88 Ⓐ Ⓑ Ⓒ Ⓓ
9 Ⓐ Ⓑ Ⓒ Ⓓ	49 Ⓐ Ⓑ Ⓒ Ⓓ	89 Ⓐ Ⓑ Ⓒ Ⓓ
10 Ⓐ Ⓑ Ⓒ Ⓓ	50 Ⓐ Ⓑ Ⓒ Ⓓ	90 Ⓐ Ⓑ Ⓒ Ⓓ
11 Ⓐ Ⓑ Ⓒ Ⓓ	51 Ⓐ Ⓑ Ⓒ Ⓓ	91 Ⓐ Ⓑ Ⓒ Ⓓ
12 Ⓐ Ⓑ Ⓒ Ⓓ	52 Ⓐ Ⓑ Ⓒ Ⓓ	92 Ⓐ Ⓑ Ⓒ Ⓓ
13 Ⓐ Ⓑ Ⓒ Ⓓ	53 Ⓐ Ⓑ Ⓒ Ⓓ	93 Ⓐ Ⓑ Ⓒ Ⓓ
14 Ⓐ Ⓑ Ⓒ Ⓓ	54 Ⓐ Ⓑ Ⓒ Ⓓ	94 Ⓐ Ⓑ Ⓒ Ⓓ
15 Ⓐ Ⓑ Ⓒ Ⓓ	55 Ⓐ Ⓑ Ⓒ Ⓓ	95 Ⓐ Ⓑ Ⓒ Ⓓ
16 Ⓐ Ⓑ Ⓒ Ⓓ	56 Ⓐ Ⓑ Ⓒ Ⓓ	96 Ⓐ Ⓑ Ⓒ Ⓓ
17 Ⓐ Ⓑ Ⓒ Ⓓ	57 Ⓐ Ⓑ Ⓒ Ⓓ	97 Ⓐ Ⓑ Ⓒ Ⓓ
18 Ⓐ Ⓑ Ⓒ Ⓓ	58 Ⓐ Ⓑ Ⓒ Ⓓ	98 Ⓐ Ⓑ Ⓒ Ⓓ
19 Ⓐ Ⓑ Ⓒ Ⓓ	59 Ⓐ Ⓑ Ⓒ Ⓓ	99 Ⓐ Ⓑ Ⓒ Ⓓ
20 Ⓐ Ⓑ Ⓒ Ⓓ	60 Ⓐ Ⓑ Ⓒ Ⓓ	100 Ⓐ Ⓑ Ⓒ Ⓓ
21 Ⓐ Ⓑ Ⓒ Ⓓ	61 Ⓐ Ⓑ Ⓒ Ⓓ	101 Ⓐ Ⓑ Ⓒ Ⓓ
22 Ⓐ Ⓑ Ⓒ Ⓓ	62 Ⓐ Ⓑ Ⓒ Ⓓ	102 Ⓐ Ⓑ Ⓒ Ⓓ
23 Ⓐ Ⓑ Ⓒ Ⓓ	63 Ⓐ Ⓑ Ⓒ Ⓓ	103 Ⓐ Ⓑ Ⓒ Ⓓ
24 Ⓐ Ⓑ Ⓒ Ⓓ	64 Ⓐ Ⓑ Ⓒ Ⓓ	104 Ⓐ Ⓑ Ⓒ Ⓓ
25 Ⓐ Ⓑ Ⓒ Ⓓ	65 Ⓐ Ⓑ Ⓒ Ⓓ	105 Ⓐ Ⓑ Ⓒ Ⓓ
26 Ⓐ Ⓑ Ⓒ Ⓓ	66 Ⓐ Ⓑ Ⓒ Ⓓ	106 Ⓐ Ⓑ Ⓒ Ⓓ
27 Ⓐ Ⓑ Ⓒ Ⓓ	67 Ⓐ Ⓑ Ⓒ Ⓓ	107 Ⓐ Ⓑ Ⓒ Ⓓ
28 Ⓐ Ⓑ Ⓒ Ⓓ	68 Ⓐ Ⓑ Ⓒ Ⓓ	108 Ⓐ Ⓑ Ⓒ Ⓓ
29 Ⓐ Ⓑ Ⓒ Ⓓ	69 Ⓐ Ⓑ Ⓒ Ⓓ	109 Ⓐ Ⓑ Ⓒ Ⓓ
30 Ⓐ Ⓑ Ⓒ Ⓓ	70 Ⓐ Ⓑ Ⓒ Ⓓ	110 Ⓐ Ⓑ Ⓒ Ⓓ
31 Ⓐ Ⓑ Ⓒ Ⓓ	71 Ⓐ Ⓑ Ⓒ Ⓓ	111 Ⓐ Ⓑ Ⓒ Ⓓ
32 Ⓐ Ⓑ Ⓒ Ⓓ	72 Ⓐ Ⓑ Ⓒ Ⓓ	112 Ⓐ Ⓑ Ⓒ Ⓓ
33 Ⓐ Ⓑ Ⓒ Ⓓ	73 Ⓐ Ⓑ Ⓒ Ⓓ	113 Ⓐ Ⓑ Ⓒ Ⓓ
34 Ⓐ Ⓑ Ⓒ Ⓓ	74 Ⓐ Ⓑ Ⓒ Ⓓ	114 Ⓐ Ⓑ Ⓒ Ⓓ
35 Ⓐ Ⓑ Ⓒ Ⓓ	75 Ⓐ Ⓑ Ⓒ Ⓓ	115 Ⓐ Ⓑ Ⓒ Ⓓ
36 Ⓐ Ⓑ Ⓒ Ⓓ	76 Ⓐ Ⓑ Ⓒ Ⓓ	116 Ⓐ Ⓑ Ⓒ Ⓓ
37 Ⓐ Ⓑ Ⓒ Ⓓ	77 Ⓐ Ⓑ Ⓒ Ⓓ	117 Ⓐ Ⓑ Ⓒ Ⓓ
38 Ⓐ Ⓑ Ⓒ Ⓓ	78 Ⓐ Ⓑ Ⓒ Ⓓ	118 Ⓐ Ⓑ Ⓒ Ⓓ
39 Ⓐ Ⓑ Ⓒ Ⓓ	79 Ⓐ Ⓑ Ⓒ Ⓓ	119 Ⓐ Ⓑ Ⓒ Ⓓ
40 Ⓐ Ⓑ Ⓒ Ⓓ	80 Ⓐ Ⓑ Ⓒ Ⓓ	120 Ⓐ Ⓑ Ⓒ Ⓓ

CUT HERE

CUT HERE

Practice Test 0041

Directions: Each of the questions or statements below is followed by four suggested answers or completions. Select the one that is best in each case. You have two hours to answer 120 multiple-choice questions.

1. The literary works below were written during which of the following periods in British literature?

Isabella by Keats

Prometheus Unbound by Shelley

Don Juan by Byron

   A. Renaissance
   B. Romantic
   C. Modern
   D. Harlem

Questions 2–3 are about the following excerpt from a Robert Frost poem.

Two roads diverged in a yellow wood,
And sorry I could not travel both
And be one traveler, long I stood
And looked down one as far as I could
To where it bent in the undergrowth;

2. Which of the following is the correct title of the poem from which this excerpt is taken?

   A. "The Long and Winding Road"
   B. "The Road Less Traveled"
   C. "Life Is a Road"
   D. "The Road Not Taken"

3. Which of the following describes the rhyme scheme and meter of this excerpt?

   I.   abaab
   II. Iambic pentameter
   III. Couplet
   IV. Trochaic septameter

   A. All of the above
   B. I
   C. I, II
   D. I, IV

GO ON TO THE NEXT PAGE

Questions 4–6 are based on this opening scene from Shakespeare's *Macbeth*.

FIRST WITCH: When shall we three meet again?
In thunder, lightning, or in rain?
SECOND WITCH: When the hurleyburley's done,
When the battle's lost and won.
THIRD WITCH: That will be ere the set of sun.
FIRST WITCH: Where the place?
SECOND WITCH: Upon the heath.
THIRD WITCH: There to meet with Macbeth.
FIRST WITCH: I come, Graymalkin.
ALL: Paddock calls. Anon!
Fair is foul, and foul is fair.
Hover through the fog and filthy air.

4. Who or what is Graymalkin in this scene?

    A. A sentry

    B. One of the witches

    C. A familiar in the form of a toad

    D. An evil servant in the form of a cat

5. Which of the following is synonymous with the word *heath*?

    A. Moor

    B. Desert

    C. Valley

    D. Mountain

6. What does the term *ere* mean in the line "That will be ere the set of the sun"?

    A. Before

    B. After

    C. During

    D. Until

Questions 7–8 are based on the following excerpt from Alfred Lord Tennyson's poem "The Lady Shallot."

> On either side the river lie
> Long fields of barley and of rye,
> That clothe the wold and meet the sky;
> And thro' the field the road runs by
> To many-tower'd Camelot;
> And up and down the people go,
> Gazing where the lilies blow
> Round an island there below,
> The island of Shallot.

7. Which of the following best describes the versification of the lines above?

A. Iambic pentameter
B. Iambic tetrameter
C. Anapestic pentameter
D. Anapestic tetrameter

8. This poem contains an allusion to Malory's *Le Morte D'Arthur*. Which of the following words in this excerpt alludes to this work from the Middle English period?

A. Island
B. Lilies
C. Wold
D. Camelot

Questions 9–10 are based on the following excerpt from Elie Wiesel's *Night*.

The Hungarian lieutenant went around with a basket and retrieved the last possessions from those who chose not to go on tasting the bitterness of fear.

"There are eighty of you in the car," the German officer added. "Anyone who goes missing, you will all be shot, like dogs."

9. *Night* is written as a(n) _____.

A. Documentary
B. Elegy
C. Biography
D. Memoir

10. In the excerpt above, which of the following best describes the purpose or type of writing?

A. Scholarly
B. Personal
C. Persuasive
D. Editorial

GO ON TO THE NEXT PAGE

11. Which of the following best describes the writing process?

    A. Stagelike

    B. Developmental

    C. Exclusionary

    D. Recursive

Questions 12–13 are based on the poem "Harlem" by Langston Hughes, reprinted below.

What happens to a dream deferred?
Does it dry up
Like a raisin in the sun?
Or fester like a sore—
And then run?
Does it stink like rotten meat?
Or crust and sugar over—
like a syrupy sweet?
Maybe it just sags
like a heavy load.
Or does it explode?

12. Which of the following best describes the theme of this poem?

    A. Life in the city can be fraught with peril and delight.

    B. Dreams really do come true.

    C. Postponing one's deepest-held desires may lead to destruction.

    D. Good things come to those who wait.

13. Which of the following best describes the versification of the poem above?

    A. Free verse

    B. Iambic pentameter

    C. Couplet

    D. Haiku

14. Which of the following authors is associated with the Victorian period of British literature?

    A. Shakespeare

    B. Whitman

    C. Dickens

    D. Emerson

Questions 15–17 are based on the following excerpt from Shirley Jackson's "The Lottery."

The lottery was conducted—as were the square dances, the teen club, the Halloween program—by Mr. Summers who had time and energy to devote to civic activities. He was a round-faced, jovial man and he ran the coal business, and people were sorry for him because he had no children and his wife was a scold. When he arrived in the square, carrying the black wooden box, there was a murmur of conversation among the villagers, and he waved and called "Little late today, folks." The postmaster, Mr. Graves, followed him, carrying a three-legged stool, and the stool was put in the center of the square and Mr. Summers set the black box down on it. The villagers kept their distance, leaving a space between themselves and the stool. And when Mr. Summers said, "Some of you fellows want to give me a hand?" there was a hesitation before two men, Mr. Martin and his oldest son, Baxter, came forward to hold the box steady on the stool while Mr. Summers stirred up the papers inside it.

15. Based on your reading of the excerpt above and your previous reading of "The Lottery," which of the following best describes the ultimate purpose of this town's lottery?

    A. To award a monetary prize

    B. To stone a person to death

    C. To recognize the award-winning townspeople

    D. To elect town officials

16. In a short story such as "The Lottery," brief _____ prose is used to give readers a glimpse of an event or life experience.

    A. Historical

    B. Poetic

    C. Nonfiction

    D. Fictional

17. Which of the following terms best describes the use of the word *lottery* in this short story?

    A. Moral

    B. Irony

    C. Hyperbole

    D. Simile

18. Which of the following names the "legend" of Washington Irving's *The Legend of Sleepy Hollow*?

    A. Satchmo

    B. Rip van Winkle

    C. Tam O'Shanter

    D. The Headless Horseman

19. Each of the following novels is paired with its author EXCEPT

    A. *Peyton Place,* Hawthorne

    B. *Pride and Prejudice*, Austen

    C. *Waiting for Godot,* Beckett

    D. *The Catcher in the Rye,* Salinger

GO ON TO THE NEXT PAGE

20. Of the lines below, which ones contain alliteration?

    I.   If ever man were loved by wife, then thee;

    II. Or all the riches that the East doth hold

    III. Then while we live, in love let's so persevere

    IV. That when we live no more, we may live ever

    A. I

    B. I, II

    C. I, II, III

    D. All of the above

Questions 21–25 are based on an excerpt from Chapter 59 of Dickens' *Great Expectations,* the final chapter.

Estella was the next to break the silence that ensued between us.

"I have very often hoped and intended to come back, but have been prevented by many circumstances. Poor, poor old place!"

The silvery mist was touched with the first rays of the moonlight, and the same rays touched the tears that dropped from her eyes. Not knowing that I saw them, and setting herself to get the better of them, she said quietly:

"Were you wondering, as you walked along, how it came to be left in this condition?"

"Yes, Estella."

"The ground belongs to me. It is the only possession I have not relinquished. Everything else has gone from me, little by little, but I have kept this. It was the subject of the only determined resistance I made in all the wretched years."

"Is it to be built on?"

"At last it is. I came here to take leave of it before its change. And you," she said, in a voice of touching interest to a wanderer, "you live abroad still?"

"Still."

"And do well, I am sure?"

"I work pretty hard for a sufficient living, and therefore—Yes, I do well."

"I have often thought of you," said Estella.

"Have you?"

"Of late, very often. There was a long hard time when I kept far from me, the remembrance, of what I had thrown away when I was quite ignorant of its worth. But, since my duty has not been incompatible with the admission of that remembrance, I have given it a place in my heart."

"You have always held your place in my heart," I answered.

And we were silent again, until she spoke.

"I little thought," said Estella, "that I should take leave of you in taking leave of this spot. I am very glad to do so."

"Glad to part again, Estella? To me, parting is a painful thing. To me, the remembrance of our last parting has been ever mournful and painful."

"But you said to me," returned Estella, very earnestly, 'God bless you, God forgive you!' And if you could say that to me then, you will not hesitate to say that to me now—now, when suffering has been stronger than all other teaching, and has taught me to understand what your heart used to be. I have been bent and broken, but—I hope—into a better shape. Be as considerate and good to me as you were, and tell me we are friends."

"We are friends," said I, rising and bending over her, as she rose from the bench.

"And will continue friends apart," said Estella.

I took her hand in mine, and we went out of the ruined place; and, as the morning mists had risen long ago when I first left the forge, so, the evening mists were rising now, and in all the broad expanse of tranquil light they showed to me, I saw no shadow of another parting from her.

21. Dickens' concluding line of *Great Expectations* includes imagery of evening mists, tranquil light, and no shadow when Estella parted. Which of the following best summarizes the author's meaning in the closing of the novel?

A. Pip will always regret losing Estella.
B. The dark mists, the evening, and the shadow signify the anger Pip still holds for Estella.
C. Pip is at peace with his relationship with Estella and can let her go.
D. Pip had great expectations for his home and Estella that never came to fruition.

22. The house that is referred to in this excerpt is known as _____ House in *Great Expectations*.

A. Tara
B. Satis
C. Havisham
D. Bleak

23. This final chapter of *Great Expectations* is best known as which of the following?

A. Denouement
B. Climax
C. Suspense
D. Plot

24. Which of the following is the correct MLA-format citation for the book *Great Expectations*?

A. Dickens, C. Great expectations. New York: Random House, 1907.
B. Dickens, C. (1907). Great Expectations. New York: Random House.
C. Dickens, Charles. Great Expectations. New York: Random House, 1907.
D. Dickens, Charles. *Great expectations*. New York; Random House, 1907.

25. Which of the following is the correct APA-format citation for the book *Great Expectations*?

A. Charles Dickens, Great Expectations. New York: Random House, 1907.
B. Dickens, C. (1907). *Great expectations*. New York: Random House.
C. Dickens, C. (1907). *Great Expectations*. New York: Random House
D. Dickens, Charles. (1907). *Great expectations*. New York: Random House.

26. Which of the following lines from a Sylvia Plath poem do NOT contain an example of onomatopoeia?

I. sharded in black, like beetles
II. It stuck in a barb wire snare.
   Ich, ich, ich, ich.
III. Chuffing me off like a Jew,
IV. oozing the glue drops

A. II, III, IV
B. All of the above
C. I, II
D. I

GO ON TO THE NEXT PAGE

Questions 27–28 are based on the following excerpt.

> I have heard that guilty creatures sitting at a play
> Have, by the very cunning of the scene,
> Been struck so to the soul that presently
> They have proclaimed their malefactions.

27. Which of the following Shakespearean tragedies contains a play within a play in which the villainous king is invited to *The Mousetrap* to see a reenactment of the murder of his brother?

    A. *Hamlet*
    B. *Macbeth*
    C. *Julius Caesar*
    D. *King Richard III*

28. Which villainous character is meant to proclaim his "malefactions"?

    A. Polonius
    B. Macbeth
    C. Claudius
    D. Caesar

Questions 29–31 are based on the following excerpt from the Declaration of Independence.

When in the Course of human events, it becomes necessary for one people to dissolve the political bands which have connected them with another, and to assume among the powers of the earth, the separate and equal situation to which the Laws of Nature and of Nature's God entitle them, a decent respect to the opinions of mankind requires that they should declare the causes which impel them to the separation.

29. Which of the following authors wrote the first draft of the Declaration of Independence?

    A. George Washington
    B. Thomas Jefferson
    C. Patrick Henry
    D. John Hancock

30. Which of the following best describes the meaning of the phrase "to dissolve the political bands which have connected them with another"?

    A. To seek a resolution to the political nature of a conflict
    B. To sever political ties with England
    C. To seek a change in the political structure of the homeland
    D. To seek religious freedom

31. The phrase "a decent respect to the opinions of mankind" works persuasively because it appeals to the reader's sense of _____.

    A. Audience
    B. Propriety
    C. Rationale
    D. Manhood

Questions 32–35 are based on the following passage from *Gulliver's Travels* by Jonathan Swift.

We arrived at Lisbon, Nov. 5, 1715. At our landing, the Captain forced me to cover myself with his Cloak, to prevent the Rabble from crouding about me. I was conveyed to his own House, and at my earnest Request, he led me to the highest Room backwards. I conjured him to conceal from all Persons what I had told him of the *Houyhnhnms,* because the least Hint of such a Story would not only draw Numbers of People to see me, but probably put me in Danger of being imprisoned, or burned by the Inquisition. The Captain persuaded me to accept a Suit of Cloaths newly made; but I would not suffer the Taylor to take my Measure; however, Don Pedro being almost of my Size, they fitted me well enough. He accoutred me with other Necessaries, all new, which I aired for twenty-four Hours before I would use them.

32. Which of the following best describes this excerpt from *Gulliver's Travels*?

   A. Realistic fiction
   B. Lyrical poetry
   C. Prose in comparison-and-contrast structure
   D. Prose in chronological sequence

33. Which of the following best describes the meaning of the phrase "would not suffer the tailor to take my measure"?

   A. Because of Gulliver's personality, he does not have the patience for the tailor.
   B. Due to Gulliver's size, the tailor would not be equipped to prepare a suit for Gulliver.
   C. Gulliver did not want the tailor to go to the trouble of measuring him.
   D. The tailor would suffer if he took Gulliver's measurement.

34. In which of the following periods was *Gulliver's Travels* written and first published?

   A. Early 1700s
   B. Early 1800s
   C. Early 1900s
   D. Early 1600s

35. If a student makes several errors like those in the sentence below, the teacher should plan for more instruction in _____.

One sunny morning sixty-seven years ago Southern New England was going well until everything changed.

   A. Verb tense
   B. Syntax
   C. Paraphrasing
   D. Comma usage

36. Each of the following pairs are homophones, EXCEPT

   A. sell/cell
   B. read/read
   C. waist/waste
   D. witch/which

GO ON TO THE NEXT PAGE

37. Which of the following is the best example of a rhetorical question?

    A. Can you help me locate the main office?

    B. Do you need anything else to help make your lesson more effective?

    C. Do we really expect that schools will be funded by property taxes alone?

    D. Do you think you will pass the Praxis II exam?

38. One phonological feature of African American Vernacular English (also known as Black English) is _____.

    A. The use of sporting expressions such as "bowled over" to mean "taken by surprise" and *football* to mean "soccer"

    B. The pronunciation of the final *-ng* in one-syllable words: *sing* becomes *sin* or *ring* becomes *rin*

    C. The realization of the final *-ng* in two-syllable words: *wedding* becomes *weddin* or *nothing* becomes *nufin*

    D. The use of the word *ja* in place of the word *yes,* as in "You're alright, ja?"

39. In the quote "To err is human; to forgive is divine," which of the following rhetorical devices is used?

    A. Persuasion

    B. Rhetorical question

    C. Parallel structure

    D. Emotive language

40. Abraham Lincoln is attributed as having said, "You can fool some of the people all of the time, and all of the people some of the time, but you cannot fool all of the people all of the time." Which of the following rhetorical devices was President Lincoln using?

    A. Simile

    B. Hyperbole

    C. Metaphor

    D. Repetition

Questions 41–42 are based on this excerpt from Maya Angelou's "Inaugural Poem, January 20, 1993."

> The horizon leans forward,
> Offering you space to place new steps of change.
> Here, on the pulse of this fine day
> You may have the courage
> To look up and out upon me, the
> Rock, the River, the Tree, your country.

41. In this first two lines of this stanza, which literary device is used?

    A. Personification

    B. Myth

    C. Hubris

    D. Irony

42. Which of the following best describes the rhetorical device used in the final line of this stanza?

    A. The "rule of three"

    B. Argument

    C. Capitulation

    D. Sound patterns

43. During which period did the British Romantics such as Keats, Shelley, and Byron write?

    A. 1880–1930
    B. 1780–1840
    C. 1660–1700
    D. 1900–2000

Questions 44–46 are based on this excerpt from William Shakespeare's Sonnet 18.

Shall I compare thee to a summer's day?
Thou art more lovely and more temperate:
Rough winds do shake the darling buds of May,
And summer's lease hath all too short a date:
Sometime too hot the eye of heaven shines,
And often is his gold complexion dimm'd;
And every fair from fair sometime declines,
By chance, or nature's changing course untrimm'd;
But thy eternal summer shall not fade,
Nor lose possession of that fair thou ow'st,
Nor shall death brag thou wander'st in his shade,
When in eternal lines to time thou grow'st;
So long as men can breathe, or eyes can see,
So long lives this, and this gives life to thee.

44. Which of the following is another name for this Shakespearean sonnet?

    A. Ode
    B. Elegy
    C. Epic poem
    D. Lyric poem

45. Of the following choices, which of the following describe the metrics of Shakespeare's Sonnet 18?

    I. 14 lines
    II. Iambic pentameter
    III. Approximately ten syllables per line
    IV. Iambic couplet

    A. I
    B. II
    C. I, II, III
    D. All of the above

46. Which of the following best describes this sonnet's rhyme scheme?

    A. baba; dcdc; fefe; gg
    B. abab; cdcd; efef; gg
    C. aabb; ccdd; eeff; gg
    D. three quatrains and two couplets

GO ON TO THE NEXT PAGE

Questions 47–48 are based on the following excerpt from Amy Tan's *The Joy Luck Club*.

My daughter has put me in the tiniest of rooms in her new house.

"This is the guest bedroom," Lena said in her proud American way.

I smiled. But to Chinese ways of thinking, the guest bedroom is the best bedroom, where she and her husband sleep. I do not tell her this. Her wisdom is like a bottomless pond. You throw stones in and they sink into the darkness and dissolve. Her eyes looking back do not reflect anything.

47. The sentence "Her wisdom is like a bottomless pond" includes which of the following literary devices or figurative language?

    A. Rhetorical question

    B. Personification

    C. Metaphor

    D. Simile

48. Which of the following is the best interpretation of the line "Her wisdom is like a bottomless pond"?

    A. Her daughter's wisdom is fluid and never-ending or bottomless.

    B. Her daughter is reflective and pensive.

    C. Her daughter does not learn from subtle and less-than-subtle attempts to teach her.

    D. Her daughter is not bright and may have learning disabilities.

Question 49 is based on this haiku poem by Raizan.

You rice-field maidens!

The only things not muddy

Are the songs you sing.

49. Haiku is often written in 17 syllables with three lines divided into _____.

    A. 5, 7, 5 syllables

    B. 3, 7, 7 syllables

    C. 5, 7, 5 words

    D. 5, 7, 7 words

50. Which of the following is best described as a cliché?

    A. You can't teach an old dog new tricks.

    B. My grandmother passed away last April.

    C. The Holocaust victims were executed in a concentration camp.

    D. Agent Orange was a chemical used during the Vietnam War.

Questions 51–52 are based on Thomas Hardy's poem "To a Lady."

Now that my page upcloses, doomed, maybe,
Never to press thy cosy cushions more,
Or wake thy ready Yeas as heretofore,
Or stir thy gentle vows of faith in me:
Knowing thy natural receptivity,
I figure that, as flambeaux banish eve,
My sombre image, warped by insidious heave
Of those less forthright, must lose place in thee.
So be it. I have borne such. Let thy dreams
Of me and mine diminish day by day,
And yield their space to shine of smugger things;
Till I shape to thee but in fitful gleams,
And then in far and feeble visitings,
And then surcease. Truth will be truth alway.

51. The poet's use of the word *upcloses* indicates which of the following meanings?

    A. His feelings have died.

    B. He is up close and personal with this woman.

    C. His book is complete.

    D. His relationship is coming to an end.

52. Which of the following rhetorical devices does Hardy use in the last line of this poem?

    A. Rhetorical question

    B. Repetition

    C. Extended metaphor

    D. Contrast

53. Which of the following lines contains an allusion?

    A. "Men are April when they woo, December when they wed."

    B. "Knaves and robbers can obtain only what was before possessed by others."

    C. Town Manager Kern is a "man for all seasons."

    D. The couple had a bliss-filled marriage.

GO ON TO THE NEXT PAGE

Questions 54–55 are based on an excerpt from *The Scarlet Letter.*

The effect of the symbol—or rather, of the position in respect to society that was indicated by it—on the mind of Hester Prynne herself, was powerful and peculiar. All the light and graceful foliage of her character had been withered up by this red-hot brand, and had long ago fallen away, leaving a bare and harsh outline, which might have been repulsive, had she possessed friends or companions to be repelled by it.

54. Which of the following best describes the main conflict in *The Scarlet Letter*?

    A. Person versus nature

    B. Person versus person

    C. Person versus society

    D. Person versus fate

55. Which of the following authors wrote *The Scarlet Letter*?

    A. Edwards

    B. Emerson

    C. Hawthorne

    D. Miller

Questions 56–57 are based on this final excerpt from Ibsen's play *A Doll's House.*

NORA.
That's right. Now it is all over. I have put the keys here. The maids know all about everything in the house—better than I do. Tomorrow, after I have left her, Christine will come here and pack up my own things that I brought with me from home. I will have them sent after me.

HELMER.
All over! All over!—Nora, shall you never think of me again?

NORA.
I know I shall often think of you, the children, and this house.

HELMER.
May I write to you, Nora?

NORA.
No—never. You must not do that.

HELMER.
But at least let me send you—

NORA.
Nothing—nothing—

HELMER.
Let me help you if you are in want.

NORA.
No. I can receive nothing from a stranger.

HELMER.
Nora—can I never be anything more than a stranger to you?

NORA. (taking her bag)
Ah, Torvald, the most wonderful thing of all would have to happen.

HELMER.
Tell me what that would be!

NORA.
Both you and I would have to be so changed that—. Oh, Torvald, I don't believe any longer in wonderful things happening.

HELMER.
But I will believe in it. Tell me! So changed that—?

NORA.
That our life together would be a real wedlock. Goodbye. (She goes out through the hall.)

HELMER. (sinks down on a chair at the door and buries his face in his hands)
Nora! Nora! (Looks round, and rises.) Empty. She is gone. (A hope flashes across his mind.) The most wonderful thing of all—?

(The sound of a door shutting is heard from below.)

56. Ibsen's play *A Doll's House* popularized which of the following types of drama?

   A. Realist
   B. Romantic
   C. Existentialist
   D. Neoclassical

57. The character Nora possesses which of the following character traits at some point in the play?

   I. Silly
   II. Feminist
   III. Serious
   IV. Open-minded

   A. I, III
   B. All of the above
   C. III, IV
   D. I, II

GO ON TO THE NEXT PAGE

58. From which of the following works by the playwright Oscar Wilde is the excerpt below?

Morning-room in Algernon's flat in Half-Moon Street. The room is luxuriously and artistically furnished. The sound of a piano is heard in the adjoining room.

[Lane is arranging afternoon tea on the table, and after the music has ceased, Algernon enters.]

Algernon. Did you hear what I was playing, Lane?

Lane. I didn't think it polite to listen, sir.

Algernon. I'm sorry for that, for your sake. I don't play accurately—anyone can play accurately—but I play with wonderful expression. As far as the piano is concerned, sentiment is my forte. I keep science for Life.

Lane. Yes, sir.

Algernon. And, speaking of the science of Life, have you got the cucumber sandwiches cut for Lady Bracknell?

Lane. Yes, sir. [Hands them on a salver.]

Algernon. [Inspects them, takes two, and sits down on the sofa.] Oh! . . . by the way, Lane, I see from your book that on Thursday night, when Lord Shoreman and Mr. Worthing were dining with me, eight bottles of champagne are entered as having been consumed.

Lane. Yes, sir; eight bottles and a pint.

Algernon. Why is it that at a bachelor's establishment the servants invariably drink the champagne? I ask merely for information.

  A. *A Streetcar Named Desire*
  B. *Flowers for Algernon*
  C. *The Importance of Being Earnest*
  D. *Utopia*

59. Which of the following literary devices is used in the opening line of this excerpt from Michael Ondaatje's novel *The English Patient*?

Now his face is a knife. The weeping from shock and horror contained, seeing everything, all those around him, in a different light. Night could fall between them, fog could fall, and the young man's dark brown eyes would reach the new revealed enemy.

My brother told me. Never turn your back on Europe. The deal makers. The contract makers. The map drawers. Never trust Europeans he said.

  A. Canto
  B. Simile
  C. Caesura
  D. Metaphor

Question 60 is based on the excerpt below.

The Commissioner went away, taking three or four of the soldiers with him. In the many years in which he had toiled to bring civilization to different parts of Africa he had learned a number of things. One of them was that a District Commissioner must never attend to such undignified details as cutting a hanged man from a tree. Such attention would give the natives a poor opinion of him.

60. Which of the following is the primary setting of Chinua Achebe's *Things Fall Apart*?

   A. Nigeria
   B. Post-colonial America
   C. South Africa
   D. Egypt

Questions 61–62 are based on the following excerpt from the play *Pygmalion* by George Bernard Shaw.

THE FLOWER GIRL [to Pickering, as he passes her] Buy a flower, kind gentleman. I'm short for my lodging.

PICKERING. I really haven't any change. I'm sorry [he goes away].

HIGGINS [shocked at girl's mendacity] Liar. You said you could change half-a-crown.

THE FLOWER GIRL [rising in desperation] You ought to be stuffed with nails, you ought. [Flinging the basket at his feet] Take the whole blooming basket for sixpence.

The church clock strikes the second quarter.

HIGGINS [hearing in it the voice of God, rebuking him for his Pharisaic want of charity to the poor girl] A reminder. [He raises his hat solemnly; then throws a handful of money into the basket and follows Pickering].

THE FLOWER GIRL [picking up a half-crown] Ah—ow—ooh! [Picking up a couple of florins] Aaah—ow—ooh! [Picking up several coins] Aaaaaah—ow—ooh! [Picking up a half-sovereign] Aasaaaaaaaaah—ow—ooh!!!

FREDDY [springing out of a taxicab] Got one at last. Hallo! [To the girl] Where are the two ladies that were here?

THE FLOWER GIRL. They walked to the bus when the rain stopped.

FREDDY. And left me with a cab on my hands. Damnation!

THE FLOWER GIRL [with grandeur] Never you mind, young man. I'm going home in a taxi. [She sails off to the cab. The driver puts his hand behind him and holds the door firmly shut against her. Quite understanding his mistrust, she shows him her handful of money]. Eightpence ain't no object to me, Charlie. [He grins and opens the door]. Angel Court, Drury Lane, round the corner of Micklejohn's oil shop. Let's see how fast you can make her hop it. [She gets in and pulls the door to with a slam as the taxicab starts].

FREDDY. Well, I'm dashed!

61. Which of the following is the primary setting of *Pygmalion*?

   A. Contemporary France
   B. Modern-day Africa
   C. Puritan times in New England
   D. Great Britain

GO ON TO THE NEXT PAGE

62. After hearing the church bell, Higgins reflects that he may have expressed a "Pharisaic want of charity" toward the Flower Girl. Which of the following best defines the word *Pharisaic* in this play?

    A. A member of an ancient Jewish sect

    B. Hypocritically self-righteous

    C. Pragmatic

    D. A kinglike leader of ancient Egypt

Questions 63–64 are based on this excerpt from T. S. Eliot's poem "The Waste Land."

April is the cruelest month, breeding
Lilacs out of the dead land, mixing
Memory and desire, stirring
Dull roots with spring rain.
Winter kept us warm, covering
Earth in forgetful snow, feeding
A little life with dried tubers.

63. T. S. Eliot wrote during which of the following periods?

    A. Nationalist Period 1828–1836

    B. Modern Period 1900–1945

    C. Colonial Period 1630–1760

    D. Puritan Period 1625–1660

64. Which of the following literary devices is used in the first few lines of this literary work?

    A. Syntax

    B. Structure

    C. Personification

    D. Denouement

Questions 65–69 are based on the following excerpt from William Shakespeare's play *Hamlet.*

HAMLET: O that this too too sullied flesh would melt,
Thaw, and resolve itself into a dew!
Or that the Everlasting had not fixed
His canon 'gainst self-slaughter! O God, God,
How weary, stale, flat, and unprofitable
Seem to me all the uses of this world!
Fie on't, ah fie! 'tis an unweeded garden
That grows to seed; things rank and gross in nature
Possess it merely. That it should come to this!
But two months dead, nay, not so much, not two.
So excellent a king, that was to this
Hyperion to a satyr; so loving to my mother
That he might not beteem the winds of heaven
Visit her face too roughly. Heaven and earth,
Must I remember? Why, she would hang on him
As if increase of appetite had grown
By what it fed on.

65. Which of the following best describes the phrase "'tis an unweeded garden that grows to seed"?

   A. A simile comparing Hamlet to his mother
   B. A metaphor comparing Hamlet's mother to Eden
   C. A metaphor comparing Hamlet's appetite to a garden
   D. A simile comparing the king's death to heaven and hell

66. To whom is Hamlet referring in the line "But two months dead, nay, not so much, not two"?

   A. Fortinbras
   B. Queen Gertrude
   C. King Claudius
   D. King Hamlet

67. Which of the following best describes *Hamlet*?

   A. Comedy
   B. Tragedy
   C. History
   D. Sonnet

68. This excerpt from *Hamlet* uses which of the following rhetorical devices?

   A. Sarcasm
   B. Praise
   C. Appeal to emotion
   D. Counterpoints

69. Which of the following is the best interpretation of the line "that was to this Hyperion to a satyr"?

   A. It alludes to an entertainment industry giant.
   B. It alludes to an incomplete poem by Keats.
   C. It alludes to a star in the universe.
   D. It alludes to the mythical god of the sun.

70. The author of *Beowulf* is _____.

   A. Racine
   B. Socrates
   C. Ulysses
   D. Unknown

Question 71 is based on the following excerpt from Plato's *The Republic*.

The result, then, is that more plentiful and better-quality goods are more easily produced if each person does one thing for which he is naturally suited, does it at the right time, and is released from having to do any of the others.

71. Which of the following best summarizes Plato's point in this passage?

   A. Each person must do the work that fits his or her own strengths.
   B. Every man for himself.
   C. A philosopher must choose wisely.
   D. A farmer's work is never done.

GO ON TO THE NEXT PAGE

72. Which of the following terms can be defined as using language persuasively or pleasingly?

   A. Personification

   B. Rhetoric

   C. Tone

   D. Point of view

73. Which of the following lines contains a simile?

   A. "Mine eyes have seen the glory of the coming of the Lord:"

   B. "Woodman, spare that tree! Touch not a single bough!"

   C. "Away to the window I flew like a flash."

   D. "My candle burns at both ends; it will not last the night;"

74. The following poem by Edward Lear is known as a _____.

There was a Young Lady whose eyes,
Were unique as to colour and size;
When she opened them wide,
People all turned aside,
And started away in surprise.

   A. Ballad

   B. Canto

   C. Ode

   D. Limerick

75. Which of the following authors wrote *The Catcher in the Rye*?

   A. Alex Haley

   B. John Updike

   C. J. D. Salinger

   D. Sylvia Plath

76. In which of the following periods was *The Catcher in the Rye* written?

   A. 20th-century British literature

   B. Contemporary U.S. literature

   C. American Renaissance period

   D. British Victorian period

Questions 77–78 are based on the following excerpt from the poem "The Love Song of J. Alfred Prufrock" by T. S. Eliot.

No! I am not Prince Hamlet, nor was meant to be;
Am an attendant lord, one that will do
To swell a progress, start a scene or two,
Advise the prince; no doubt, an easy tool,
Deferential, glad to be of use,
Politic, cautious, and meticulous;
Full of high sentence, but a bit obtuse;
At times, indeed, almost ridiculous—
Almost, at times, the Fool.

I grow old... I grow old...
I shall wear the bottoms of my trousers rolled.

Shall I part my hair behind? Do I dare to eat a peach?
I shall wear white flannel trousers, and walk upon the beach.
I have heard the mermaids singing, each to each.

I do not think that they will sing to me.

77. Which of the following is the best interpretation of the poet's meaning in this excerpt?

    A.   Prufrock is paralyzed to act, specifically to eat a peach.

    B.   Prufrock is contemplating murder, like Hamlet.

    C.   Prufrock is afraid of growing old.

    D.   Prufrock is a man in love with a mermaid.

78. Which of the following best describes the mode in which T. S. Eliot writes in this poem?

    A.   Classicalist

    B.   Realist

    C.   Fragmentalist

    D.   Modernist

79. A high school English teacher wants to effectively open a lesson on *Hamlet*. Which of the following is most likcly to motivate adolescent readers?

    A.   An analysis of the play by a famous English author

    B.   A homework assignment to read Act I

    C.   A round-robin read-aloud in which students take turns reading the play without time to practice

    D.   A discussion about seeking the truth in students' lives and personal experiences

80. Which of the following cognates is most DIFFERENT in meaning and usage from its original Latin root?

    A.   Facile

    B.   Facilitate

    C.   Faction

    D.   Facility

81. Which of the following are examples of correlative conjunctions?

    A.   and/but

    B.   not only/but also

    C.   after/before

    D.   since/then

82. Which of the following is an appropriate revision-stage activity during the writing process?

    A.   Peer conferencing

    B.   Peer cditing

    C.   Teacher editing

    D.   Prewriting

GO ON TO THE NEXT PAGE

83. Which of the following is the best definition of a writing rubric?

    A. A frame story

    B. A writing scoring guide

    C. A description of a writing assignment

    D. A part of a manuscript or book

84. Which of the following correctly cites a source using MLA-format guidelines?

    A. Golding wrote in his opening line of Lord of the Flies, "The boy with fair hair lowered himself down the last few feet of rock and began to pick his way toward the lagoon" (7).

    B. Golding wrote in his opening line of Lord of the Flies, "The boy with fair hair lowered himself down the last few feet of rock and began to pick his way toward the lagoon" (7).

    C. Golding wrote in his opening line of Lord of the Flies, "The boy with fair hair lowered himself down the last few feet of rock and began to pick his way toward the lagoon" (Golding, 7).

    D. Golding wrote in his opening line of *Lord of the Flies*, "The boy with fair hair lowered himself down the last few feet of rock and began to pick his way toward the lagoon." (Golding, 7)

85. Which of the following plays by Harold Pinter is seen as an extended metaphor for society in the 1950s, with Stanley representing "angry young men" and his antagonists representing repressive conformists?

    A. *The Birthday Party*

    B. *The Iceman Cometh*

    C. *A Doll's House*

    D. *Waiting for Godot*

86. Consider the following sentence:

The Commander's conceited wife rambled on about her upcoming move from one military base to another and was heard to say, "The move is eminent."

The wife's error is known as (a) _____?

    A. Cliché

    B. Slang

    C. Malapropism

    D. Metaphor

87. Which of the following authors and works represents the Colonial period of literature?

    A. Anne Bradstreet's *The Tenth Muse Lately Sprung Up in America*

    B. Thomas Hardy's *Winter Words*

    C. Washington Irving's *Rip van Winkle*

    D. Ben Franklin's *The Contrast*

88. Which of the following characters is the protagonist of the work cited?

    A. Claudius in *Hamlet*

    B. Nanny in *Their Eyes Were Watching God*

    C. Chillingsworth in *The Scarlet Letter*

    D. Odysseus in *The Odyssey*

89. Which of the following is the definition of the denouement in a literary work?

    A. The conflict or problem
    B. The solution or outcome
    C. The setting, such as time and place
    D. The plot or events in the story

90. Which of the following strategies is used in the following excerpt from W. E. B. DuBois' "Advice to a Black Schoolgirl"?

Ignorance is a cure for nothing. Get the very best training possible and the doors of opportunity will fly open before you as they are flying before thousands of your fellows. On the other hand every time a colored person neglects an opportunity, it makes it more difficult for others of the race to get such an opportunity. Do you want to cut off the chances of the boys and girls of tomorrow?

    A. Appeal to emotion
    B. Appeal to authority
    C. Extended metaphor
    D. Counterpoints

Questions 91–94 are based on the following excerpt from Jesse Jackson's speech to the Democratic National Convention on July 20, 1988.

. . . We meet tonight at the crossroads, a point of decision.

Shall we expand, be inclusive, find unity and power; or suffer division and impotence?

We come to Atlanta, the cradle of the old South, the crucible of the new South. Tonight, there is a sense of celebration, because we are moved, fundamentally moved from racial battlegrounds by law, to economic common ground. Tomorrow we will challenge to move to higher ground.

Common ground! Think of Jerusalem—the intersection where many trails met. A small village that became the birthplace of three great religions—Judaism, Christianity and Islam.

91. Which of the following is the best meaning of Jackson's line "Atlanta, . . . the crucible of the new South"?

    A. Atlanta is the place where racial tensions heated up and created change.
    B. Atlanta's people represent the new South.
    C. Atlanta is the place where people come together, share ideas, and create new hope for the future.
    D. Atlanta is the capital of Georgia and the center of change for the democracy.

92. In this passage, Jackson suggests moving to higher ground. Which of the following is the higher ground to which Jackson is referring?

    A. A battleground
    B. An ethical and just understanding
    C. Heaven
    D. Common ground

GO ON TO THE NEXT PAGE

93. Which of the following best describes the rhetorical strategy Jackson uses in the line ". . . Jerusalem—the intersection where the trails met"?

    A. Alliteration

    B. Allusion

    C. Prose

    D. Appeal to emotion

94. Jackson's line "Shall we expand, be inclusive, find unity and power; or suffer division and impotence?" is characterized by which of the following?

    A. Simile

    B. Personification

    C. Rhetorical question

    D. Extended metaphor

95. When a story is written from an omniscient point of view, which of the following statements is true?

    A. The narrator compares two unlike things.

    B. The story is told from the point of view of one of the characters.

    C. The story is told by someone outside of the story.

    D. The narrator is free to tell the story from any and all characters' points of view.

96. A poem written in a quintet contains _____.

    A. A five-line stanza

    B. Five stanzas

    C. Five syllables

    D. Parts for five actors

Questions 97–99 are based on the following excerpt from *1984*.

On each landing, opposite the lift-shaft, the poster with the enormous face gazed from the wall. It was one of those pictures which are so contrived that the eyes follow you about when you move. BIG BROTHER IS WATCHING YOU, the caption beneath it ran.

97. The author's use of the phrase "lift-shaft" exemplifies which of the following rhetorical features?

    A. Tone

    B. Diction

    C. Attitude

    D. Sarcasm

98. The author's description of the poster with the enormous face and the message BIG BROTHER IS WATCHING YOU is meant to _____.

    A. Appeal to all readers

    B. Appeal to authority

    C. Appeal to the reader's emotions

    D. Appeal to the reader's sense of self

99. Which of the following authors wrote *1984*?

    A. Orwell

    B. Osmond

    C. Ormstrong

    D. O'Henry

Questions 100–101 are based on this excerpt from John Steinbeck's *The Grapes of Wrath*.

To the red country and part of the gray country of Oklahoma, the last rains came gently, and they did not cut the scarred earth. The plows crossed and recrossed the rivulet marks. The last rains lifted the corn quickly and scattered weed colonies and grass along the sides of the roads so that the gray country and dark red country began to disappear under a green cover.

100. Which of the following best describes the setting of *The Grapes of Wrath*?

    A. 1900s Industrial Revolution in the Midwestern United States

    B. 1930s Dust Bowl in the Midwestern United States

    C. 1890s Gold Rush

    D. 1930s pre–World War I England and the United States

101. "The last rains" symbolizes which of the following in *The Grapes of Wrath*?

    A. The end of the California Gold Rush and the beginning of a drought

    B. The end of the rainy season

    C. The beginning of a drought and the end of seasonable weather

    D. The beginning of the Dust Bowl and the end of many farmers' livelihoods

102. In which of the following literary periods was *Le Morte d'Arthur* written?

    A. Middle English period

    B. Elizabethan period

    C. Romantic period

    D. Victorian period

GO ON TO THE NEXT PAGE

Questions 103–104 are based on the following excerpt from *Sonnets from the Portuguese.*

Beloved, thou hast brought me many flowers
Plucked in the garden, all the summer through,
And winter, and it seemed as if they grew
In this close room, nor missed the sun and showers.
So, in the like name of that love of ours,
Take back these thoughts which here unfolded too,
And which on warm and cold days I withdrew
From my heart's ground. Indeed, those beds and bowers
Be overgrown with bitter weeds and rue,
And wait thy weeding; yet here's eglantine,
Here's ivy!—take them, as I used to do
Thy flowers, and keep them where they shall not pine.
Instruct thine eyes to keep their colours true,
And tell thy soul, their roots are left in mine.

103. Which of the following metric is used in the sonnet above?

    A. Trochaic pentameter

    B. Iambic quintet

    C. Iambic pentameter

    D. Anapestic pentameter

104. Which of the following authors wrote *Sonnets from the Portuguese*?

    A. Emily Dickinson

    B. Elizabeth Barrett Browning

    C. T. S. Eliot

    D. George Eliot

Questions 105–106 are based on the following excerpt from D. H. Lawrence's essay *Nathaniel Hawthorne and The Scarlet Letter.*

Nathaniel Hawthorne writes romance.

And what's romance? Usually, a nice little tale where you have everything As You Like It, where rain never wets your jacket and gnats never bite your nose and it's always daisy-time. *As You Like It* and *Forest Lovers*, etc. *Morte d'Arthur.*

Hawthorne obviously isn't this kind of romanticist: though nobody has muddy boots in *The Scarlet Letter,* either.

But there is more to it. *The Scarlet Letter* isn't a pleasant, pretty romance. It is a sort of parable, an earthly story with a hellish meaning.

All the time there is this split in the American art and art-consciousness. On the top it is as nice as pie, goody-goody and lovey-dovey. Like Hawthorne being such a blue-eyed darling, in life, and Longfellow and the rest such sucking-doves. Hawthorne's wife said she 'never saw him in time', which doesn't mean she saw him too late.

105. Which of the following is the best definition of a parable?

    A. A brief story that illustrates a point

    B. A story with a contradictory message or statement

    C. A fictional work meant to tell a story

    D. A story meant to teach a moral lesson

106. Longfellow and Hawthorne were considered _____.

    A. Existentialists

    B. Transcendentalists

    C. Communists

    D. Anarchists

107. Which of the following works is from the Middle English period 1066–1550?

    A. Chaucer's *Canterbury Tales*

    B. Shakespeare's sonnets

    C. Goethe's *Faust*

    D. Homer's *The Iliad*

108. Dorothy Parker's poem "Guinevere at Her Fireside" is from her collection of poems titled _____.

    A. *The Arthurian Legend*

    B. *Enough Rope*

    C. *Death and Taxes*

    D. *The New Yorker Collection*

109. Langston Hughes wrote his poem "Po' Boy Blues" using _____.

    A. Iambic pentameter

    B. Free verse

    C. Authentic setting and meaning

    D. Idioms and dialect from African American Vernacular English

110. Tory participates in basketball, softball and playing the piano.

This sentence can be improved by _____.

    A. Adding "playing" before basketball

    B. Deleting "playing the" and adding " lessons" after piano

    C. Deleting "playing"

    D. Adding a comma after "softball"

111. Consider the following sentences:

Jimmy and Austin were the highest scorers in the basketball game. He enjoyed the recognition of his accomplishment from the coach and his teammates.

Which of the following grammatical errors is the primary problem in the second sentence above?

    A. Pronoun reference

    B. Subject-verb agreement

    C. Verb tense

    D. Coordinating pronoun

GO ON TO THE NEXT PAGE

112. Sociolinguistics is the study of language as it relates to _____.

    A. Semantics

    B. Social skills

    C. Society

    D. Psychology

113. Which of the following activities is LEAST likely to occur during the publishing stage of the writing process?

    A. Examining a book to learn about the features of the publication

    B. Preparing a cover and title page

    C. Using the Internet to search for writing ideas

    D. Writing an acknowledgment section

114. In which of the following sources is a reader MOST likely to find an aphorism from Benjamin Franklin?

    A. Dictionary

    B. *Bartlett's Familiar Quotations*

    C. Encyclopedia

    D. Thesaurus

115. Which of the following is an appropriate greeting in a business letter?

    A. Dear Sir or Madam:

    B. Dear Sir or Madam

    C. Dear Mary,

    D. Hi, Mr. Stevens:

116. Which of the following activities is MOST likely to occur in the prewriting stage of the writing process?

    A. Listing topics

    B. Sharing a draft with a peer

    C. Reading the draft to the teacher

    D. Correcting spelling errors

117. The word *restroom* is a(n) _____ for the toilet room.

    A. Elegy

    B. Anapestic

    C. Aphorism

    D. Euphemism

118. Concrete poetry is a poetic form in which

    A. Formal structure is foremost.

    B. Stanzas and couplets are used.

    C. Shape and visual effects are emphasized.

    D. Onomatopoeia is emphasized.

119. Diction is best defined as _____.

    A. Proficient use of the dictionary

    B. An exact quotation

    C. Disregard for meaning with an emphasis on pronunciation

    D. Careful word choice to communicate effectively

120. The emotional atmosphere created by the author is known as the _____ of a literary work.

    A. Setting

    B. Mood

    C. Plot

    D. Denouement

Answers and Explanations

		Answer Key	
Question	*Answer*	*Content Category*	*Where to Get More Help*
1.	B	Reading and Understanding Text	Chapter 4
2.	D	Reading and Understanding Text	Chapter 4
3.	C	Reading and Understanding Text	Chapter 4
4.	D	Reading and Understanding Text	Chapter 4
5.	A	Reading and Understanding Text	Chapter 4
6.	A	Language and Linguistics	Chapter 5
7.	B	Language and Linguistics	Chapter 5
8.	D	Composition and Rhetoric	Chapter 6
9.	D	Composition and Rhetoric	Chapter 6
10.	B	Composition and Rhetoric	Chapter 6
11.	D	Composition and Rhetoric	Chapter 6
12.	C	Composition and Rhetoric	Chapter 6
13.	A	Reading and Understanding Text	Chapter 4
14.	C	Reading and Understanding Text	Chapter 4
15.	B	Reading and Understanding Text	Chapter 4
16.	D	Reading and Understanding Text	Chapter 4
17.	B	Reading and Understanding Text	Chapter 4
18.	D	Reading and Understanding Text	Chapter 4
19.	A	Reading and Understanding Text	Chapter 4
20.	D	Reading and Understanding Text	Chapter 4
21.	C	Language and Linguistics	Chapter 5
22.	B	Language and Linguistics	Chapter 5
23.	A	Composition and Rhetoric	Chapter 6
24.	C	Composition and Rhetoric	Chapter 6
25.	B	Composition and Rhetoric	Chapter 6
26.	D	Composition and Rhetoric	Chapter 6
27.	A	Reading and Understanding Text	Chapter 4
28.	C	Reading and Understanding Text	Chapter 4
29.	B	Reading and Understanding Text	Chapter 4
30.	B	Reading and Understanding Text	Chapter 4

Question	Answer	Content Category	Where to Get More Help
31.	B	Reading and Understanding Text	Chapter 4
32.	D	Reading and Understanding Text	Chapter 4
33.	C	Reading and Understanding Text	Chapter 4
34.	A	Reading and Understanding Text	Chapter 4
35.	D	Language and Linguistics	Chapter 5
36.	B	Language and Linguistics	Chapter 5
37.	C	Composition and Rhetoric	Chapter 6
38.	C	Composition and Rhetoric	Chapter 6
39.	C	Composition and Rhetoric	Chapter 6
40.	D	Composition and Rhetoric	Chapter 6
41.	A	Composition and Rhetoric	Chapter 6
42.	A	Reading and Understanding Text	Chapter 4
43.	B	Reading and Understanding Text	Chapter 4
44.	D	Reading and Understanding Text	Chapter 4
45.	A	Reading and Understanding Text	Chapter 4
46.	B	Reading and Understanding Text	Chapter 4
47.	D	Reading and Understanding Text	Chapter 4
48.	C	Reading and Understanding Text	Chapter 4
49.	A	Reading and Understanding Text	Chapter 4
50.	A	Language and Linguistics	Chapter 5
51.	D	Language and Linguistics	Chapter 5
52.	B	Composition and Rhetoric	Chapter 6
53.	C	Composition and Rhetoric	Chapter 6
54.	C	Reading and Understanding Text	Chapter 4
55.	C	Reading and Understanding Text	Chapter 4
56.	A	Reading and Understanding Text	Chapter 4
57.	B	Reading and Understanding Text	Chapter 4
58.	C	Reading and Understanding Text	Chapter 4
59.	D	Reading and Understanding Text	Chapter 4
60.	A	Reading and Understanding Text	Chapter 4
61.	D	Reading and Understanding Text	Chapter 4
62.	B	Composition and Rhetoric	Chapter 6
63.	B	Composition and Rhetoric	Chapter 6

(continued)

	Answer Key *(continued)*		
Question	*Answer*	*Content Category*	*Where to Get More Help*
64.	C	Language and Linguistics	Chapter 5
65.	C	Language and Linguistics	Chapter 5
66.	D	Composition and Rhetoric	Chapter 6
67.	B	Composition and Rhetoric	Chapter 6
68.	C	Composition and Rhetoric	Chapter 6
69.	D	Reading and Understanding Text	Chapter 4
70.	D	Reading and Understanding Text	Chapter 4
71.	A	Reading and Understanding Text	Chapter 4
72.	B	Reading and Understanding Text	Chapter 4
73.	C	Reading and Understanding Text	Chapter 4
74.	D	Reading and Understanding Text	Chapter 4
75.	C	Reading and Understanding Text	Chapter 4
76.	B	Reading and Understanding Text	Chapter 4
77.	A	Reading and Understanding Text	Chapter 4
78.	D	Reading and Understanding Text	Chapter 4
79.	D	Language and Linguistics	Chapter 5
80.	C	Language and Linguistics	Chapter 5
81.	B	Composition and Rhetoric	Chapter 6
82.	A	Composition and Rhetoric	Chapter 6
83.	B	Composition and Rhetoric	Chapter 6
84.	B	Composition and Rhetoric	Chapter 6
85.	A	Composition and Rhetoric	Chapter 6
86.	C	Reading and Understanding Text	Chapter 4
87.	A	Reading and Understanding Text	Chapter 4
88.	D	Reading and Understanding Text	Chapter 4
89.	B	Reading and Understanding Text	Chapter 4
90.	A	Reading and Understanding Text	Chapter 4
91.	A	Reading and Understanding Text	Chapter 4
92.	D	Reading and Understanding Text	Chapter 4
93.	B	Reading and Understanding Text	Chapter 4
94.	C	Language and Linguistics	Chapter 5
95.	D	Language and Linguistics	Chapter 5

Question	Answer	Content Category	Where to Get More Help
96.	A	Composition and Rhetoric	Chapter 6
97.	B	Composition and Rhetoric	Chapter 6
98.	C	Composition and Rhetoric	Chapter 6
99.	A	Reading and Understanding Text	Chapter 4
100.	B	Reading and Understanding Text	Chapter 4
101.	D	Reading and Understanding Text	Chapter 4
102.	A	Reading and Understanding Text	Chapter 4
103.	C	Reading and Understanding Text	Chapter 4
104.	B	Reading and Understanding Text	Chapter 4
105.	D	Reading and Understanding Text	Chapter 4
106.	B	Reading and Understanding Text	Chapter 4
107.	A	Reading and Understanding Text	Chapter 4
108.	C	Reading and Understanding Text	Chapter 4
109.	D	Language and Linguistics	Chapter 5
110.	B	Language and Linguistics	Chapter 5
111.	A	Language and Linguistics	Chapter 5
112.	C	Language and Linguistics	Chapter 5
113.	C	Composition and Rhetoric	Chapter 6
114.	B	Composition and Rhetoric	Chapter 6
115.	A	Composition and Rhetoric	Chapter 6
116.	A	Composition and Rhetoric	Chapter 6
117.	D	Reading and Understanding Text	Chapter 4
118.	C	Composition and Rhetoric	Chapter 6
119.	D	Composition and Rhetoric	Chapter 6
120.	B	Composition and Rhetoric	Chapter 6

1. B. Keats, Shelley, and Byron are all Romantic period authors in British literary history.

2. D. This excerpt is from the first stanza of Robert Frost's famous poem "The Road Not Taken."

3. C. This excerpt is an example of a five-line stanza, so you can rule out choice A immediately because it is not written in couplets. The rhyme scheme is abaab, so choices B, C, and D are viable options. Next, you have to identify the metrical feet of the poem. An iambic metrical foot begins with an unstressed syllable followed by a stressed syllable. A trochaic metrical foot begins with a stressed syllable followed by an unstressed syllable. Each line of this excerpt begins with an unstressed syllable and contains five feet, indicating that choice C, iambic pentameter, is the credited response.

4. D. Graymalkin is the evil servant of the first witch. In this period, this creature was known as a "familiar," which is synonymous with "evil servant." The toad is the familiar to the second witch, and this creature's name is Paddock.

5. **A.** A heath or moor is a large expanse of land covered with low-growing shrubs such as heather and other varieties of evergreens.

6. **A.** The word *ere* in Elizabethan-period English means "before."

7. **B.** Iambic tetrameter is the versification of the poem "The Lady Shallot" by Alfred Lord Tennyson. A poem written in iambic tetrameter is written with an unstressed first syllable followed by a stressed second syllable, for a total of four feet.

8. **D.** Camelot is the setting of *Le Morte d'Arthur* by Malory and cues the reader to the allusion to this famous work from the Middle English period.

9. **D.** *Night* is a memoir written by Elie Wiesel that offers a firsthand account of the Jewish people's horrific ordeal and his miraculous escape from death during the Holocaust.

10. **B.** Of the choices given, *Night* can best be described as personal writing, a form of writing meant to express innermost thoughts, feelings, and responses.

11. **D.** The writing process is a recursive process in which the writer moves through the stages of writing in a unique sequence. The term *recursive* signifies that each writer's process is not linear—going directly from one prescribed stage to another—rather, the writing process is unique to each writer and is based on that writer's distinct needs.

12. **C.** Hughes' poem "Harlem" is commonly referred to as "Dream Deferred." In this poem, the dream that is deferred, or "put off," could be lost or destroyed. Lines such as "fester in the sun" and "stink like rotten meat" support this interpretation of the theme.

13. **A.** This poem uses the poetic form free verse, in which a poem contains lines with an irregular metrical pattern and line length.

14. **C.** Charles Dickens wrote during the Victorian period of British literary history, approximately 1840–1900. He is the author of many works, including *Great Expectations* and *Oliver Twist*.

15. **B.** The lottery referred to in Jackson's short story involves an annual event in which the citizens of the town select one member to be stoned to death.

16. **D.** A short story is a brief fictional prose that succinctly portrays a life event or experience.

17. **B.** The title "The Lottery" is ironic in that one thinks of a lottery as something that is won. In this lottery, the "winner" is the one chosen to die.

18. **D.** *The Legend of Sleepy Hollow,* a short story whose main character is Ichabod Crane, is about the legend of a headless horseman who lost his head to a cannonball and rides to find his lost head.

19. **A.** *Peyton Place* was written by Grace Metalious in 1957, not by Hawthorne.

20. **D.** Each of the selected lines from Anne Bradstreet's poem "To My Dear and Loving Husband" contains at least one example of alliteration—the repetition of initial consonant sounds (not necessarily the same letter).

21. **C.** The imagery of the tranquility of nightfall and Pip's not envisioning a shadow of another parting with Estella signifies his ability to let his loss of her love go and be at peace with the ending of their relationship.

22. **B.** Satis House is the mansion in which Estella lived her entire childhood with Miss Habersham, who preferred that no light enter the house.

23. **A.** The denouement of a literary work follows the events after the story's climax and serves as the conclusion. The word *denouement* is derived from the Old French term *denoer,* meaning "to untie."

24. **C.** The proper MLA citation of Dickens' *Great Expectations* is:

Dickens, Charles. <u>Great Expectations</u>. New York: Random House, 1907.

25. **B.** The proper APA citation of Dickens' *Great Expectations* is:

Dickens, C. (1907). *Great expectations*. New York: Random House.

26. D. "Sharded in black, like beetles" from Plath's poem "Old Ladies' Home" is the only set of lines that does not contain onomatopoeia—the use of sound words to suggest meaning.

27. A. *Hamlet* contains at least one play within a play, the primary of which is referred to in this passage. Hamlet invites actors to perform a play he has written, called *The Mousetrap,* that contains parallels to Claudius' marriage to Hamlet's mother and Claudius' murder of his brother, King Hamlet.

28. C. Claudius is the villainous man who plays many roles in Hamlet's life—uncle, stepfather, king, traitor, enemy—and is the intended audience of *The Mousetrap,* the play that Hamlet consigns to be performed at the castle in an effort to expose Claudius' evil acts.

29. B. The Declaration of Independence was first penned by Thomas Jefferson as a member of a committee with John Adams and Benjamin Franklin.

30. B. The meaning of the phrase "to dissolve the political bands which have connected them with another" is best paraphrased in choice B, to sever political ties with England.

31. B. The author respectfully sets a purpose for this declaration based on "a decent respect to the opinions of mankind." This rhetorical strategy persuades the reader to read on and respectfully consider this declaration.

32. D. This excerpt from *Gulliver's Travels* can best be described as prose in chronological sequence. The narrator tells the reader about his arrival in Lisbon, his welcoming at the Captain's home, and his efforts to be clothed properly and comfortably.

33. C. The term *suffer* is used often in *Gulliver's Travels* to express discomfort or trouble.

34. A. Jonathan Swift was born in 1667. *Gulliver's Travels* was first published anonymously in 1726.

35. D. The student's most important error is in comma usage. This issue should be the teacher's first priority; lessons on word choice and sentence construction could follow.

36. B. The words *read* and *read* are not homophones because they are not pronounced the same way. For example, consider the following sentences using *read* and *read:*

I *read* the newspaper yesterday.

I will *read* the newspaper tomorrow.

37. C. A rhetorical question is one that the speaker does not truly want answered.

38. C. African American English Vernacular (AAEV) has many features, including the pronunciation of two-syllable words that end in *-ng* as "weddin" for *wedding* or "nuffin" for *nothing*.

39. C. This quote uses parallel structure as a rhetorical device.

40. D. Lincoln, one of the United States' great orators, used repetition in this quote to make his point effectively.

41. A. Personification is a literary device in which nature, in this example, is represented as having human traits, such as "leans forward" and "offering you space."

42. A. Angelou uses the "rule of three" to bring together the three images in her poem—a rock, a river, and a tree.

43. B. The British Romantic period of literature was 1780–1840.

44. D. A sonnet is a lyric poem with a formal structure. Lyric poems are usually short and often personal.

45. A. This sonnet has 14 lines written in iambic pentameter, which means that each line has 14 syllables, with the stressed syllable or accent on every second syllable.

46. B. The Shakespearean sonnet's rhyme scheme is abab, cdcd, efef, gg, with three quatrains followed by a couplet.

47. D. This line from Tan's *The Joy Luck Club* contains a simile, which is a comparison using *like* or *as.*

48. C. The mother describes her daughter's wisdom as a bottomless pond. She then states that if you throw stones at the pond—meaning if you criticize, correct, or teach the daughter something—it sinks into a bottomless place. Furthermore, the "American ways" daughter's eyes do not reflect anything, meaning that she does not appear to learn or understand the subtleties that her mother is trying to teach her.

49. A. Traditional haiku poetry is made up of three lines containing 5, 7, and 5 syllables.

50. A. Clichés are phrases that are used so often that they lose their expressive power.

51. D. Hardy uses the metaphor of a book and its pages to convey the message of this poem, which is that this relationship is coming to an end.

52. B. Hardy repeats the word *truth* for emphasis and persuasion.

53. C. The allusion "man for all seasons" comes from Thomas More, the author of *Utopia,* who was sent to prison and executed. He was considered a man for all seasons for courageously holding firm to his beliefs.

54. C. The central conflict in *The Scarlet Letter* is best described as person versus society. Hester Prynne, the main character in the story, has a problem with an element of society; specifically, she has committed adultery and is forced to wear a scarlet letter on her dress at all times.

55. C. The author of *The Scarlet Letter* is Nathaniel Hawthorne, who completed this classic novel in 1850.

56. A. In the mid-1800s, a time of revolution in Europe, writers like Ibsen began to challenge the romantic traditions that were in vogue at the time. Ibsen, a writer from Norway, is credited with mastering and popularizing realist drama.

57. B. Nora is an immature, silly young woman at the opening of the play. By the end, she has grown into a serious, open-minded woman who rejects the traditional roles available to a woman during this time—housewife, mother, dependent.

58. C. This opening scene is from *The Importance of Being Earnest* by Oscar Wilde.

59. D. The metaphor "his face was a knife" is used in this passage to express the depth of the character's anger and his piercing stare.

60. A. *Things Fall Apart* takes place in Nigeria.

61. D. *Pygmalion* takes place in Great Britain.

62. B. Higgins' use of the term *Pharisaic* is best defined as hypocritically self-righteous. Higgins regrets his behavior toward the lower-class Flower Girl and offers her much of the change in his pocket as a sign of his repentance.

63. B. T. S. Eliot wrote his most famous poem, "The Waste Land," during the Modern Period, 1900–1945.

64. C. Personification is used to describe the month of April with human characteristics, such as cruelty and the ability to breed.

65. C. In this scene, Hamlet is despondent over his father's death and his mother's hasty marriage to his uncle. Hamlet uses the metaphor of an unweeded garden to compare his mother to an Eden ruined.

66. D. Hamlet is referring to his father, King Hamlet.

67. B. *Hamlet* is one of Shakespeare's great tragedies.

68. C. This excerpt from *Hamlet* uses an appeal to emotion to convey the author's message. We are to feel pity and empathy for Prince Hamlet.

69. D. This allusion to the mythical god of the sun as compared to a cowardly beast contrasts Old Hamlet and the new King Claudius.

70. D. The author of *Beowulf* is unknown.

71. A. Plato suggests that each person must do the work that fits his or her own strengths. For example, he goes on to say that philosophers rule, warriors fight, farmers produce, etc.

72. B. Rhetoric can be defined as the use of language in a persuasive or pleasing way.

73. C. This line from Clement C. Moore's *A Visit from Saint Nicholas* contains the simile "like a flash."

74. D. This limerick by Edward Lear is a humorous verse form of five anapestic lines with the rhyme scheme aabba.

75. C. J. D. Salinger is the author of *The Catcher in the Rye.*

76. B. *The Catcher in the Rye* was published in 1951 in the United States.

77. A. Prufrock's name is meant to elicit the image of a prude in a frock who is incapable of action, specifically to eat a peach in the presence of high-society women.

78. D. T. S. Eliot is the foremost poet who wrote in the Modernist style.

79. D. A discussion about seeking the truth in students' lives and personal experiences activates students' prior knowledge and experiences about the central theme of *Hamlet.*

80. C. *Faction*—a group of persons forming a cohesive, often contentious group—is the word least related to the Latin cognate *facilis,* which means "easy."

81. B. Correlative conjunctions are used only in pairs and include not only/but also, neither/nor, and either/or.

82. A. During a peer conference, students read their writing to hear their ideas aloud and receive feedback from an initial audience. This is an appropriate revision-stage activity in which students re-see their writing to potentially strengthen and change the piece.

83. B. A rubric is a writing scoring guide used to provide feedback to students and to help students assess their writing.

84. B. The proper MLA citation is choice B because it contains an underline for the book title and only the page number in parentheses since the author's name appears in the sentence.

85. A. *The Birthday Party* is one of Harold Pinter's most famous plays and contains an extended metaphor.

86. C. A malapropism is the unintentional misuse of a word that is confused with one that sounds similar. The commander's wife meant to say that the move was *imminent* (pending), not *eminent* (distinguished).

87. A. Anne Bradstreet's *The Tenth Muse Lately Sprung Up in America* was written in 1650.

88. D. Odysseus is the central character in the epic *The Odyssey.*

89. B. The denouement is the tying up of loose ends in a story, leading to the outcome or resolution.

90. A. W. E. B. DuBois effectively uses the rhetorical device of appeal to emotion to persuade the young schoolgirl not to give up and to attend to her studies.

91. A. In the 1960s, Atlanta was the place where racial tensions heated up and created change. Jackson makes an analogy to a crucible, a vessel made of materials that are resistant to heat for the purpose of mixing chemicals.

92. D. In this speech, Jackson is suggesting that the people move to higher ground, that of a common ground, in which all people build interpersonal relationships and understanding.

93. B. Jackson's reference to Jerusalem in the speech is meant to allude to the Bible and to appeal emotionally to the listener.

94. C. Jackson uses a rhetorical question, one that he does not actually want answered, to motivate his listeners and persuade them of the importance of his message.

95. D. In the omniscient point of view, the narrator is free to tell the story from any and all characters' perspectives.

96. A. A quintet contains a five-line stanza.

97. B. Orwell, a British author who wrote the novel *1984,* displays his use of diction by choosing such phrases as "lift-shaft."

98. C. BIG BROTHER IS WATCHING YOU is used as a rhetorical strategy to appeal to the reader's emotions.

99. A. George Orwell, a British author, wrote *1984* in 1948.

100. B. Steinbeck chose the setting of the 1930s Dust Bowl in the Midwestern United States for his novel *The Grapes of Wrath.*

101. D. The phrase "the last rains" evokes an image of the beginning of the Dust Bowl and the end of many farmers' livelihoods.

102. A. *Le Morte d'Arthur* was written in the Middle English period (1066–1550).

103. C. An English sonnet is traditionally written in iambic pentameter.

104. B. Elizabeth Barrett Browning wrote *Sonnets from the Portuguese,* a collection of 44 love sonnets to her husband, Robert Browning.

105. D. A parable is a story meant to teach a moral lesson. Hester Prynne's scarlet letter is meant to symbolize shame, but she integrates it into who she is, empowering her to find her own identity and inner strength.

106. B. Transcendentalist authors like Longfellow and Hawthorne were dedicated to the belief that the divine can be found everywhere.

107. A. Chaucer's *Canterbury Tales* is from the Middle English period of British literature.

108. C. *Death and Taxes* is perhaps the most famous collection of poetry by Dorothy Parker.

109. D. Hughes captured the beauty of African American English Vernacular through his authentic and careful use of idioms and dialect.

110. B. By deleting "playing the" and adding "lessons" after "piano," the sentence now contains proper parallelism.

111. A. The second sentence has a problem with the pronoun *he.* It is unclear to the reader whether Jimmy or Austin received recognition from the coach and teammates.

112. C. Sociolinguistics is the study of language as it relates to society, including class, race, and gender.

113. C. In the publication stage of the writing process, a writer is LEAST likely to use the Internet to search for writing ideas. This task is more likely to occur during the prewriting stage.

114. B. *Bartlett's Familiar Quotations* is the foremost print and online source of famous quotations.

115. A. "Dear Sir or Madam:" is an appropriate greeting in a business letter.

116. A. Listing writing topics is an excellent prewriting activity.

117. D. A euphemism is a polite way to discuss a topic that may bring about discomfort.

118. C. Concrete poetry emphasizes shape and visual effects to create meaning.

119. D. One meaning of the word *diction* is careful word choice to communicate effectively.

120. B. The emotional atmosphere created by the author is the mood of a literary work.

English Language, Literature, and Composition: Essays (0042)

This chapter includes one full-length practice test for the Praxis II: English Language, Literature, and Composition: Essays (0042) test. This practice test will give you a sense of the format of the test and help you determine which content areas you need to study. You also may want to practice your pacing while taking this full-length practice test. Remember, you will have a total of two hours to complete this test—approximately 30 minutes for each of the four essay questions.

After you complete the practice test, score your answers and use the explanations to assess content areas to study in Part II of this book. You may want to complete, or at least review, the full-length practice tests in Chapters 8, 10, 11, and 12 to help you determine further content areas to study. Even though these additional practice tests are written for other Praxis II: English Content Knowledge tests, the topics of the questions—Reading and Understanding Text, Language and Linguistics, Composition and Rhetoric, and Teaching English—remain virtually the same.

Ready? Find yourself a quiet place to work with no interruptions, get your pencils or pens ready, take a look at the clock, and begin your practice test.

Practice Test 0042

Essay I

Interpreting Literature: Poetry

Directions: Read the following poem, "To My Dear and Loving Husband" by Anne Bradstreet, carefully. Then discuss how Bradstreet uses metrics, alliteration, and parallelism in the poem. Be sure to cite at least THREE specific examples from the poem to support your points about Bradstreet's use of metrics, alliteration, and parallelism. Write your answer on a separate sheet of paper.

To My Dear and Loving Husband

If ever two were one, then surely we.
If ever man were loved by wife, then thee.
If ever wife was happy in a man,
Compare with me, ye women, if you can.
I prize thy love more than whole Mines of gold
Or all the riches that the East doth hold.
My love is such that rivers cannot quench,
Nor ought but love from thee, give recompense.
Thy love is such I can no way repay,
The heavens reward thee manifold, I pray.
Then while we live, in love let's so persevere
That when we live no more, we may live ever.

Essay II

Interpreting Literature: Prose

Directions: Read carefully the following excerpt from *Moby Dick* by Herman Melville. Then, in your own words, identify Melville's central idea in the passage and discuss how he uses characterization and symbolism to clarify his central idea. Write your answer on a separate sheet of paper.

CHAPTER 1

Loomings.

Call me Ishmael. Some years ago—never mind how long precisely—having little or no money in my purse, and nothing particular to interest me on shore, I thought I would sail about a little and see the watery part of the world. It is a way I have of driving off the spleen and regulating the circulation. Whenever I find myself growing grim about the mouth; whenever it is a damp, drizzly November in my soul; whenever I find myself involuntarily pausing before coffin warehouses, and bringing up the rear of every funeral I meet; and especially whenever my hypos get such an upper hand of me, that it requires a strong moral principle to prevent me from deliberately stepping into the street, and methodically knocking people's hats off—then, I account it high time to get to sea as soon as I can. This is my substitute for pistol and ball. With a philosophical flourish Cato throws himself upon his sword; I quietly take to the ship. There is nothing surprising in this. If they but knew it, almost all men in their degree, some time or other, cherish very nearly the same feelings towards the ocean with me.

Essay III

Issues in English: Understanding Literary Issues

Directions: Read the following excerpt from Booker T. Washington's *Up from Slavery: An Autobiography* carefully. In your own words, identify the author's main idea in the excerpt and show how that method of development and the prose style (sentence structure, word choice, and figurative language) clarify and support the author's main idea. Be sure to refer to specific points from the excerpt in your essay. Write your answer on a separate sheet of paper.

Excerpt from Chapter 3, "The Struggle for an Education"

One day, while at work in the coal-mine, I happened to overhear two miners talking about a great school for coloured people somewhere in Virginia. This was the first time that I had ever heard anything about any kind of school or college that was more pretentious than the little coloured school in our town.

In the darkness of the mine I noiselessly crept as close as I could to the two men who were talking. I heard one tell the other that not only was the school established for the members of any race, but the opportunities that it provided by which poor but worthy students could work out all or a part of the cost of a board, and at the same time be taught some trade or industry.

As they went on describing the school, it seemed to me that it must be the greatest place on earth, and not even Heaven presented more attractions for me at that time than did the Hampton Normal and Agricultural Institute in Virginia, about which these men were talking. I resolved at once to go to that school, although I had no idea where it was, or how many miles away, or how I was going to reach it; I remembered only that I was on fire constantly with one ambition, and that was to go to Hampton. This thought was with me day and night.

After hearing of the Hampton Institute, I continued to work for a few months longer in the coal-mine. While at work there, I heard of a vacant position in the household of General Lewis Ruffner, the owner of the salt-furnace and coal-mine. Mrs. Viola Ruffner, the wife of General Ruffner, was a "Yankee" woman from Vermont. Mrs. Ruffner had a reputation all through the vicinity for being very strict with her servants, and especially with the boys who tried to serve her. Few of them remained with her more than two or three weeks. They all left with the same excuse: she was too strict. I decided, however, that I would rather try Mrs. Ruffner's house than remain in the coal-mine, and so my mother applied to her for the vacant position. I was hired at a salary of $5 per month.

I had heard so much about Mrs. Ruffner's severity that I was almost afraid to see her, and trembled when I went into her presence. I had not lived with her many weeks, however, before I began to understand her. I soon began to learn that, first of all, she wanted everything kept clean about her, that she wanted things done promptly and systematically, and that at the bottom of everything she wanted absolute honesty and frankness. Nothing must be sloven or slipshod; every door, every fence, must be kept in repair.

I cannot now recall how long I lived with Mrs. Ruffner before going to Hampton, but I think it must have been a year and a half. At any rate, I here repeat what I have said more than once before, that the lessons that I learned in the home of Mrs. Ruffner were as valuable to me as any education I have ever gotten anywhere else. Even to this day I never see bits of paper scattered around a house or in the street that I do not want to pick them up at once. I never see a filthy yard that I do not want to clean it, a paling off of a fence that I do not want to put it on, an unpainted or unwhitewashed house that I do not want to pain or whitewash it, or a button off one's clothes, or a grease-spot on them or on a floor, that I do not want to call attention to it.

GO ON TO THE NEXT PAGE

Essay IV

Issues in English: Literary Issues and Literary Texts

Directions: A writer's characterization depicts the main character's move from powerlessness to inner strength and personal growth. Choose TWO works from the list below and then write a well-organized essay in which you SUPPORT the statement above. Be sure to develop your thesis using specific references to the elements of the two works you choose (e.g., point of view, theme, plot, character, style). Write your answer on a separate sheet of paper.

- Mark Twain's *The Adventures of Huckleberry Finn*
- Toni Morrison's *Beloved*
- Alice Walker's *The Color Purple*
- Michael Ondaatje's *The English Patient*
- Piri Thomas' *Down These Mean Streets*
- Zora Neale Hurston's *Their Eyes Were Watching God*

Answers and Explanations

Essay I

Here is an example of an essay that could be scored as a 3:

Anne Bradstreet, an American Puritan period poet, effectively uses alliteration, parallelism, and metrics in her poem "To My Dear and Loving Husband" to convey her message of love for her husband. In this poem, Bradstreet writes about the depth of her love for her husband in a time in which women were required not to show their emotions outwardly, to dress conservatively, and to repress urges of pleasure and passion. It is within this context that Bradstreet's poem is analyzed.

Throughout the poem, Bradstreet uses alliteration to develop an upbeat sense of musical rhythm. Examples of alliteration include then/thee, while/we, and live/love/let's. Each of these alliterative pairs invites the reader into the poet's heart as she writes about her life and her love, and implores her husband to "let us" continue to love for the remainder of their lives. Bradstreet uses parallelism in the opening of the poem to entice and to challenge the reader to compare the depth of her love for her husband with the love in "ye women['s]" life. The first three lines of the poem begin with "if ever" and build to a challenge for other women to compare their love with the poet's:

> If ever two were one, then surely we.
> If ever man were lov'd by wife, then thee.
> If ever wife was happy in a man,
> Compare with me, ye women, if you can.

The love that Bradstreet holds for her husband is more prized "than whole Mines of gold" and "all the riches that the East doth hold." In this heroic couplet, the poet posits that her love is more valuable than gold or all of the riches of the Far East. She also uses parallelism in the final couplet of the poem in which she repeats the words "we live." She closes with a challenge to her husband—to live and love so deeply that when they die their love will live on forever. The heroic couplets, which contain end rhyme and are written in iambic pentameter, provide a sense of rhythmic joy and celebration of this great love. In summary, Anne Bradstreet is defiantly disobeying the norms of her Puritan time and sharing her heartfelt passion and love for her "dear and loving husband."

Essay II

Here is an example of an essay that could be scored as a 3:

Melville opens <u>Moby Dick</u> with what has become one of the most recognizable and famous lines in American literature—"Call me Ishmael." His use of characterization and symbolism in this passage, and throughout the work, convey his central message. Ishmael is Everyman, a simple man and an observer, who will narrate the story as a subordinate character. Ishmael appeals to all people and states that "almost all men in their degree, some time or other, cherish nearly the same feelings towards the ocean with me." The reader learns that Ishmael turns to the sea when he finds himself "growing grim about the mouth" or considering his mortality or angrily lashing out at people. Ishmael uses the sea as a place to re-center himself and to reflect, as so many people do.

<u>Moby Dick</u> is a novel that has allegorical features—there is both a literal level of meaning and a deeper, inferential meaning. Specifically in this passage, Melville uses references to the Bible and to a Roman politician and philosopher. "Call me Ishmael" evokes an image of the biblical Ishmael, the son of Abraham who is cast out after the birth of Isaac. Ishmael casts out to the sea at every opportunity. Melville also refers to the Roman politician and philosopher Cato the Younger, who was a violent opponent to Julius Caesar and who attempted suicide by thrusting a sword in his belly. Ishmael states that "Cato throws himself upon his sword," whereas Ishmael quietly goes to sea in times of trouble. The reader is led to infer that these biblical and historical images will provide a deeper understanding of the central themes Melville has planned in <u>Moby Dick</u>.

Essay III

Here is an example of an essay that could be scored as a 3:

Booker T. Washington writes persuasively and passionately about his ambition to overcome poverty by obtaining an education in this excerpt from "The Struggle for an Education." The author's main idea is that his most valuable lessons learned were not found in the halls of Hampton Normal and Agricultural Institute, but were acquired in a most unlikely place—the home of Mrs. Ruffner, a "Yankee" woman from Vermont and the wife of the coalmine owner.

In the first three paragraphs, the reader learns that Booker, who works in a coalmine, strives to escape from his life of poverty by obtaining an education at Hampton, a school the author refers to as the place that "must be the greatest place on earth." To show the depth of his passion and his perseverance, the author compares Hampton to heaven and metaphorically states that "I was on fire constantly with one ambition, and that was to go to Hampton." The reader senses that Booker must have achieved his goal based on his adept use of language, employing words and phrases such as "pretentious" and "noiselessly crept," although at this point in the essay's development, we are left to wonder and imagine how Booker achieved this goal with so many roadblocks before him.

In the final three paragraphs of the excerpt, the reader learns that Booker does indeed achieve his goal for an education at Hampton; although, ironically, he learns his most valuable lessons in the home of the coalmine owner's wife, Mrs. Ruffner. The depth of Booker's inner strength and ambition is revealed in his risky decision to leave his position in the coalmine to work in the home of a "master" so strict and severe that "few remained with her for more than two weeks." The author not only remains in this position for approximately a year and a half, but also learns that hard work, attention to detail, and promptness pay off in his studies and in life. This excerpt demonstrates the author's main point that formal education is an important goal to achieve, but life's most valuable lessons are learned in the everyday, practical interactions we experience through hard work and perserverance.

Essay IV

Here is an example of an essay that could be scored as a 3:

In Hurston's Their Eyes Were Watching God and Walker's The Color Purple, the main characters, Janie and Celie, respectively, are introduced to the reader as powerless African American women in very difficult circumstances whose journeys in life lead them to find inner strength and personal growth. In this essay, I will offer specific comparisons of characterization, theme, and story elements to support the statement above.

The main characters in both novels share several character traits that lead them to find themselves as women of strength, dignity, and worthiness. Janie is introduced to the reader as a 16-year-old African American girl living in Eatonville, Florida. She is raised by her nanny to believe that she is a very special person, although Janie's biological mother was the product of rape by a white slave master. The small-town community in which they live shuns Janie because she appears to think she's better than other schoolgirls and women; she has light brown skin and braided long hair, and she is better dressed than other girls her age. Janie is given away to marry a potato farmer many years older than her. Celie is introduced to the reader as a 14-year-old African American girl living in Macon County, Georgia. Her mother has died, and she is forced to care for her younger siblings and to tolerate being raped by a man she calls Pa, although we learn later in the novel that he is not her biological father. Celie is described as homely and is given away to marry a man Celie refers to only as Mr. _____ until much later in the novel. Both young women begin their lives in loveless marriages and view themselves as powerless at the start of each novel.

Two themes The Color Purple and Their Eyes Were Watching God share involve God and independence. In both novels, God appears to be viewed by Janie and Celie as a higher power who represents life and love. Hurston's title Their Eyes Were Watching God seems to refer to Janie's lifelong pursuit for love and fulfillment. While Janie develops from a powerless young girl to a woman blessed with love and happiness, she is reminded that her God is the higher power who controls her love and happiness. This is evident when Janie's true love, Tea Cake, dies in a hurricane, a force of nature. The Color Purple is written in the form of a series of letters, many of which are addressed to God. In Celie's view, God is identified in nature—in the color purple, in the trees, in everything. Celie finds true happiness as she develops from a powerless young girl to a woman secure in her existence within the world.

Finally, each author uses the story elements dialect and figurative language to help the reader see the main character's journey from powerlessness to inner strength and personal growth. Dialect is used in each novel to make each character come to life. In Their Eyes Were Watching God, Hurston captures the various subdialects of the people of Eatonville with notable expertise and accuracy. The dialects of the "porch sitters," the migrant workers, and the townspeople of Eatonville capture the nuances of oral communication by these people and suggest the social stratification in this small town. In The Color Purple, Walker uses Southern African American dialect to help the reader imagine Celie as a real, honest, and endearing woman. Near the end of the novel, Celie has grown to be secure with herself and comes to realize that she is content in her life. Walker uses dialect to describe Shug when she returns to live with Celie as looking like a "moving star." This use of dialect and misuse of the term "movie star" is endearing, real, and ironic. Celie probably does view Shug as a heavenly object and a gift from God.

In conclusion, in Zora Neale Hurston's Their Eyes Were Watching God and Alice Walker's The Color Purple, the authors show the main characters' journeys from desperate circumstances filled with powerlessness to fulfilled lives replete with personal empowerment and mature growth.

English Language, Literature, and Composition: Pedagogy (0043)

This chapter includes one full-length practice test for the Praxis II: English Language, Literature, and Composition: Pedagogy (0043) test. This practice test will give you a sense of the format of the test and help you determine which content areas you need to study. You also may want to practice your pacing while taking this full-length practice test. Remember, you will have a total of one hour to answer two constructed-response questions. Each constructed response represents half of your test score.

After you complete the practice test, review your answers and use the sample responses to assess content areas to study in Part II of this book. You may want to complete, or at least review, the full-length practice tests in Chapters 8, 9, 11, and 12 to determine further content areas to study. Even though these additional practice tests are written for other English Content Knowledge tests, the topics of the questions—Teaching Literature and Responding to Student Writing—overlap with the content categories discussed throughout this book.

You've read many great works of literature, you've critically analyzed literature in many courses, and you've studied the constructed-response format (see Chapter 1) and the content (see Chapters 4–7) in this book. You're ready to practice for the actual exam! Find a place to work for one hour with no interruptions, take a look at your watch, pick up your pen, and begin.

Practice Test 0043

Constructed Response I: Teaching Literature

Directions: This constructed response presents a list of literary works commonly taught at the secondary level and asks you to respond to a three-part question. You are to write a short answer for each of the three parts. Be sure to answer all parts of the question. Write your answers on a separate sheet of paper.

Assume you are teaching literature to an 11th-grade class. Your overall goal is to help your students recognize and understand key literary features of the works they read. Your choices of literary works to use as parts of this unit are the following:

- Nathaniel Hawthorne, *The Scarlet Letter*
- Joseph Heller, *Catch-22*
- Arthur Miller, *The Crucible*
- Kurt Vonnegut, *Slaughterhouse Five*
- William Shakespeare, *Hamlet*

Choose ONE of the works listed above. Select a work that you know well enough to identify and cite examples of its key literary features. For example, you may identify and cite examples of specific characterization and narration methods, characteristics of the genre or subgenre, specific literary devices, or specific poetic techniques. Once you have chosen ONE of the literary works, answer the following three-part question.

1. Identify and describe TWO literary features key to the work that you have chosen for your 11th-grade literature unit. In your response:
   - Be specific about what you want your students to know about each literary feature.
   - Include specific examples from the literary work that are relevant to each feature.
   - Describe how knowledge of these literary features is appropriate to teach in an 11th-grade classroom.

2. Identify and describe TWO challenges to understanding this work that you anticipate your 11th-grade students might have. In your response:

   ■ Explain why each challenging aspect of this text is likely to cause trouble for 11th-grade students.

   ■ Include specific examples from the literary work that are relevant to each challenging aspect.

3. Describe TWO instructional activities that you would use to teach this literary work to your 11th-grade English students. Be sure to incorporate either the literary features you described in part 1 or the challenging aspects you described in part 2. In your response:

   ■ Offer clear, well-formulated activities that actively involve students.

   ■ Explain how each activity helps students understand the literary features (from part 1) and/or the challenging aspect of the work (from part 2).

   ■ Describe activities that are appropriate for 11th-grade students.

Constructed Response II: Responding to Student Writing

Directions: This constructed response asks you to read an authentic piece of student writing and then assess its strengths and weaknesses, identify errors in conventions of standard written English, and design a follow-up assignment that addresses those strengths and weaknesses. You are to write a short answer for each of the four parts of the question. Be sure to answer all parts of the question. Write your answers on a separate sheet of paper.

In this exercise, you will answer questions about a student's writing sample. Some questions will ask about "strengths," "weaknesses," and "errors in conventions of standard written English." Below are examples of how these terms should be understood for the purpose of this test question. You may find it helpful to refer to these examples when you write your constructed response, although you may introduce your own examples.

Examples of strengths and weaknesses in writing:

■ Sense of voice

■ Paragraph organization

■ Essay organization

■ Sentence variety and complexity

■ Sense of audience

Examples of errors in conventions of standard written English:

■ Misplaced semicolons or commas

■ Unparallel construction

■ Run-on sentences

■ Sentence fragments

■ Subject-verb agreement errors

■ Verb tense inconsistency

■ Pronoun/antecedent agreement errors

Question: A 12th-grade English class was assigned to write an essay examining characterization in *Hamlet* as depicted in the text and in two film versions of the play. What follows is a student response to this assignment. It is a final draft. Read this response carefully.

Claudius: The Character People Love to Hate

Like the world today the play <u>Hamlet</u> by William Shakespeare contains many different individuals who are portrayed and defined through their own personal characteristics. Hamlets uncle Claudius is the type of character that everyone loves to hate. He not only puts himself into deceitful situations but he also drags others into these situations with him. Claudius flaws are the characteristics that define his personality. He is conniving, arrogant, and un-
(5)   abashed through the entirety of the play. Though one of these characteristics alone would make a person out to be appalling, these three characteristics put together make Claudius into the absolute vile character and man that he is.

Claudius is a man of great power who has little to no respect for others. He is very smart, but he uses his intelligence for evil and in turn he is extremely conniving. From the beginning Claudius is weaving his web of lies and deceit. Throughout the play he is constantly using his intelligence to hatch devious and murderous plans against his
(10)   own family to better himself. In order to save himself from the truth that is about to be reveled, Claudius plots with Laertes to kill his own nephew Hamlet; he tells Laertes that,

"No place indeed should murder sanctuarize;/ Revenge should have no bounds. But, good Laertes,/ Will you do this? Keep close within your chamber./ Hamlet, returned, shall know you are come home./ We'll put on those shall praise your excellence/ And set a double varnish on the fame" (IV, vii,145-150).
(15)   Through his deceitful ways and constant scheming Claudius actions characterize him as conniving and as the type of man who just does not care about being that way.

While being conniving Claudius also portrays himself as being an extremely arrogant individual. Claudius murders, commits adultery, and lies all while acting as if there is nothing wrong with it. He feels no guilt, and even when he tries to confess his sins he cannot. "My words fly up, my thoughts remain below;/ Words without thoughts
(20)   never to heaven go" (III, iv, 101-102). He himself, states that even though his is praying for forgiveness his heart just is not there so the forgiveness is unwanted and unobtainable. He continually commits what most would see as crimes and they just do not seem to phase him. After his brother's funeral, his arrogance is seen through the comments he is making to his grieving nephew. Claudius plays off his brother's murder to Hamlet, as just the circle of life by saying, "But you must know your father lost a father./ That father lost, lost his" (I, ii, 92-93). Through this
(25)   he is basically telling Hamlet to get over it because everyone loses a father at some point. Claudius is unable to learn from his past because he blinds himself from seeing the error of his ways. This trait will ultimately lead to Claudius demise.

Though he is extremely sneaky Claudius is also unabashed. He has no problem just coming out and saying what is on his mind so that he can manipulate others into doing his dirty work. After Polonius is killed, Claudius taunts
(30)   his son Laertes by being extremely forward and manipulative in saying, "Laertes, was your father dear to you?/ Or are you like the painting of sorrow,/ A face without a heart?" (IV, vii, 122-124). By being so unabashed, he is able to convince Laertes to kill Hamlet to avenge his fathers death in order to prove that he truly loved him. Though being unabashed may be good in a few situations Claudius incorporates the trait into his everyday life so that he can control others around him and get away with the actions he takes to gain further power.
(35)   In the 2000 Ethan Hawke version of *Hamlet* there are similarities between the movie and the play in relation to the character, Claudius. In the movie Claudius is also portrayed as a snide, arrogant man who will do anything and everything to get what he wants and where he wants. I feel that this character was matched to the T, and the actor did a great job with all of the tough situations that come about. Though you are able to visualize the character while reading the play, the actor from the movie really brings Claudius to life, making it easier to comprehend the true
(40)   villain that he is. The scene in the movie where Claudius is telling Laertes how the murder would go down was one of the major similarities that stuck out to me. This scene plays a very important role in the story and I feel that even though the words were still the same, the actors and writers got the emotions behind the scene perfectly. If this scene had been played with less emotion it would not have worked and one of the main correlations from play to movie would have been lost.

GO ON TO THE NEXT PAGE

(45)   Though there were some great similarities between the play and the movie there were also a couple differences. In the play Claudius is violent towards Hamlet but instead of pursuing the violence himself he has others do it for him. However, in the movie Claudius takes a personal role in more of the violence against Hamlet, especially in the scene where they are in the laundry mat and he punches Hamlet. Even though this does not happen in the play it did add more to the fact that Claudius is ruthless and arrogant. Another difference came at the end where Gertrude

(50) drinks the poison and dies. In the play, Claudius seemed extremely upset, but in the movie he did not even seem phased by her death. I felt this was odd because the whole premise of the play is based on the fact that he killed his brother to gain the queen and the kingdom, yet in the movie when she dies he seems fine with it.

      Claudius is a character of many layers. Around every turn in the play there was another surprise surrounding his character that went along with his traits of being conniving, arrogant, and unabashed. He never seemed to change

(55) or grow making him susceptible to many enemies, even those in his own family. The characteristics of Claudius are not that uncommon among people but the fact that he has all three traits playing against him makes him a character that most love to hate.

4. Identify ONE significant strength (give specific examples and line references) and explain how this strength contributes to the paper's effectiveness. Do NOT discuss the student's ability to follow conventions of standard written English (e.g., grammar and punctuation) in your response.

5. Identify ONE significant weakness (give specific examples and line references) and explain how this weakness interferes with the paper's effectiveness. Do NOT discuss the student's ability to follow conventions of standard written English (e.g., grammar and punctuation) in your response.

6. Identify TWO specific errors in conventions of standard written English in the student's writing (quote from the narrative and give specific line references). For each error, identify the type of error that was made.

7. Based on this student's writing sample, describe ONE follow-up assignment you would give to help improve the student's writing ability. Explain how you would address the strength (from part 4) and/or the weakness (from part 5). Your follow-up assignment should NOT address errors in conventions of standard written English (e.g., grammar and punctuation).

Answers and Explanations

Constructed Response I

The following suggested responses would earn full credit:

1. <u>Hamlet</u> by William Shakespeare uses dramatic irony and imagery throughout the play to convey meaning in this tragedy about seeking truth. Each of these literary elements is important to help 11th-grade students gain deeper understanding of this rich and complex text. Dramatic irony—events in which the reader sees a character's errors, but the character does not—is certainly a hallmark of Shakespeare's genius. For example, Polonius hides behind the curtain in Queen Gertrude's bedroom to silently observe Hamlet's madness and to trap him. Instead, Polonius himself is silenced and trapped when Hamlet impulsively murders him when he hears something behind the bedroom curtain. A second example of dramatic irony occurs at the end of the play when Claudius adds poison to the goblet with the intent to use it on Hamlet if his first plan of attack—the rapier—is ineffective. Instead, Claudius' wife, Queen Gertrude, drinks from the goblet in a gesture of love and admiration for her son Hamlet. As a teacher, it is important to take the time to discuss examples of dramatic irony and ask the students to identify further examples of irony in the play.

   Shakespeare uses the imagery of a garden in several of his plays, including <u>Hamlet</u>. Early in the play, as Hamlet is grieving the death of his father and the hasty remarriage of his mother to his Uncle Claudius, Hamlet refers to his mother as an "unweeded garden." By saying this Hamlet is condemning his mother's lust and marriage so soon after the death of her husband and believes she is "rank and gross in nature." He is repulsed by and angry with her. Hamlet's love, Ophelia, is often associated with flowers in the play to symbolize her beauty, her virginity, and, in the end, her loss of sanity. Hamlet tells Ophelia "to get thee to a nunnery" in a scene filled with sexual innuendo and her "deflowering." As Ophelia loses her sanity and moves toward her ultimate suicide, she gives flowers, or her love, herself sexually, to counteract the loss of her ability to love her father and Hamlet. When Ophelia is found drowned in the river, she is surrounded by flowers. These examples of imagery embedded in the challenging language of Shakespeare's play <u>Hamlet</u> are essential elements to teach 11th-graders that they can read to enjoy the subtlety of language and can find their own examples of imagery in future readings of literary works.

2. Two challenges to 11th-graders' understanding of <u>Hamlet</u> include the Elizabethan Era language and the subtlety of the irony in the play. Shakespeare's English is complex for students to understand without guidance from the teacher at first. For example, in the opening of the play, in which the night watchmen call out, "Who's there," and another replies, "Stand and unfold yourself," a literal reader of the text might think that the request was to unfold yourself, such as stand up from a sitting position, or even more literally be stymied by how a person can be unfolded. In this example, the first meaning of the phrase "stand up and unfold yourself" is a request to identify yourself. On a deeper level, Shakespeare is setting the stage for the major theme of the play—seeking the truth. Clearly, many high school seniors may need the English teacher's support to find the first-level meaning and each of the deeper meanings one line of dialogue may contain in this play. Irony is a second challenge for many 11th-grade readers of <u>Hamlet</u>. Dramatic irony is often used to add comedic elements to the play and can be misinterpreted if taken figuratively. For example, in the scene in which Hamlet tells Ophelia "to get thee to a nunnery," he uses sexual innuendo to communicate his love for Ophelia and his need to protect her from the pain of what he is going through. Several lines are meant to be both humorous and serious. He really does want her to protect herself from him, but he also would love to have her for himself. Hamlet tells Ophelia to be "as chaste as ice," and if she must marry, then marry a fool, because wise men know what women will do to ruin them, referring to his mother's marriage.

3. One instructional activity to teach understanding of Elizabethan-era English is to preteach common words and their meanings (and perhaps multiple meanings) through a variety of approaches. First, to engage students, the teacher could lead a lesson on Shakespearean language insults and help students appropriately and humorously insult one another. Building on this vocabulary knowledge, the teacher would then begin a close reading of the text with the students and identify the meanings of words and phrases that present a challenge. These words and phrases could be added to a Shakespearean word wall around the room and in a personal dictionary that students keep with their <u>Hamlet</u> materials.

To teach irony, one instructional activity would be to have students act out scenes first with the literary meaning and then with the more subtle, ironic, and fuller meaning of the scene. Students could be divided into "figurative players," "dramatic irony players," and "the all-knowing audience." Each group could provide an interpretation of the current scene, and the teacher could facilitate the whole-class discussion of the scene. Each of these activities is appropriate for 11th-graders, as they actively engage students as young adult learners who can maturely and creatively interpret Shakespearean texts collaboratively.

Constructed Response II

The following suggested responses would earn full credit:

4. One strength of this student's essay is the description of Claudius' character traits in <u>Hamlet</u>. The essay opens with an introductory statement summarizing three main character traits of Claudius—conniving, arrogant, and unabashed. Then the student clearly offers examples of each character trait, specifically and accurately referring to the text. For example, in lines 18–21, the student author provides an example of Claudius' conniving nature and his inability to confess his sins. She cites the text, "My words fly up, my thoughts remain below," with citation and explanation after the quote. The student author transitions to the second character trait smoothly with the sentence, "Though he is extremely sneaky, Claudius is also unabashed" (line 28). She closes with a summary of the three character traits discussed in the essay and ends effectively with the conclusion, "The fact that he has all three traits playing against him makes him a character that most love to hate" (lines 56–57).

5. One significant weakness occurs in the discussion of the film version of <u>Hamlet</u>. While the student's discussion of Claudius' character traits as they are found in the text are detailed, text-specific, and accurate, the references to Claudius' character traits as found in the film version are vague and appear opinion-based. For example, the student writes in lines 37–38, "I feel this character was matched to a T, and the actor did a great job with all of the tough situations that come about." This statement does not provide a clear, specific example of one of the three character traits discussed so well earlier in the essay; rather, the student's recall appears vague, and her opinion about the casting of the actor in the film does not offer literary or film criticism about characterization.

6. One consistent error in conventions is comma usage. A second error is usage of the apostrophe to show possession. The student writer consistently omits a necessary comma after introductory phrases and clauses. For example, in line 15 she writes, "Through his deceitful ways and constant scheming Claudius actions characterize him as conniving . . . ," and in line 35 she writes "In the 2000 Ethan Hawke version of <u>Hamlet</u> there are similarities . . . ." In each example, the writer has omitted a comma after an introductory phrase. A second error in conventions is the student's omission of an apostrophe to show possession. In line 15, she omits an apostrophe after Claudius' name, "Through his deceitful ways and constant scheming, Claudius actions characterize him . . . ," and in lines 26–27 she states, "This trait will ultimately lead to Claudius demise." It is important to note that the student does use an apostrophe to show possession correctly in line 22, "After his brother's funeral . . . ."

7. Based on this student's writing sample, one follow-up assignment I would give to improve her writing ability would be to build on the strength of the structure, content, and literary analysis of the text and teach the student how to continue this high-quality work when citing nonprint texts, such as the 2000 Ethan Hawke version of <u>Hamlet</u>. To this end, I would offer her a viewing guide to take notes during repeat viewings of the film. For the first viewing, I would seek impressions similar to what she offered in this essay. For the second (or subsequent) viewing of the film, I would ask the student to return to particular scenes in which Claudius demonstrates his conniving, arrogant, and unabashed character. The student, the class, and I would discuss the similarities and differences of these traits as demonstrated in the film. I would ask the student writer to take careful notes on her viewing guide and cite the act and scene number using the text as a guide. Next, I would help the student organize her citations of the film examples within the existing structure of her essay. For example, in the second paragraph, I would suggest that the student add an example or two from the film to support or contrast her depiction of Claudius' conniving nature. After teaching this rhetorical technique, I would ask the student if she thinks this technique strengthens her essay, and if so I would suggest that she add specific film citations to paragraphs 3 and 4 and then suggest that she can now delete paragraphs 5 and 6. Her final paragraph 7 could remain as originally written because it is a strong conclusion paragraph. This guided instruction would support the student by replacing vague, opinion-based examples with rich, specific, nonprint text citations.

Teaching Foundations: English (0048)

This chapter includes one full-length practice test for the Praxis II: Teaching Foundations: English (0048) test. This practice test will give you a sense of the format of the test and help you determine which content areas you need to study. You also may want to practice your pacing while taking this full-length practice test. Remember, you will have a total of four hours to complete this test, which is made up of 50 multiple-choice questions and two constructed-response questions.

After you complete the practice test, score your answers and use the explanations to assess content areas to study in Part II of this book. You may want to complete, or at least review, the full-length practice tests in Chapters 8, 9, 10, and 12 to determine further content areas to study. Even though these additional practice tests are written for other English Content Knowledge tests, the broad topics of the questions—Reading and Understanding Text, Language and Linguistics, Composition and Rhetoric, and Teaching English—remain virtually the same.

Specifically, the Teaching Foundations: English test covers information from the following content categories: Human Development; Addressing Learning Differences and Special Needs; Working with English Learners; Reading Instruction; Assessment of Student Progress; Classroom Management Techniques; Teaching Methods in English, Middle/Junior High Level; and Teaching Methods in English, High School Level. You also must be familiar with the *Content Standards for California Public Schools* for grades 7–12.

It's time to set yourself up in a quiet place with no interruptions, get your pencils ready, take a look at the clock, and begin your practice test.

(Remove this sheet and use it to mark your answers to the multiple-choice questions.)

Answer Sheet

1 Ⓐ Ⓑ Ⓒ Ⓓ	21 Ⓐ Ⓑ Ⓒ Ⓓ	41 Ⓐ Ⓑ Ⓒ Ⓓ
2 Ⓐ Ⓑ Ⓒ Ⓓ	22 Ⓐ Ⓑ Ⓒ Ⓓ	42 Ⓐ Ⓑ Ⓒ Ⓓ
3 Ⓐ Ⓑ Ⓒ Ⓓ	23 Ⓐ Ⓑ Ⓒ Ⓓ	43 Ⓐ Ⓑ Ⓒ Ⓓ
4 Ⓐ Ⓑ Ⓒ Ⓓ	24 Ⓐ Ⓑ Ⓒ Ⓓ	44 Ⓐ Ⓑ Ⓒ Ⓓ
5 Ⓐ Ⓑ Ⓒ Ⓓ	25 Ⓐ Ⓑ Ⓒ Ⓓ	45 Ⓐ Ⓑ Ⓒ Ⓓ
6 Ⓐ Ⓑ Ⓒ Ⓓ	26 Ⓐ Ⓑ Ⓒ Ⓓ	46 Ⓐ Ⓑ Ⓒ Ⓓ
7 Ⓐ Ⓑ Ⓒ Ⓓ	27 Ⓐ Ⓑ Ⓒ Ⓓ	47 Ⓐ Ⓑ Ⓒ Ⓓ
8 Ⓐ Ⓑ Ⓒ Ⓓ	28 Ⓐ Ⓑ Ⓒ Ⓓ	48 Ⓐ Ⓑ Ⓒ Ⓓ
9 Ⓐ Ⓑ Ⓒ Ⓓ	29 Ⓐ Ⓑ Ⓒ Ⓓ	49 Ⓐ Ⓑ Ⓒ Ⓓ
10 Ⓐ Ⓑ Ⓒ Ⓓ	30 Ⓐ Ⓑ Ⓒ Ⓓ	50 Ⓐ Ⓑ Ⓒ Ⓓ
11 Ⓐ Ⓑ Ⓒ Ⓓ	31 Ⓐ Ⓑ Ⓒ Ⓓ	
12 Ⓐ Ⓑ Ⓒ Ⓓ	32 Ⓐ Ⓑ Ⓒ Ⓓ	
13 Ⓐ Ⓑ Ⓒ Ⓓ	33 Ⓐ Ⓑ Ⓒ Ⓓ	
14 Ⓐ Ⓑ Ⓒ Ⓓ	34 Ⓐ Ⓑ Ⓒ Ⓓ	
15 Ⓐ Ⓑ Ⓒ Ⓓ	35 Ⓐ Ⓑ Ⓒ Ⓓ	
16 Ⓐ Ⓑ Ⓒ Ⓓ	36 Ⓐ Ⓑ Ⓒ Ⓓ	
17 Ⓐ Ⓑ Ⓒ Ⓓ	37 Ⓐ Ⓑ Ⓒ Ⓓ	
18 Ⓐ Ⓑ Ⓒ Ⓓ	38 Ⓐ Ⓑ Ⓒ Ⓓ	
19 Ⓐ Ⓑ Ⓒ Ⓓ	39 Ⓐ Ⓑ Ⓒ Ⓓ	
20 Ⓐ Ⓑ Ⓒ Ⓓ	40 Ⓐ Ⓑ Ⓒ Ⓓ	

CUT HERE

Practice Test 0048

Multiple-Choice Questions

Directions: Each of the questions or statements below is followed by four possible answers or completions. Select the one that is best in each case. There are 50 multiple-choice questions in this part of the test.

1. According to Erikson's theory of human development, adolescents ages 12–18 work to resolve which of the following conflicts?

   A. Peers versus parents
   B. Identity versus role confusion
   C. Social versus academic
   D. Guilt versus isolation

2. Jimmy is a tenth-grader who enjoys basketball, music, and acting out skits from literature. If asked to work alone at his seat for an extended period, Jimmy often fidgets, gets up to sharpen his pencil, or turns to talk with a peer. Which of the following best describes Jimmy's learning style?

   A. Musical
   B. Visual
   C. Auditory
   D. Kinesthetic

3. Mr. LaBarbara believes that students need clear guidelines and expectations for homework. He does not allow any late homework, although he allows students to show him their homework the next day for no credit. For students who complete homework on time, he gives full credit. In addition, students who complete homework receive one extra-credit point for every five homework assignments completed. Which of the following principles of learning and teaching guides Mr. LaBarbara's practice?

   A. Intrinsic motivation
   B. Rewards
   C. Operant conditioning
   D. Structure

4. Mrs. Gagliardi and her 11th-grade English students enjoy their discussions of the King Arthur legend. Mrs. Gagliardi prefers to help her students come to their own interpretations of the text through open-ended questions and by exposing her students to a variety of viewpoints on the legend's meaning. Mrs. Gagliardi is using which of the following theories to guide her educational practice?

   A. Moral development
   B. Behaviorism
   C. Authoritarianism
   D. Constructivism

GO ON TO THE NEXT PAGE

145

5. Miss Cavallaro is a first-year teacher of tenth-grade English. She feels successful in her knowledge of content, her ability to plan lessons, and her interactions with colleagues. She has reflected on her instruction and realizes that her students frequently talk off task, especially during independent assignments. Which of the following suggestions would be most helpful to Miss Cavallaro in this situation?

    A. Give the teacher "look," create incentive systems, and provide individual help to students.
    B. Offer after-school help, give students detention, and speak individually with students.
    C. Create incentive systems, refer students to the principal's office, and use more wait time.
    D. Call the students' parents, initiate a special-education referral, and offer after-school help.

6. Which of the following theories espouses offering adequate support or scaffolding to enable students to perform challenging tasks with success?

    A. Social learning theory
    B. Behaviorist learning theory
    C. Motivation theory
    D. Classical theory

7. Pedro is a student who is new to the United States and just recently began to speak English. Spanish is his native language. Which of the following behaviors does a student often engage in when thought and new language acquisition first come together?

    A. Babbling
    B. Self-talk
    C. Simultaneous play
    D. Zone of proximal development

8. Mrs. Reynolds has asked her 11th-grade students to free-write in their journals for five minutes. Which of the following best describes this activity?

    A. Wait time
    B. Norm-referenced assessment
    C. Lecture
    D. All pupil response

9. Prior to assigning a short-story writing project, an English teacher can do which of the following to prepare the students for success?

    A. Proofread
    B. Revise
    C. Watch a film
    D. Prewrite

Questions 10–11 are based on the following excerpt from Jesse Jackson's speech to the Democratic National Convention on July 20, 1988.

. . . We meet tonight at the crossroads, a point of decision.

Shall we expand, be inclusive, find unity and power; or suffer division and impotence?

We come to Atlanta, the cradle of the old South, the crucible of the new South. Tonight, there is a sense of celebration, because we are moved, fundamentally moved from racial battlegrounds by law, to economic common ground. Tomorrow we will challenge to move to higher ground.

Common ground! Think of Jerusalem—the intersection where many trails met. A small village that became the birthplace of three great religions—Judaism, Christianity and Islam.

10. Which of the following best describes the rhetorical strategy Jackson uses in the line "Jerusalem—the intersection where the trails met"?

   A. Alliteration
   B. Allusion
   C. Prosidy
   D. Appeal to emotion

11. Jackson's line "Shall we expand, be inclusive, find unity and power; or suffer division and impotence?" is called which of the following?

   A. Allusion
   B. Personification
   C. Extended metaphor
   D. Rhetorical question

12. Which of the following is a type of story that includes people, things, or actions that represent an idea or generalization about life?

   A. Allegory
   B. Biography
   C. Ballad
   D. Analogy

13. Mrs. Wildes opens her lesson on *The Giver* with a series of questions that have no right or wrong answer. The questions are meant to inspire discussion and debate on issues related to themes in the novel. Which of the following is the name of this instructional technique?

   A. Anticipation guide
   B. Post-test
   C. Story map
   D. Concrete experience

14. Structure cues, also known as grapho-phonic cues, are being used in which of the following situations?

   A. Jimmy skips a difficult word in *The Adventures of Huckleberry Finn* to try to figure out its meaning.
   B. Matt reads a chapter of *The Iliad* and then summarizes what he's read.
   C. Tory sounds out the word *yisgadal* in *Night*.
   D. Jim comes upon a passage in the newspaper that is about basketball, a topic he knows a lot about.

GO ON TO THE NEXT PAGE

15. Which of the following types of assessment helps inform an English teacher's day-to-day instruction?

    A. Summative assessment
    B. Formative assessment
    C. Norm-referenced assessment
    D. Achievement assessment

16. Brian is a freshman in high school with Down's syndrome. He receives his English, mathematics, and science instruction in a self-contained special-education room. He attends regular classes with his grade-level peers for all other subjects, including physical education and lunch. Which of the following describes the instructional setting for Brian's educational programming?

    A. Self-contained classroom
    B. School-to-work program
    C. Private school setting
    D. Least restrictive environment

17. Maria is participating in a class taught entirely in English even though she has just moved to the United States from Central America. Her lessons are offered in simplified English so that she can learn both English and the academic content. Which of the following best describes the type of instruction Maria is receiving?

    A. Primary language not English instruction
    B. English immersion instruction
    C. English as a second language instruction
    D. Ebonics

18. Which of the following public laws mandates the regulation and formulation of Individualized Education Plans for students with identified learning differences?

    A. ADA
    B. NCLB
    C. Section 504 of the Rehabilitation Act
    D. P. L. 94-142

19. Which of the following provides a solid rationale for having "with-it-ness" during small-group work?

    A. The teacher is aware of students who are struggling or are off task.
    B. More students have time to think and respond.
    C. The teacher can focus on the small-group work.
    D. Fewer students have time to complete the work.

20. Mrs. McGuire assigns her students a portion of a chapter to read and respond to for homework. When the students return to class, they work in small groups with students who had read the remainder of the chapter. The students discuss and make sense of their reading. Which of the following is the name for this instructional strategy?

    A. Think-pair-share
    B. Student Teams Achievement Division
    C. Advance organizer
    D. Jigsaw

21. Melissa and Sarah are visual and auditory learners who show multiple intelligences in the verbal-linguistic and musical areas. Which of the following instructional resources would most likely meet their learning styles?

   A.   Whiteboard and markers
   B.   Books
   C.   Multimedia/technology
   D.   Art supplies

Questions 22–23 are based on the following scenario.

Ms. Salvatore is a special-education resource teacher who provides services identified with IEPs in Mrs. Kern's heterogeneously grouped seventh-grade English classroom. Mrs. Kern has just completed a lesson on *The Outsiders* and has asked her students to complete a character-analysis activity in small groups. Ms. Salvatore helps any student who needs the support but pays particular to the students identified as having special needs. One student, Shea, appears to be having difficulty getting along with the students in his group and quickly becomes angry. Shea has been diagnosed with an emotional problem and has a behavior intervention plan to support him.

22. Ms. Salvatore and Mrs. Kern work together in

   A.   An Individualized Education Plan
   B.   An inclusion program
   C.   A resource room
   D.   A self-contained room

23. Students with identified emotional problems usually benefit from which of the following supports?

   A.   Structured choices and a positive environment
   B.   Unlimited choices and a supportive environment
   C.   No-tolerance policies and a strict environment
   D.   Strict rules and self-contained classrooms

24. If a teacher wants to ask lower-level questions, which of the following types of questions from Bloom's taxonomy would she use?

   A.   Comprehension and discussion
   B.   Analysis and synthesis
   C.   Knowledge and literal
   D.   Open-ended and reflective

25. Josh's family situation—living with a single mother who is dependent on alcohol and drugs—makes it difficult for him to succeed in school. Josh is the provider for his family at the young age of 13, and he is the authoritative voice for his younger siblings. Josh helps his siblings complete homework; he fixes dinner; he organizes all the school papers and even signs permission slips. Josh has a difficult time in school when he is treated "like a baby" and is told what to do by teachers and other authority figures. Which of the following best describes Josh's difficulty in school?

   A.   Josh may have learning disabilities.
   B.   Josh may be experiencing a cultural mismatch between home and school.
   C.   Josh is from a minority ethnic group.
   D.   Josh has a behavior problem.

GO ON TO THE NEXT PAGE

26. Which of the following federal laws protects a student's rights and prohibits discrimination on the basis of disability?

    A. Section 504 of the Rehabilitation Act

    B. IEP

    C. Due Process Law

    D. Americans with Disabilities Act (ADA)

Questions 27–28 are based on the following passage.

Dee is a new student in Mrs. Meyer's ninth-grade English class. Mrs. Meyer learns from Dee's school records that she has recently moved to the United States from Cambodia and that her family speaks Vietnamese at home. Dee has been nearly silent in the classroom during this first month of school, and Mrs. Meyer would like to get to know Dee's literacy and educational needs better. Mrs. Meyer has three other students who speak both Vietnamese and English in her class this year and hopes that the students can help her teach Dee.

27. Which of the following best describes Dee's current language/literacy status?

    A. Primary language not English

    B. Alliterate

    C. Mentally handicapped

    D. Developmentally delayed

28. Which of the following strategies will best help Dee as she learns English in Mrs. Meyer's classroom?

    A. Conduct whole-group discussions and hope that Dee learns English.

    B. Provide Dee with a hall pass to meet with the librarian to find books she can read.

    C. Give Dee the opportunity to talk with peers in small groups.

    D. Send home notes to Dee's parents to help them understand how important it is for Dee to learn English.

29. Mrs. Josephson is a ninth-grade English teacher who is teaching her nonfluent students of English to understand a short story. Which of the following approaches would be LEAST effective for Mrs. Josephson's students?

    A. Have students take turns repeat-reading in pairs.

    B. Have students take turns reading aloud passages from the short story to the whole class.

    C. Have students ask preview-and-predict questions prior to reading silently.

    D. Have students work in cooperative learning groups to read the short story.

30. Mrs. Dougherty has several students in her class who are English language learners. She strives to teach English at an appropriate level for her students, and she teaches in English between 70 and 90 percent of the time. Which of the following describes the program Mrs. Dougherty uses?

    A. Ebonics

    B. Structured English immersion

    C. Phonics approach

    D. Total physical approach

31. Which of the following instructional strategies is most likely to benefit an English language learner?

   I. Preteach vocabulary.

   II. Provide an overview of the lesson prior to instruction.

   III. Assign silent reading followed by a chapter test.

   IV. Allow time for small-group discussion.

   A. I, II, III
   B. I, II, IV
   C. I
   D. I, III

32. Miss Ellsworth is teaching *A Separate Peace* to her tenth-grade students in a diverse urban high school. Several of her students are recent immigrants to the United States and speak more than one language. *A Separate Peace* is set in New England during World War II, and Miss Ellsworth is concerned that all of her students may not be familiar with the cultural context of the work. Which of the following openings to the lesson would be most effective for all of Miss Ellsworth's students?

   A. Who can tell us about World War II?
   B. How many of you have read *A Separate Peace* before?
   C. The next book we'll read is about Phineas and Gene, who are attending a boys' boarding school in New England. Have any of you been to New England or to a boarding school? What do you think it is like?
   D. The next book we'll read is about conflict. We all experience conflict in our lives—such as arguments with siblings and friends or larger conflicts such as war. Think about a small or large conflict you have experienced and then turn to your partner and discuss your conflict.

33. Nishita is a gifted 12th-grader who accurately and thoroughly completes her assignments 30 minutes earlier than her peers. Recently, Nishita appears bored with her schoolwork and is spending time visiting with classmates while they are trying to complete their work. Nishita also has started to forget to hand in her classwork. Which of the following instructional strategies may be most helpful to Nishita?

   A. Cooperative learning
   B. Jigsaw
   C. Curriculum compacting
   D. Curriculum chunking

34. Mrs. Horton is teaching a reading lesson to her tenth-grade students. She has already discussed the story's structure. Next, she would like her students to identify the story's main characters, setting, and basic plot elements. Which of the following graphic organizers would be most helpful in Mrs. Horton's lesson?

   A. Story map
   B. Sequence chart
   C. Hierarchical array
   D. Venn diagram

35. Which of the following is an important comprehension strategy that involves teaching students to use a double-entry notebook or SQ3R to comprehend written materials that can be incorporated into lessons?

   A. Reinforcing and providing recognition
   B. Identifying similarities and differences
   C. Creating nonlinguistic representations
   D. Summarizing and note-taking

GO ON TO THE NEXT PAGE

36. A question to which a reader can find the answer by rereading and reviewing the text is known as a _____ question.

    A. Stop and think
    B. Right there
    C. Synthesis
    D. Rhetorical

37. Mrs. Manning strives to respond to the wide range of abilities of her eighth-grade learners by using methods such as tiered instruction and flexible grouping. Mrs. Manning is

    A. Directing instruction
    B. Sequencing instruction
    C. Differentiating instruction
    D. Demonstrating instruction

38. Which of the following activities is most likely to improve a student's reading fluency?

    A. Attending a community theater performance
    B. Performing a minor role in the school play
    C. Participating in readers' theater
    D. Participating in theater of the absurd

39. Which of the following types of writing are examples of workplace writing?

    A. Memos and friendly letters
    B. Journals and personal narratives
    C. Resumes and business letters
    D. Cover letters and editorials

40. Which of the following words is known as a portmanteau word?

    A. Fedora
    B. Gardening
    C. Basketball
    D. Ebonics

41. Effective classroom managers have a keen sense of awareness about all that is going on in the classroom simultaneously. Kounin calls this ability

    A. With-it-ness
    B. Perception
    C. Professionalism
    D. Behavior modification

42. One approach to classroom management centers on effective lesson planning as the best way to manage classroom behavior. The teacher begins the lesson with an anticipatory set to help the students connect their background knowledge and experiences with the new information in the lesson. Next, the teacher models and provides guided practice for the new information to be learned. At the close of the lesson, the teacher provides opportunities for independent and extended practice. This approach is known as

    A. Hunter's model
    B. Canter's model
    C. Glasser's model
    D. Jones's model

43. Mrs. Burt likes to have a friendly relationship with her students and brings a laissez-faire approach to classroom management. For example, she prefers that her students take charge of classroom procedures, and she allows them to go to the restroom, use the classroom telephone, or visit other teachers' classrooms whenever they want to. Between teaching lessons, Mrs. Burt uses the Internet to order from catalogs and check her e-mail while the students work on assignments. Based on this situation, which of the following is NOT a strength of Mrs. Burt's classroom management approach?

   A. Viewing diversity as positive and enriching

   B. Understanding her role as a classroom manager and leader

   C. Understanding her own culture

   D. Valuing the importance of empowering learners

44. Which of the following cooperative learning grouping practices involves an individual student completing his or her work and then teaming with another student to assess the work and discuss content?

   A. Group investigation

   B. Student-Team-Academic-Discussion

   C. Whole-group instruction

   D. Partner check

45. When Mr. Byrd's students act off task, he writes their names on the chalkboard as a warning. If a student continues to choose to misbehave, he assigns detention or sends the student to the discipline office. Which of the following theories of classroom management most likely guides Mr. Byrd's approach?

   A. Assertive discipline

   B. Choice theory

   C. Hunter's model

   D. Constructivism

46. Mrs. Munroe, a ninth-grade teacher, holds class meetings to discuss conflicts that arise in the classroom. She focuses on behaviors rather than students to help her students resolve conflicts. Her classroom management philosophy is based on which of the following theories?

   A. Canter's assertive discipline theory

   B. Glasser's control or choice theory

   C. Kounin's management plan theory

   D. Hunter's direct instruction theory

47. Prior to calling on students to respond to his questions about *Julius Caesar,* Mr. Haskell asks students to think, pair with other students to discuss ideas, and then raise hands to share responses. Mr. Haskell is using which of the following modifications to his lesson to help all students succeed?

   A. Inquiry, response, inquiry

   B. Hands-on experiences

   C. Direct instruction

   D. Cooperative learning

48. A teacher with a laissez-faire approach to classroom management

   A. Uses discussion to determine rules with students

   B. Uses rewards and punishments to change student behavior

   C. Establishes no rules and allows students to do what they want

   D. Establishes rules and allows students to do what they want

GO ON TO THE NEXT PAGE

49. A reading lesson plan that is organized with direct instruction, guided practice, and independent practice is likely to provide which of the following to students?

    A. Scaffolding

    B. Fluency instruction

    C. Grade-level expectations

    D. Vocabulary development

50. As part of the district's assessment plan, Miss Britton gives a criterion-referenced assessment to her 11th-graders at the end of her rhetoric unit. Which of the following types of information will Miss Britton most likely get from this assessment?

    A. Each student's grade-level equivalent as compared to other 11th-graders in the district

    B. Each student's attainment of the goals and objectives of the unit

    C. A better understanding of the students' attitudes about English

    D. Each student's percentile rank in English language arts performance on the rhetoric unit

Constructed Response I: Teaching Methods in English, Middle/Junior High Level

Directions: There are FOUR parts to this constructed-response question. Given the student learning goal and grade level indicated below, you are to develop an appropriate instructional sequence (i.e., lesson plan) and then analyze specific elements of your plan. The suggested amount of time for this question is 80 minutes.

Student learning goal: Analyze the differences in structure and purpose between various categories of informational materials (e.g., textbooks and newspapers) (Grade 7, Reading Comprehension 2.1).

Grade level: Grade 7

The class is made up of 26 students: 16 boys and 10 girls.

Part 1: Instructional sequence

Describe a lesson plan that you would use to help students meet the student learning goal stated above. You can use a bulleted list or outline form. Be certain that the content and instructional approaches you suggest are appropriate for the stated grade level. Your instructional sequence can be structured for a single class day or for a span of a few days. In your lesson plan:

- Include one group activity that requires active student participation.

- Identify one reading skill or strategy that students must use to be successful in the lesson, and include an activity in your lesson plan to help students improve this reading strategy or skill.

- Include three assessment activities: 1) prior to instruction, 2) during instruction, and 3) after instruction to evaluate whether students achieved the learning goal.

Part 2: Group activity

Describe ONE of the group activities from your lesson plan. Be sure to provide sufficient detail in your description and explain what the teacher will do, what the students will do, and why the activity contributes to the student learning goal.

Part 3: Strengthening reading abilities

Describe why you chose the reading skill or strategy included in your lesson plan. Be sure to explain why this reading strategy or skill is important to the students' achievement of the lesson goal and why your activity would be effective for improving the skill.

Part 4: Assessment

Describe ONE of the three assessment activities that you included in your lesson plan (prior to instruction, during instruction, and after instruction). Be sure to describe how the assessment would provide evidence of the degree to which the students have achieved the learning goal.

Constructed Response II: Teaching Methods in English, High School Level

Directions: There are FOUR parts to this constructed-response question. Given the student learning goal and grade level indicated below, you are to develop an appropriate instructional sequence (i.e., lesson plan) and then analyze specific elements of your plan. The suggested amount of time for this question is 80 minutes.

Student learning goal: Students will analyze characteristics of subgenres (e.g., satire, parody, allegory) that are used in poetry, novels, and short stories (Grades 11–12, Writing, 1.3).

Grade level: Grade 12

The class is made up of 30 students: 10 boys and 20 girls.

Part 1: Instructional sequence

Describe a lesson plan that you would use to help students meet the student learning goal stated above. You can use a bulleted list or outline form. Be certain that the content and instructional approaches you suggest are appropriate for the stated grade level. Your instructional sequence can be structured for a single class day or for a span of a few days. In your lesson plan:

- Include one group or participatory activity that requires active student participation.
- Identify one reading skill that students must use to be successful in the lesson, and include an activity in your lesson plan to help students improve this reading skill.
- Include three assessment activities: 1) prior to instruction, 2) during instruction, and 3) after instruction to evaluate whether students achieved the learning goal.

Part 2: Group or participatory activity

Describe ONE of the group activities from your lesson plan. Be sure to provide sufficient detail in your description and explain what the teacher will do, what the students will do, and why the activity contributes to the student learning goal.

Part 3: Strengthening writing abilities

Describe why you chose the reading skill included in your lesson plan. Be sure to explain why this reading skill is important to the students' achievement of the lesson goal and why your activity would be effective for improving the skill.

Part 4: Assessment

Describe ONE of the three assessment activities that you included in your lesson plan (prior to instruction, during instruction, after instruction). Be sure to describe how the assessment would provide evidence of the degree to which the students have achieved the learning goal.

Answers and Explanations

Multiple-Choice Questions

Answer Key			
Question	Answer	Content Category	Where to Get More Help
1.	B	Teaching English	Chapter 7, Human Development section
2.	D	Teaching English	Chapter 7, Human Development section
3.	C	Teaching English	Chapter 7, Human Development section
4.	D	Teaching English	Chapter 7, Human Development section
5.	A	Teaching English	Chapter 7, Human Development section
6.	A	Teaching English	Chapter 7, Human Development section
7.	B	Teaching English	Chapter 7, Human Development section
8.	D	Composition and Rhetoric	Chapter 6, Elements of Teaching Writing section
9.	D	Composition and Rhetoric	Chapter 6, Elements of Teaching Writing section
10.	B	Composition and Rhetoric	Chapter 6, Elements of Teaching Writing section
11.	D	Composition and Rhetoric	Chapter 6, Elements of Teaching Writing section
12.	C	Reading and Understanding Text	Chapter 4, Teaching Reading and Text Interpretation section
13.	A	Reading and Understanding Text	Chapter 4, Teaching Reading and Text Interpretation section
14.	C	Reading and Understanding Text	Chapter 4, Teaching Reading and Text Interpretation section
15.	B	Reading and Understanding Text	Chapter 4, Teaching Reading and Text Interpretation section
16.	D	Teaching English	Chapter 7, Addressing Learning Differences and Special Needs section

Question	Answer	Content Category	Where to Get More Help
17.	B	Teaching English	Chapter 7, Addressing Learning Differences and Special Needs section
18.	D	Teaching English	Chapter 7, Addressing Learning Differences and Special Needs section
19.	A	Teaching English	Chapter 7, Addressing Learning Differences and Special Needs section
20.	D	Teaching English	Chapter 7, Addressing Learning Differences and Special Needs section
21.	C	Teaching English	Chapter 7, Addressing Learning Differences and Special Needs section
22.	B	Teaching English	Chapter 7, Addressing Learning Differences and Special Needs section
23.	A	Teaching English	Chapter 7, Addressing Learning Differences and Special Needs section
24.	C	Teaching English	Chapter 7, Addressing Learning Differences and Special Needs section
25.	B	Language and Linguistics	Chapter 5, Principles of Language Acquisition and Development section
26.	D	Language and Linguistics	Chapter 5, Principles of Language Acquisition and Development section
27.	A	Language and Linguistics	Chapter 5, Principles of Language Acquisition and Development section
28.	C	Language and Linguistics	Chapter 5, Principles of Language Acquisition and Development section
29.	B	Language and Linguistics	Chapter 5, Principles of Language Acquisition and Development section
30.	B	Language and Linguistics	Chapter 5, Principles of Language Acquisition and Development section
31.	B	Language and Linguistics	Chapter 5, Principles of Language Acquisition and Development section
32.	D	Language and Linguistics	Chapter 5, Principles of Language Acquisition and Development section

(continued)

Question	Answer	Content Category	Where to Get More Help
		Answer Key *(continued)*	
33.	C	Reading and Understanding Text	Chapter 4, Teaching Reading and Text Interpretation section
34.	A	Reading and Understanding Text	Chapter 4, Teaching Reading and Text Interpretation section
35.	D	Reading and Understanding Text	Chapter 4, Teaching Reading and Text Interpretation section
36.	B	Reading and Understanding Text	Chapter 4, Teaching Reading and Text Interpretation section
37.	C	Reading and Understanding Text	Chapter 4, Teaching Reading and Text Interpretation section
38.	C	Reading and Understanding Text	Chapter 4, Teaching Reading and Text Interpretation section
39.	C	Reading and Understanding Text	Chapter 4, Teaching Reading and Text Interpretation section
40.	D	Reading and Understanding Text	Chapter 4, Teaching Reading and Text Interpretation section
41.	A	Teaching English	Chapter 7, Classroom Management Techniques section
42.	A	Teaching English	Chapter 7, Classroom Management Techniques section
43.	B	Teaching English	Chapter 7, Classroom Management Techniques section
44.	D	Teaching English	Chapter 7, Classroom Management Techniques section
45.	A	Teaching English	Chapter 7, Classroom Management Techniques section
46.	B	Teaching English	Chapter 7, Classroom Management Techniques section
47.	D	Teaching English	Chapter 7, Classroom Management Techniques section
48.	C	Teaching English	Chapter 7, Classroom Management Techniques section
49.	A	Reading and Understanding Text	Chapter 4, Teaching Reading and Text Interpretation section
50.	B	Teaching English	Chapter 7, Assessment of Student Progress section

1. **B.** According to Erikson's stages of human development, adolescents ages 12–18 work to resolve the conflict of identity versus role confusion. Adolescents consider the roles they play in the adult world and initially experience a sense of role confusion. Eventually, most adolescents achieve a sense of identity—a better understanding of who they are and how they can contribute to the adult world.

2. **D.** A kinesthetic learner learns by doing. Movement, interaction, and hands-on activities are a must for this type of learner.

3. **C.** Mr. LaBarbara's practice is guided by an understanding of Skinner's theory of operant conditioning. Operant conditioning is a form of learning in which a learning response increases in frequency when followed by reinforcement.

4. **D.** Constructivism is theoretical perspective on learning that suggests learners create or construct knowledge from their experiences. Rather than provide the interpretation of the literature, Mrs. Gagliardi fosters a sense of inquiry and helps her students discover their own meaning based on specific references to the text.

5. **A.** Miss Cavallaro should first attempt to handle this discipline problem within the classroom; therefore, choice A is the credited response. The teacher can first try to give a "look," or a stern glance; create incentive systems; and provide additional help. If these efforts fail, then Miss Cavallaro may want to seek outside supports for the classroom discipline problems she is experiencing.

6. **A.** Social learning theory focuses on the concept that people learn from observing others.

7. **B.** Self-talk is a behavior that students often engage in when thought and language first come together. Secondary teachers may see this behavior in students who are learning English for the first time.

8. **D.** A free-write is an activity that elicits all pupil response in that all students work simultaneously and have an equal opportunity to participate.

9. **D.** The prewriting stage of the writing process gives students an opportunity to brainstorm ideas for the short-story assignment with the teacher's guidance.

10. **B.** Jackson's reference to Jerusalem in the speech is meant to allude to the Bible and appeal emotionally to the listener.

11. **D.** Jackson uses a rhetorical question, one that he does not actually want answered, to motivate his listeners and persuade them of the importance of his message.

12. **C.** A ballad is a short poem composed of short verses intended to be sung or recited.

13. **A.** Mrs. Wildes uses an anticipation guide to open the lesson on *The Giver*. This short questionnaire prompts the students to debate and discuss issues related to the book prior to reading.

14. **C.** Structure cues are used when a student sounds out a word and uses visual and phonics cues to determine how to pronounce or read a word.

15. **B.** Formative assessment is used before or during instruction to inform instructional planning and enhance student achievement.

16. **D.** Brian is receiving instruction in his least restrictive environment. He needs a higher level of support in mathematics and science; therefore, he attends a self-contained classroom for these lessons. He does not need as much support in other subjects, so he attends those classes with his grade-level peers.

17. **B.** English immersion instruction consists of classroom discourse conducted in English only, even if students speak other languages. The teacher offers simplified English so that Maria can learn both English and the academic content.

18. **D.** Public Law 94-142 mandates that students with documented learning differences have Individualized Education Plans (IEP).

19. **A.** With-it-ness is a classroom strategy that teachers use to be aware of all that is happening while students are working (or not!). This strategy is particularly useful for students who may be struggling or off task. The teacher can intervene, reteach, or prompt students so that they are actively learning.

20. **D.** Jigsaw is a cooperative learning structure in which students are responsible for only a portion of a task and then work together with the students who have the remainder of the information. In this way, the task is "jigsawed."

21. **C.** Auditory and visual learners benefit from the use of such instructional resources as multimedia and technology. Students with verbal-linguistic and musical intelligences also are likely to learn well with multimedia resources.

22. **B.** An inclusion program for special-education students typically provides supports for students in as many general-education classes as possible, such as this scenario with Ms. Salvatore and Mrs. Kern's class. Usually, the special-education teacher works in the general-education teacher's classroom to provide supports to students with IEPs and offer expertise and assistance.

23. **A.** Students with emotional and/or behavioral problems usually respond well to structured choices and a positive, supportive classroom environment. The teacher must strive to maintain a balanced perspective about the student and focus on the student's efforts at self-control and self-discipline. Answer choices A, B, and C all suggest control and rigidity, which often result in an escalation of the student's emotional or behavioral issues rather than the more desirable de-escalation of behavior problems in the classroom.

24. **C.** Lower-level questions in Bloom's taxonomy include knowledge and literal questions.

25. **B.** Josh may be experiencing a cultural mismatch between home and school. At home, he is playing the role of an adult, being the caregiver for his mother and siblings. At school, he is required to switch to a more age-appropriate role, but one that is not a part of his cultural experiences.

26. **D.** The Americans with Disabilities Act prohibits discrimination against students on the basis of disability.

27. **A.** Based on the passage, Dee's language/literacy status is best described as primary language not English (PLNE). Mrs. Meyer can support Dee by building on her culture, supporting Dee's language/literacy proficiency in her primary language (Vietnamese), and offering opportunities for Dee to work in small groups. It is common for PLNE students to remain nearly silent in the classroom for several months until they gain proficiency in English.

28. **C.** Students who are learning a new language benefit from opportunities to speak in small groups with peers. Small groups give students more opportunities to interact and take risks with language when the whole class is not listening.

29. **B.** Students who are nonfluent in English can read silently and comprehend with some proficiency before they can read aloud proficiently; therefore, choice B is the least likely to be supportive for nonfluent English readers.

30. **B.** Structured English immersion programs emphasize instruction in English between 70 and 90 percent of the school day and prioritize teaching at the students' language level proficiency.

31. **B.** English language learners will benefit from all of the instructional strategies except silent reading followed by a chapter test. While silent reading is expected at some point, the reading should be accompanied by preteaching of vocabulary and key concepts.

32. **D.** Teachers of English language learners should be aware that many texts contain cultural contextual information that may need to be taught to students. Teachers can start with broad, universal concepts, such as conflict in this example, and then build on students' background knowledge to teach them the necessary background information.

33. **C.** Of the choices offered, Nishita would benefit most from curriculum compacting, or determining the key components of the curriculum that must be met and offering a compacted version of the work. Students like Nishita may become bored or even develop discipline problems when the work is not challenging.

34. **A.** A story map is the best graphic organizer to present information such as characters, plot, and setting, which are also known as story elements or story grammar. A sequence chart is best used to support instruction about the beginning, middle, and ending events in a story. A hierarchical array shows the relationship between a concept/term and its related elements, which are presented below the concept or term. A Venn diagram is best used to show the similarities and differences among elements in a story.

35. **D.** Summarizing and note-taking are essential instructional strategies that teach students to better comprehend materials.

36. **B.** "Right there" questions can be answered by rereading or reviewing the text. The reader can cite a portion of the text to support his or her response. This type of question is also known as a literal-level question on Bloom's taxonomy.

37. **C.** Tiered instruction and flexible grouping are instructional methods to differentiate instruction in which the teacher plans tasks of varying complexity, with the same high standards and content expectations for all learners.

38. **C.** Readers' theater is an instructional method in which students read and reread parts of a script to improve fluency, intonation, and expression.

39. **C.** Resumes and cover letters are workplace writing examples. Other examples include memos and job applications.

40. **D.** A portmanteau word is a word that has been melded together, such as Ebonics, which is a combination of *ebony* and *phonics*.

41. **A.** Kounin calls a teacher's ability to be aware of all that is going on in the classroom simultaneously "with-it-ness." Teacher with-it-ness helps minimize student misbehavior and safety problems and maximizes student learning.

42. **A.** Hunter's model is an approach to classroom management that centers on the teacher's planning for good lessons, not managing an individual child's behavior. Hunter's model lessons include an anticipatory set, modeling, guided practice, independent practice, and extended practice.

43. **B.** Mrs. Burt appears to be having difficulty enacting and understanding the importance of her role as a leader and classroom manager. While a laissez-faire approach is effective for some teachers, Mrs. Burt's attempts to befriend her students rather than teach them reveal her lack of professionalism and misguided priorities in the classroom.

44. **D.** Partner check is a cooperative learning grouping strategy in which students work individually to complete their work and then partner with peers to check the assigned work and review the content.

45. **A.** Canter and Canter's assertive discipline approach suggests that students have a choice to behave or misbehave. The teacher's role is to guide students toward positive behavior and offer consequences for poor choices.

46. **B.** Glasser's control theory suggests that teachers discuss behaviors, not students, in class meetings. In this constructivist approach, students listen to one another and arrive at compromises to resolve conflicts.

47. **D.** Cooperative learning instructional methods, such as think-pair-share, offer students opportunities to talk to one another and support one another's higher-level thinking.

48. **C.** There are three basic classroom management styles: authoritarian, laissez-faire, and authoritative. A teacher with a laissez-faire style of classroom management does not set rules or behavior expectations.

49. **A.** Scaffolding is an instructional technique introduced by Vygotsky. The teacher models how to approach a task, breaks complex assignments into smaller parts, and offers scaffolding, or support, for student learning. When a student is ready, the teacher provides independent practice.

50. **B.** A criterion-referenced test compares a student's knowledge, as demonstrated on the test, to the goals and objectives of the curriculum.

Constructed Response I: Teaching Methods in English, Middle/Junior High Level

The following response earned a score of 4 on a 4-point scale.

Part 1: This lesson plan is designed for seventh-grade learners' ability to understand and analyze the differences in structure between textbooks and newspapers.

Lesson instructional sequence:

Opening: Tell the students that they are going to be reading to learn from both realistic fiction and newspapers. Explain that this is an important reading skill because informational texts, such as newspapers, and narrative texts, such as realistic fiction, contain many interesting and important pieces of information, but they require different types of reading.

Project a current news article from the *New York Times* on a topic that is relevant to students, such as adolescents and eating disorders. Students will be assessed prior to instruction during this opening section of the lesson to determine whether they understand the structural elements of a news article, such headlines, bylines, and the five Ws—who, what, when, where, and why. The teacher will ask the students what makes the news article interesting and understandable and try to elicit students' prior knowledge of these structural differences.

Next, the teacher will read aloud a short passage from a realistic work of fiction, such as the novel *Stick Figure* by Lori Gottlieb. Ask the students to elaborate on the features of this climactic moment in the story and discuss how this text differs from the news article.

Proceed in a similar way, alternating the use of the novel and the newspaper, to help students identify and analyze the different structures and purposes of each.

Middle: Organize the students in small, heterogeneous groups to read one of four news articles. Have each member of the group become an "expert of the day" on finding the five Ws, headings, and bylines. Alternate this role each day to ensure that all students gain experience in identifying each structural element. The students first read independently, taking margin notes (using stick-on notes) on examples of structural elements. Then the students reconvene their small group to discuss, correct, or enrich understanding of today's reading. The teacher will conduct a "during reading" assessment by sitting in on small-group discussions and evaluating individual student participation and understanding. In addition, he or she will randomly collect student news articles to review their notes.

Closing: The class reconvenes as a group to discuss each of the four news articles, their purposes, and their structural elements. The teacher will summarize findings on a large, bulletin-board–size graphic organizer so that students can recall the purposes and structural differences of this informational text when they read independently.

The students continue with this sequence of activities until the story has been completed and all chapters have been charted on the graphic organizer. After the graphic organizer is complete, the students will work in their small groups to practice orally summarizing the plot of the literary work.

Follow-up activity: Students will read and identify the purpose and structural elements of a news article independently. This homework assignment will act as the summative assessment to determine whether each individual student has achieved the learning goal.

Part 2: As briefly stated in the lesson plan, the seventh-graders will work in small, cooperative groups to read and identify the structural elements and purposes of an informational text, such as a newspaper article. The students will take turns becoming the "expert of the day" in identifying examples of the key features of a news article. The students will be held individually accountable by having to write margin notes that the teacher will check randomly. In addition, the students will be individually accountable to the group and the class when the group reports to the whole class at the end of the lesson. The teacher will also sit in to assess each group's level of performance. The students will work simultaneously to read and identify the structural elements of a news article and then discuss their findings with the small group. This activity contributes to the students' achievement of the learning goal by requiring reading, writing, speaking, listening, and thinking as individuals and as group members. The cooperative nature of the group activity offers all students an opportunity to learn.

Part 3: The reading strategy—identifying and analyzing the structural elements of an informational text—was chosen because it is a real-life and important comprehension strategy that adolescents must practice and master. In addition, this reading strategy was chosen because it usually still needs to be *taught* to seventh-graders. The inclusion of an Internet news article to activate students' prior knowledge is designed to motivate and engage all adolescent readers to open them to examine more challenging and accessible informational texts.

Part 4: The assessment planned for the middle of the lesson occurs during reading and provides a formative assessment of the student learning goal. The teacher will observe the students' participation in their small, cooperative groups and evaluate each student's level of participation and accuracy of contributions. In addition, the teacher will randomly collect the students' news articles to review the margin notes on news article features more carefully, assessing students' individual contributions as well as their content knowledge. This assessment helps hold students individually accountable in the small groups, provides the students with ongoing feedback about their progress, and enables the teacher to plan for closing discussion questions and future lessons as needed.

Constructed Response II: Teaching Methods in English, High School Level

The following response earned a score of 4 on a 4-point scale.

Part 1: This lesson plan is designed for 12th-grade learners' ability to analyze the characteristics of subgenres such as satire and parody. In addition, students will support their ideas with relevant text citations and margin notes.

Lesson instructional sequence:

Opening: Explain real-life connections and the purpose for the lesson so that students understand why they are learning this literary response strategy. Tell the students that they are going to be laughing and smiling in class for the next few weeks—reading parodies and interpreting satire. They will find themselves "getting" the subtle humor in the literary work and enjoying reading all the more.

Next, invite the whole class to the auditorium to see a parody that the teachers have written and rehearsed. This parody takes place in the senior courtyard of the school and involves various student conversations typical of this senior class. After several laughs and time for discussion, the teacher will seek student prior knowledge (prior to instruction assessment) on parody and satire, or he or she will provide information as needed.

Middle: Next, the teacher will give a brief lecture in which students take notes on the definitions and key elements of satire or parody. Then the teacher will use the overhead projector to display an excerpt of a parody from Shakespeare and walk the students through an interpretation of this parody. The teacher will help the students see the layers of meaning and the plays on words used. Next, the teacher will ask the students to work in pairs to read selected literary works that contain parody and satire. The students will make margin notes and make specific text references to the parody or satire in the piece. The teacher will select literary works with humorous parody and satire with a 12th-grade reader in mind.

Closing: The class will reconvene and discuss the examples of humor in their literary works, citing specific examples from the texts.

Follow-up assignment: Students will analyze a short story for satire or parody independently. They will be graded on their margin notes and text citations that demonstrate satire or parody in the literary work.

Part 2: One of the group activities in this lesson is designed for students to work in pairs to identify and analyze the features of parody and satire. This activity contributes directly to the students' achievement of the learning goal by giving the students opportunities to discuss the layers of meaning in a literary work and identify the characteristics of a subgenre.

Part 3: The literary response reading skill chosen for this lesson involves analyzing the characteristics of a subgenre. During prereading, the students viewed a parody performed by the teachers to activate prior knowledge on this subgenre. Next, the teacher asked the students to work in pairs to identify and analyze the features of parody and satire. Next, the students were asked to read and analyze a literary work for parody and satire independently. This particular skill is especially important for high school seniors, who are ready for higher-level thinking and the complexities of parody and satire.

Part 4: One assessment in this literary response lesson plan for 12th-graders is an informal assessment of students' margin notes and text citations. This assignment was modeled in class, taught with guided practice, and individually assessed. Students who are successful at analyzing literary works for parody and satire demonstrate three or more accurate examples in the text based on specific text citations. Students who are not successful will review their work with the teacher and have one opportunity to submit an analysis of another literary work to demonstrate competency in this learning goal.

Middle School English Language Arts (0049)

This chapter includes one full-length practice test for the Praxis II: Middle School English Language Arts (0049) test. This practice test will give you a sense of the format of the test and help you determine which content areas you need to study. You also may want to practice your pacing while taking this full-length practice test. Remember, you will have a total of two hours to complete this test, which is made up of 90 multiple-choice questions and two constructed-response questions.

After you complete the practice test, score your answers and use the explanations to assess content areas to study in Part II of this book. You may want to complete, or at least review, the full-length practice tests in Chapters 8, 9, 10, and 11 to determine further content areas to study. Even though these additional practice tests are written for other English Content Knowledge tests, the broad content categories of the questions—Reading and Understanding Text, Language and Linguistics, and Composition and Rhetoric—remain virtually the same. Note that the Teaching English content is not assessed on this test.

Let's get started. Find a quiet place to work, check the clock before you begin, and try your best.

Answer Sheet

1 Ⓐ Ⓑ Ⓒ Ⓓ	31 Ⓐ Ⓑ Ⓒ Ⓓ	61 Ⓐ Ⓑ Ⓒ Ⓓ
2 Ⓐ Ⓑ Ⓒ Ⓓ	32 Ⓐ Ⓑ Ⓒ Ⓓ	62 Ⓐ Ⓑ Ⓒ Ⓓ
3 Ⓐ Ⓑ Ⓒ Ⓓ	33 Ⓐ Ⓑ Ⓒ Ⓓ	63 Ⓐ Ⓑ Ⓒ Ⓓ
4 Ⓐ Ⓑ Ⓒ Ⓓ	34 Ⓐ Ⓑ Ⓒ Ⓓ	64 Ⓐ Ⓑ Ⓒ Ⓓ
5 Ⓐ Ⓑ Ⓒ Ⓓ	35 Ⓐ Ⓑ Ⓒ Ⓓ	65 Ⓐ Ⓑ Ⓒ Ⓓ
6 Ⓐ Ⓑ Ⓒ Ⓓ	36 Ⓐ Ⓑ Ⓒ Ⓓ	66 Ⓐ Ⓑ Ⓒ Ⓓ
7 Ⓐ Ⓑ Ⓒ Ⓓ	37 Ⓐ Ⓑ Ⓒ Ⓓ	67 Ⓐ Ⓑ Ⓒ Ⓓ
8 Ⓐ Ⓑ Ⓒ Ⓓ	38 Ⓐ Ⓑ Ⓒ Ⓓ	68 Ⓐ Ⓑ Ⓒ Ⓓ
9 Ⓐ Ⓑ Ⓒ Ⓓ	39 Ⓐ Ⓑ Ⓒ Ⓓ	69 Ⓐ Ⓑ Ⓒ Ⓓ
10 Ⓐ Ⓑ Ⓒ Ⓓ	40 Ⓐ Ⓑ Ⓒ Ⓓ	70 Ⓐ Ⓑ Ⓒ Ⓓ
11 Ⓐ Ⓑ Ⓒ Ⓓ	41 Ⓐ Ⓑ Ⓒ Ⓓ	71 Ⓐ Ⓑ Ⓒ Ⓓ
12 Ⓐ Ⓑ Ⓒ Ⓓ	42 Ⓐ Ⓑ Ⓒ Ⓓ	72 Ⓐ Ⓑ Ⓒ Ⓓ
13 Ⓐ Ⓑ Ⓒ Ⓓ	43 Ⓐ Ⓑ Ⓒ Ⓓ	73 Ⓐ Ⓑ Ⓒ Ⓓ
14 Ⓐ Ⓑ Ⓒ Ⓓ	44 Ⓐ Ⓑ Ⓒ Ⓓ	74 Ⓐ Ⓑ Ⓒ Ⓓ
15 Ⓐ Ⓑ Ⓒ Ⓓ	45 Ⓐ Ⓑ Ⓒ Ⓓ	75 Ⓐ Ⓑ Ⓒ Ⓓ
16 Ⓐ Ⓑ Ⓒ Ⓓ	46 Ⓐ Ⓑ Ⓒ Ⓓ	76 Ⓐ Ⓑ Ⓒ Ⓓ
17 Ⓐ Ⓑ Ⓒ Ⓓ	47 Ⓐ Ⓑ Ⓒ Ⓓ	77 Ⓐ Ⓑ Ⓒ Ⓓ
18 Ⓐ Ⓓ Ⓒ Ⓓ	48 Ⓐ Ⓑ Ⓒ Ⓓ	78 Ⓐ Ⓑ Ⓒ Ⓓ
19 Ⓐ Ⓑ Ⓒ Ⓓ	49 Ⓐ Ⓑ Ⓒ Ⓓ	79 Ⓐ Ⓑ Ⓒ Ⓓ
20 Ⓐ Ⓑ Ⓒ Ⓓ	50 Ⓐ Ⓑ Ⓒ Ⓓ	80 Ⓐ Ⓑ Ⓒ Ⓓ
21 Ⓐ Ⓑ Ⓒ Ⓓ	51 Ⓐ Ⓑ Ⓒ Ⓓ	81 Ⓐ Ⓑ Ⓒ Ⓓ
22 Ⓐ Ⓑ Ⓒ Ⓓ	52 Ⓐ Ⓑ Ⓒ Ⓓ	82 Ⓐ Ⓑ Ⓒ Ⓓ
23 Ⓐ Ⓑ Ⓒ Ⓓ	53 Ⓐ Ⓑ Ⓒ Ⓓ	83 Ⓐ Ⓑ Ⓒ Ⓓ
24 Ⓐ Ⓑ Ⓒ Ⓓ	54 Ⓐ Ⓑ Ⓒ Ⓓ	84 Ⓐ Ⓑ Ⓒ Ⓓ
25 Ⓐ Ⓑ Ⓒ Ⓓ	55 Ⓐ Ⓑ Ⓒ Ⓓ	85 Ⓐ Ⓑ Ⓒ Ⓓ
26 Ⓐ Ⓑ Ⓒ Ⓓ	56 Ⓐ Ⓑ Ⓒ Ⓓ	86 Ⓐ Ⓑ Ⓒ Ⓓ
27 Ⓐ Ⓑ Ⓒ Ⓓ	57 Ⓐ Ⓑ Ⓒ Ⓓ	87 Ⓐ Ⓑ Ⓒ Ⓓ
28 Ⓐ Ⓑ Ⓒ Ⓓ	58 Ⓐ Ⓑ Ⓒ Ⓓ	88 Ⓐ Ⓑ Ⓒ Ⓓ
29 Ⓐ Ⓑ Ⓒ Ⓓ	59 Ⓐ Ⓑ Ⓒ Ⓓ	89 Ⓐ Ⓑ Ⓒ Ⓓ
30 Ⓐ Ⓓ Ⓒ Ⓓ	60 Ⓐ Ⓑ Ⓒ Ⓓ	90 Ⓐ Ⓑ Ⓒ Ⓓ

CUT HERE

Practice Test 0049

Multiple-Choice Questions

Directions: Each of the questions or statements below is followed by four possible answers or completions. Select the one that is best in each case. There are 90 multiple-choice questions in this part of the test.

1. Which of the following pairs of characters appears in Shakespeare's *A Midsummer Night's Dream*?

   A. Romeo and Juliet
   B. Hermia and Robin Goodfellow
   C. Caesar and Calpurnia
   D. Gertrude and Claudius

2. *The Giver, 1984,* and *The Lord of the Rings* can all be classified as belonging to which of the following genres?

   A. Realistic fiction
   B. Poetry
   C. Historical fiction
   D. Science fiction

3. The setting of *Fahrenheit 451* is_____.

   A. 1984
   B. The 21st century
   C. The 24th century
   D. The 1950s

Questions 4–5 are based on the following excerpt from Elie Wiesel's *Night*.

The door of the car slid aside. A German officer stepped in accompanied by a Hungarian lieutenant, acting as his interpreter.

"From this moment on, you are under the authority of the German Army. Anyone who still owns gold, silver or watches must hand them over now. Anyone who will be found to have kept any of these will be shot on the spot. Secondly, anyone who is ill should report to the hospital car. That's all."

The Hungarian lieutenant went around with a basket and retrieved the last possessions from those who chose not to go on tasting the bitterness of fear.

"There are eighty of you in the car," the German officer added. "Anyone who goes missing, you will all be shot, like dogs."

4. *Night* is written as a(n) _____.

   A. Documentary
   B. Elegy
   C. Biography
   D. Memoir

GO ON TO THE NEXT PAGE

5. Which of the following best describes the purpose or type of writing in the excerpt above?

    A. Personal writing

    B. Scholarly writing

    C. Persuasive writing

    D. Editorial writing

6. Tituba, a character in Arthur Miller's play *The Crucible,* says, "My Betty be hearty soon?" Which of the following best describes Tituba's use of language?

    A. Dialect

    B. Phonology

    C. Pragmatics

    D. Grammatical error

7. The following sentence is a _____ sentence.

I look forward to teaching, and I plan to teach middle school English because I love literature.

    A. Compound

    B. Compound/complex

    C. Complex

    D. Simple

8. Which of the following terms can be defined as using language persuasively or pleasingly?

    A. Personification

    B. Point of view

    C. Tone

    D. Rhetoric

9. Which of the following criteria should be used when evaluating Internet sources for a research paper?

    I. Author

    II. Accuracy

    III. Purpose of the site

    IV. Access

    A. I

    B. I, II

    C. I, II, IV

    D. All of the above

10. Which of the following correctly cites a source using MLA-format guidelines?

    A. Golding wrote in his opening line of Lord of the Flies, "The boy with fair hair lowered himself down the last few feet of rock and began to pick his way toward the lagoon" (7).

    B. Golding wrote in his opening line of Lord of the Flies, "The boy with fair hair lowered himself down the last few feet of rock and began to pick his way toward the lagoon" (7).

    C. Golding wrote in his opening line of Lord of the Flies, "The boy with fair hair lowered himself down the last few feet of rock and began to pick his way toward the lagoon" (Golding, 7).

    D. Golding wrote in his opening line of *Lord of the Flies*, "The boy with fair hair lowered himself down the last few feet of rock and began to pick his way toward the lagoon." (Golding, 7)

11. When a writer considers the _____ for a piece, he or she considers who else will read it and what background knowledge the reader might need to understand the point of the writing.

   A. Grade
   B. Publisher
   C. Location
   D. Audience

Questions 12–13 are based on Shakespeare's Sonnet 18.

Shall I compare thee to a summer's day?
Thou art more lovely and more temperate:
Rough winds do shake the darling buds of May,
And summer's lease hath all too short a date:
Sometime too hot the eye of heaven shines,
And often is his gold complexion dimmed,
And every fair from fair sometime declines,
By chance, or nature's changing course untrimmed:
But thy eternal summer shall not fade,
Nor lose possession of that fair thou ow'st,
Nor shall death brag thou wander'st in his shade,
When in eternal lines to time thou grow'st,
So long as men can breathe, or eyes can see,
So long lives this, and this gives life to thee.

12. Sonnet 18 is organized as a _____.

   A. Sequence
   B. Hierarchy
   C. Comparison
   D. Cause and effect

13. Prior to teaching Shakespeare's Sonnet 18 to her eighth-graders, Miss Judge asked her students open-ended questions about feelings evoked by summer and people they love. This prereading activity is called a(n) _____.

   A. Anticipation guide
   B. Pretest
   C. Brainstorm
   D. Graphic organizer

14. Prior to reading a news article about the 9/11 terrorist attacks, Miss Bell shows her students a replica of the World Trade Center that she saved as a memento from a trip to New York City. Miss Bell is using which of the following methods to activate prior knowledge?

   A. Concept mapping
   B. Replication
   C. Concrete experiences
   D. Semantic feature analysis

GO ON TO THE NEXT PAGE

15. Mr. Audette makes a point to model the reading strategy to be learned in a lesson, offer guided practice by using the reading strategy in class, and allow his students time to work independently while practicing the new reading strategy. Which of the following best describes the theory behind Mr. Audette's practice?

    A. Chalk and talk
    B. Scaffolding instruction
    C. Lecture
    D. Cooperative learning

16. Which of the following authors wrote *The Swiss Family Robinson*?

    A. Geoffrey Chaucer
    B. William Hill Brown
    C. Herman Hesse
    D. Johann Wyss

17. Mrs. Friedman has organized her students into literature circles with each student taking a role in the group. Which of the following roles is most likely found in a literature circle?

    A. Key grip
    B. Summarizer
    C. Leader
    D. Dictionary worker

18. Tory and Kelly are trying to compare and contrast the film of *The Wizard of Oz* and the book. Which of the following graphic organizers will best support their note-taking?

    A. Culture cluster
    B. Story map
    C. Hierarchical array
    D. Venn diagram

Questions 19–20 are based on the following passage from *Gulliver's Travels*.

We arrived at Lisbon, Nov. 5, 1715. At our landing, the Captain forced me to cover myself with his Cloak, to prevent the Rabble from crouding about me. I was conveyed to his own House, and at my earnest Request, he led me to the highest Room backwards. I conjured him to conceal from all Persons what I had told him of the *Houyhnhnms*, because the least Hint of such a Story would not only draw Numbers of People to see me, but probably, put me in Danger of being imprisoned, or burned by the Inquisition.

19. Which of the following best describes this excerpt from *Gulliver's Travels*?

    A. Prose in chronological sequence
    B. Lyrical poetry
    C. Prose in compare-and-contrast structure
    D. Realistic fiction

20. In which of the following periods was *Gulliver's Travels* written and first published?

    A. Early 1600s
    B. Early 1800s
    C. Early 1900s
    D. Early 1700s

21. Which of the following pairs are collective nouns?

    A. people and schools
    B. Mary's and John's
    C. gaggle and cache
    D. his and her

22. Which of the following is the verb tense in the sentence below?

Tory has attended Curtis Corner Middle School for sixth and seventh grade.

    A. Future
    B. Present perfect
    C. Present
    D. Past perfect

23. When a story is written from an omniscient point of view, which of the following is true?

    A. The narrator is free to tell the story from any and all characters' points of view.
    B. The story is told from the view of one character.
    C. The story is told by someone outside the story.
    D. The narrator compares two unlike things.

24. Which of the following word pairs demonstrates an analogous relationship to score: concerto?

    A. game: inning
    B. record: sound
    C. screenplay: movie
    D. music: video

25. Which of the following best describes the organization of a news article?

    A. Cause and effect
    B. Inverted pyramid
    C. Hierarchical array
    D. Problem/solution

26. Which of the following best defines an editorial?

    A. A fact-and-opinion essay
    B. A news article that covers an important current event
    C. A letter that discusses opinions held by the author
    D. A brief persuasive essay that expresses a viewpoint on a timely or important topic

27. Which of the following best summarizes the plot of *Julie of the Wolves* by Jean Craighead George?

    A. A young Eskimo girl experiences the changes forced upon her culture.
    B. A young girl lives outdoors for a year and removes herself from society's forces.
    C. A young girl is forced to survive alone after a storm kills all the other inhabitants of her island.
    D. A baby girl is abandoned and cared for by a pack of wolves.

GO ON TO THE NEXT PAGE

28. Which of the following authors wrote *The Outsiders*?

    A. Katherine Paterson
    B. Harper Lee
    C. S. E. Hinton
    D. Walter Dean Myers

29. Which of the following pairs are main characters in *The Outsiders*?

    A. Johnny and Maria
    B. Ponyboy and Dallas
    C. Tex and Sherri
    D. Jess and Leslie

30. Which of the following lines contain a metaphor?

    A. "And when I am king, as king I will be—"
    B. "All the world's a stage"
    C. "Neither a borrower nor a lender be"
    D. "How like a winter hath my absence been"

31. Which of the following best defines the literary term *mood*?

    A. A frequently occurring custom or behavior
    B. The emotional state of mind or atmosphere created by an author in a literary work
    C. The special characteristics an author uses in his or her writing
    D. The patterns of ideas organized in a literary work

32. Langston Hughes wrote his poem "Po' Boy Blues" using _____.

    A. Iambic pentameter
    B. Free verse
    C. Authentic setting and meaning
    D. Idioms and dialect from African American English

33. Which of the following activities is LEAST likely to occur during the publishing stage of the writing process?

    A. Examining a book to learn about the features of the publication
    B. Preparing a cover and title page
    C. Using the Internet to search for writing ideas
    D. Writing an acknowledgment section

34. Which of the following BEST describes the writing process?

    A. Recursive
    B. Developmental
    C. Exclusionary
    D. Step-by-step

35. Which of the following cueing strategies do readers use when they try to figure out an unknown word by thinking about what they know and what might make sense in the sentence?

    A. Vocabulary
    B. Grapho-phonics
    C. Structure
    D. Semantics

36. The root word in *exceed* and *succeed* is _____.

    A. ed
    B. ceed
    C. cce
    D. eed

37. The purpose of a response journal is for students to _____.

    A. Write a journal entry to the author
    B. Write about the author's message based on a lecture
    C. Construct meaning from their experiences and their reading of a text
    D. Write an entry that will be graded by the teacher

38. During a writing workshop, which of the following is the best role for the teacher?

    A. Check student work for spelling errors
    B. Correct quizzes
    C. Lead writing conferences
    D. Prepare for the close of the lesson

39. Which of the following is the correct MLA-format citation for the book *Great Expectations*?

    A. Dickens, C. Great expectations. New York: Random House, 1907.
    B. Dickens, C. (1907) Great Expectations. New York: Random House.
    C. Dickens, Charles. Great Expectations. New York: Random House, 1907.
    D. Dickens, Charles. *Great expectations*. New York; Random House, 1907.

40. In which of the following sources is a reader MOST likely to find an aphorism from Benjamin Franklin?

    A. Dictionary
    B. Thesaurus
    C. Encyclopedia
    D. *Bartlett's Familiar Quotations*

41. In an advertisement for legal services, a famous television attorney attests to the merits of the law firm being advertised. Which of the following persuasive techniques is being used in this advertisement?

    A. Appeal to authority
    B. Appeal to tradition
    C. Propaganda
    D. Appeal to excellence

GO ON TO THE NEXT PAGE

42. Which of the following pairs of words contains a vowel digraph?

   A. freight-believe
   B. right-ring
   C. organize-prioritize
   D. same-tame

43. Mrs. Josephson is an eighth-grade English teacher who is teaching her nonfluent students of English to understand a short story. Which of the following approaches is LEAST effective for Mrs. Josephson's students?

   A. Have students take turns repeat-reading in pairs.
   B. Have students take turns reading aloud passages from the short story to the whole class.
   C. Have students ask preview-and-predict questions prior to reading silently.
   D. Have students work in cooperative learning groups to read the short story.

44. What is the main problem or conflict in *Bridge to Terabithia* by Katherine Paterson?

   A. Person versus school
   B. Person versus person
   C. Person versus society
   D. Person versus self

45. What is the unique thing about the main character's name in the novel *Holes*?

   A. His name is a palindrome.
   B. His name is an acrostic.
   C. Her name is a palindrome.
   D. Her name is an acronym.

46. Which of the following topics are present in the novel *Holes*?

   A. Cheating, crocodiles, and the Everglades
   B. Bullying, lizards, and Camp Green Lake
   C. Dribbling, basketball, and the NBA
   D. Hiding, German soldiers, and World War II

47. Which of the following authors wrote *Holes*?

   A. Golding
   B. Myers
   C. Fleishman
   D. Sachar

48. The main character in Caroline B. Cooney's *The Voice on the Radio* is _____.

   A. Finny, a boy who attends a prep school
   B. Gene, a radio announcer
   C. Janie, a girl who was kidnapped as a child
   D. Caroline, the popular girl in school

49. Which of the following characters appears in *The Adventures of Huckleberry Finn*?

    A. Jim, a runaway slave

    B. Tim Sawyer, a mischievous friend

    C. Sam Clemens, a doctor

    D. Mrs. McGillicutty, a motherly neighbor

50. Which of the following sentences contains a dangling modifier?

    A. After earning a passing score on the Praxis II, the teacher certification office awarded her with a teaching license.

    B. The teacher certification office mailed the teaching license.

    C. The Praxis II is a teaching licensure test used in Rhode Island and is also required in Florida.

    D. In order to earn a teaching license, she had to complete an accredited program, file an application, and mail it to the teacher certification office.

51. Which of the following pairs is made up of compound words?

    A. read-read

    B. emigrate-immigrate

    C. firing-fired

    D. bumblebee-rosebush

52. Which of the following is an appropriate revision-stage activity during the writing process?

    A. Peer conferencing

    B. Peer editing

    C. Teacher editing

    D. Prewriting

53. When an advertisement includes testimony from a representative of the store who says, "For over 100 years, we have given customers the quality and service they deserve," which of the following persuasive strategies is being used?

    A. Appeal to authority

    B. Sex appeal

    C. Appeal to tradition

    D. Appeal to plain folks

54. Which of the following best describes the genre of *The Witch of Blackbird Pond*?

    A. Science fiction

    B. Realistic fiction

    C. Historical fiction

    D. Fantasy

55. *The Glory Field,* a book about an African-American family's present and past, was written by _____.

    A. Zora Neale Hurston

    B. Langston Hughes

    C. Walter Dean Myers

    D. Nikki Giovanni

GO ON TO THE NEXT PAGE

56. The narrator of *The Giver* is _____.

    A. Jonas

    B. Joseph

    C. Noah

    D. Nancy

57. Which of the following is a definition for *primary sources*?

    A. Commentaries

    B. Original documents

    C. News articles

    D. The first documents one uses in a research paper

58. Which of the following is a definition for *secondary sources*?

    A. The second documents one uses in a research paper

    B. Authentic diary entries

    C. Commentaries on primary sources

    D. Information overheard by another

59. In which novel do John and Lorraine tell the story of their lonely neighbor?

    A. *A Separate Peace* by John Knowles

    B. *The Chocolate War* by Robert Cormier

    C. *Holes* by Louis Sachar

    D. *The Pigman* by Paul Zindel

60. Which of the following is the best definition of a novel?

    A. An extended, fictional prose narrative

    B. A short, fictional prose narrative

    C. A narrative comprised of idealized events far removed from everyday life

    D. An expository text that describes one's life story

61. Which of the following characters is the protagonist in the work cited?

    A. Capulet in *Romeo and Juliet*

    B. Tom Sawyer in *The Adventures of Huckleberry Finn*

    C. Mr. Pendanski in *Holes*

    D. Ponyboy in *The Outsiders*

62. Which of the following text structures shows the relationship between events and their results?

    A. Chronological order

    B. Cause and effect

    C. Comparison

    D. Location

63. Which of the following literary terms can be defined as the turning point in a story?

    A. Falling action

    B. Climax

    C. Denouement

    D. Exposition

64. Which of the following words correctly uses a hyphen with a prefix?

    A. a-gain
    B. cross-stitch
    C. self-help
    D. selectman-elect

65. Which of the following is defined as informal speech made up of new words or expressions?

    A. Rap
    B. Cliché
    C. Slang
    D. Press conference

66. In this opening line of *Bridge to Terabithia*, the author uses which of the following literary devices?

"Ba-room, ba-room, ba-room, baripity, baripity, baripity, baripity—Good."

    A. Illusion
    B. Allusion
    C. Personification
    D. Onomatopoeia

67. Which of the following types of writing tries to prove that something is true or convince the reader to see the writer's viewpoint?

    A. Sonnet
    B. Argument
    C. Analysis
    D. Technical

68. Which of the following is a propaganda technique?

    A. News articles
    B. Poster
    C. Bandwagon
    D. Mass marketing

69. In a story told from the first person point of view, the story is told _____.

    A. By the main antagonist
    B. By someone outside the story
    C. From the perspective of an outside member of society
    D. From the perspective of one of the characters

70. Which of the following lines contains a simile?

    A. "Mine eyes have seen the glory of the coming of the Lord:"
    B. "Woodman, spare that tree! Touch not a single bough!"
    C. "My candle burns at both ends; it will not last the night;"
    D. "Away to the window I flew like a flash."

GO ON TO THE NEXT PAGE

71. Which of the following is LEAST likely to foster reading appreciation in adolescents?

    A. Round-robin reading aloud in class

    B. Helping students find "just right"–level books

    C. Conducting literature circles

    D. Finding an author or series to read

72. Which of the following lines from Shakespeare does NOT contain an insult?

    A. "Tis brief, my lord." "As woman's love."

    B. "Shall I compare thee to a summer's day?"

    C. "Tempt not too much the hatred of my spirit, for I am sick when I do look on thee."

    D. "She speaks yet she says nothing."

73. Which of the following techniques should students use to avoid plagiarism?

    I.   Paraphrase the author's words

    II.   Summarize in one's own words

    III.   Cite quotations

    IV.   Enclose borrowed words in quotation marks

    A. I

    B. I, II

    C. II, III, IV

    D. All of the above

74. The word *restroom* is a(n) _____ for the toilet room.

    A. Elegy

    B. Anapestic

    C. Aphorism

    D. Euphemism

75. Which of the following sentences contains a verb in the future tense?

    A. Matthew has attended Dean College.

    B. Matthew enrolled in Dean College for fall 2007.

    C. Matthew will attend Dean College in the fall.

    D. Matthew and Jimmy attend Dean College.

76. Which of the following types of writing captures the meaning of the person, place, or thing being written about?

    A. Scholarly writing

    B. Subject writing

    C. Workplace writing

    D. Persuasive writing

77. Abraham Lincoln is attributed with saying, "You can fool some of the people all of the time, and all of the people some of the time, but you cannot fool all of the people all of the time." Which of the following rhetorical devices was President Lincoln using?

    A. Repetition

    B. Hyperbole

    C. Metaphor

    D. Simile

78. Which of the following activities is MOST likely to appear in an argument written for a composition class?

    A. Run-on sentence

    B. Quarrel

    C. Insertion

    D. Assertion

79. Which of the following is an appropriate greeting in a business letter?

    A. Hi, Mr. Stevens:

    B. Dear Sir or Madam

    C. Dear Mary,

    D. Dear Sir or Madam:

80. Which of the following pairs of words contains at least one open syllable?

    A. careful-carefree

    B. cast-mast

    C. belong-believe

    D. carpet-rug

81. Which of the following BEST defines diction in a composition?

    A. The pronunciation of words

    B. The use and choice of words

    C. The meanings of particular words

    D. The number of syllables in a word

82. Which of the following best describes the theme of Langston Hughes' poem "Harlem"?

    A. Postponing one's deepest held desires may lead to destruction.

    B. Dreams really do come true.

    C. Life in the city can be fraught with peril and delight.

    D. Good things come to those who wait.

Questions 83–86 are based on the following excerpt from an inaugural address.

I am certain that my fellow Americans expect that on my induction into the presidency I will address them with a candor and a decision which the present situation of our Nation impels. This is preeminently the time to speak the truth, the whole truth, frankly and boldly. Nor need we shrink from honestly facing conditions in our country today. This great nation will endure as it has endured, will revive and will prosper. So, first of all, let me assert my firm belief that the only thing we have to fear is fear itself—nameless, unreasoning, unjustified terror which paralyzes needed efforts to convert retreat into advance.

83. Which of the following summarizes the topic sentence of this address?

    A. We have nothing to fear except fear itself.

    B. The president will speak candidly and decisively, as the people expect.

    C. The people should not shrink from fear or problems.

    D. The president will speak the whole truth.

GO ON TO THE NEXT PAGE

84. Which of the following is a supporting detail in the passage above?

    A. The president will speak candidly and decisively, as the people expect.

    B. The president will speak the whole truth.

    C. The people will attend the inauguration.

    D. The people have elected this president and, therefore, support him.

85. Which of the following best defines the word *preeminently* as used in the address above?

    A. Most important

    B. Right

    C. Formal

    D. Religious

86. Which of the following presidents delivered this inaugural address?

    A. Richard Nixon

    B. Jimmy Carter

    C. Franklin Delano Roosevelt

    D. John F. Kennedy

Questions 87–90 are based on the following poem, *Sonnets from the Portuguese*.

Beloved, thou hast brought me many flowers
Plucked in the garden, all the summer through,
And winter, and it seemed as if they grew
In this close room, nor missed the sun and showers.
So, in the like name of that love of ours,
Take back these thoughts which here unfolded too,
And which on warm and cold days I withdrew
From my heart's ground. Indeed, those beds and bowers
Be overgrown with bitter weeds and rue,
And wait thy weeding; yet here's eglantine,
Here's ivy!—take them, as I used to do
Thy flowers, and keep them where they shall not pine.
Instruct thine eyes to keep their colours true,
And tell thy soul, their roots are left in mine.

87. Which of the following metrics is used in the English sonnet above?

    A. Iambic pentameter

    B. Iambic quintet

    C. Trochaic pentameter

    D. Anapestic pentameter

88. Which of the following authors wrote *Sonnets from the Portuguese*?

    A. Emily Dickinson

    B. George Eliot

    C. T. S. Eliot

    D. Elizabeth Barrett Browning

89. The phrase "From my heart's ground" employs which of the following literary devices?

    A. Alliteration

    B. Metaphor

    C. Allusion

    D. Phoneme

90. Which of the following offers the most likely interpretation of the final line of the sonnet?

    A. The poet is asking her love to remain true to her.

    B. The poet has lost her love.

    C. The poet's husband has cut off the roots of a bouquet.

    D. The poet prefers wildflowers to store-bought flowers.

Constructed Response I: Literary Analysis

Directions: This short-answer, or constructed-response, question requires you to interpret a piece of literary or nonfiction text. Plan to spend approximately 15 minutes of your testing time on this question. The excerpt below is from Emily Dickinson's poem "Success." Explain how Dickinson uses homily and poetic form to convey meaning in her poem.

> Success is counted sweetest
> By those who ne'er succeed.
> To comprehend a nectar
> Requires sorest need.
>
> Not one of all the purple host
> Who took the flag to-day
> Can tell the definition,
> So clear, of victory,
>
> As he, defeated, dying,
> On whose forbidden ear
> The distant strains of triumph
> Break, agonized and clear!

Constructed Response II: Rhetorical Analysis

Directions: This short-answer, or constructed-response, question requires you to discuss the rhetorical elements of a piece of writing. Plan to spend approximately 15 minutes of your testing time on this question. Describe the major organizational and rhetorical features of this opening paragraph from Martin Luther King, Jr.'s March on Washington address. Refer directly to the excerpt to support your description of its organization.

Five score years ago, a great American, in whose symbolic shadow we stand, signed the Emancipation Proclamation. This momentous decree came as a great beacon light of hope to millions of Negro slaves who had been seared in the flames of withering injustice. It came as a joyous daybreak to end the long night of captivity.

But one hundred years later, we face the tragic fact that the Negro is still not free. One hundred years later, the life of the Negro is still sadly crippled by the manacles of segregation and the chains of discrimination. One hundred years later, the Negro lives on a lonely island of poverty in the midst of a vast ocean of material prosperity. One hundred years later, the Negro is still languished in the corners of American society and finds himself an exile in his own land. So we have come here today to dramatize an appalling condition.

Answers and Explanations

Multiple-Choice Questions

Answer Key, Questions 1–90			
Question	**Answer**	**Content Category**	**Where to Get More Help**
1.	B	Reading and Understanding Text	Chapter 4
2.	D	Reading and Understanding Text	Chapter 4
3.	C	Reading and Understanding Text	Chapter 4
4.	D	Reading and Understanding Text	Chapter 4
5.	A	Reading and Understanding Text	Chapter 4
6.	A	Language and Linguistics	Chapter 5
7.	B	Language and Linguistics	Chapter 5
8.	D	Composition and Rhetoric	Chapter 6
9.	D	Composition and Rhetoric	Chapter 6
10.	B	Composition and Rhetoric	Chapter 6
11.	D	Composition and Rhetoric	Chapter 6
12.	C	Composition and Rhetoric	Chapter 6
13.	A	Reading and Understanding Text	Chapter 4
14.	C	Reading and Understanding Text	Chapter 4
15.	B	Reading and Understanding Text	Chapter 4
16.	D	Reading and Understanding Text	Chapter 4
17.	B	Reading and Understanding Text	Chapter 4
18.	D	Reading and Understanding Text	Chapter 4
19.	A	Composition and Rhetoric	Chapter 6
20.	D	Composition and Rhetoric	Chapter 6
21.	C	Language and Linguistics	Chapter 5
22.	B	Language and Linguistics	Chapter 5
23.	A	Composition and Rhetoric	Chapter 6
24.	C	Composition and Rhetoric	Chapter 6
25.	B	Composition and Rhetoric	Chapter 6
26.	D	Composition and Rhetoric	Chapter 6
27.	A	Reading and Understanding Text	Chapter 4
28.	C	Reading and Understanding Text	Chapter 4
29.	B	Reading and Understanding Text	Chapter 4

Question	Answer	Content Category	Where to Get More Help
30.	B	Reading and Understanding Text	Chapter 4
31.	B	Reading and Understanding Text	Chapter 4
32.	D	Reading and Understanding Text	Chapter 4
33.	C	Composition and Rhetoric	Chapter 6
34.	A	Composition and Rhetoric	Chapter 6
35.	D	Language and Linguistics	Chapter 5
36.	B	Language and Linguistics	Chapter 5
37.	C	Composition and Rhetoric	Chapter 6
38.	C	Composition and Rhetoric	Chapter 6
39.	C	Composition and Rhetoric	Chapter 6
40.	D	Composition and Rhetoric	Chapter 6
41.	A	Composition and Rhetoric	Chapter 6
42.	A	Language and Linguistics	Chapter 5
43.	B	Language and Linguistics	Chapter 5
44.	D	Reading and Understanding Text	Chapter 4
45.	A	Reading and Understanding Text	Chapter 4
46.	B	Reading and Understanding Text	Chapter 4
47.	D	Reading and Understanding Text	Chapter 4
48.	C	Reading and Understanding Text	Chapter 4
49.	A	Reading and Understanding Text	Chapter 4
50.	A	Language and Linguistics	Chapter 5
51.	D	Language and Linguistics	Chapter 5
52.	A	Composition and Rhetoric	Chapter 6
53.	C	Composition and Rhetoric	Chapter 6
54.	C	Reading and Understanding Text	Chapter 4
55.	C	Reading and Understanding Text	Chapter 4
56.	A	Reading and Understanding Text	Chapter 4
57.	B	Composition and Rhetoric	Chapter 6
58.	C	Composition and Rhetoric	Chapter 6
59.	D	Reading and Understanding Text	Chapter 4
60.	A	Composition and Rhetoric	Chapter 6
61.	D	Composition and Rhetoric	Chapter 6
62.	B	Composition and Rhetoric	Chapter 6

(continued)

Question	Answer	Content Category	Where to Get More Help
		Answer Key, Questions 1–90 *(continued)*	
63.	B	Composition and Rhetoric	Chapter 6
64.	C	Language and Linguistics	Chapter 5
65.	C	Language and Linguistics	Chapter 5
66.	D	Composition and Rhetoric	Chapter 6
67.	B	Composition and Rhetoric	Chapter 6
68.	C	Composition and Rhetoric	Chapter 6
69.	D	Reading and Understanding Text	Chapter 4
70.	D	Reading and Understanding Text	Chapter 4
71.	A	Reading and Understanding Text	Chapter 4
72.	B	Reading and Understanding Text	Chapter 4
73.	C	Reading and Understanding Text	Chapter 4
74.	D	Language and Linguistics	Chapter 5
75.	C	Language and Linguistics	Chapter 5
76.	B	Composition and Rhetoric	Chapter 6
77.	A	Composition and Rhetoric	Chapter 6
78.	D	Composition and Rhetoric	Chapter 6
79.	D	Language and Linguistics	Chapter 5
80.	C	Language and Linguistics	Chapter 5
81.	B	Composition and Rhetoric	Chapter 6
82.	A	Composition and Rhetoric	Chapter 6
83.	B	Composition and Rhetoric	Chapter 6
84.	B	Composition and Rhetoric	Chapter 6
85.	A	Composition and Rhetoric	Chapter 6
86.	C	Reading and Understanding Text	Chapter 4
87.	A	Reading and Understanding Text	Chapter 4
88.	D	Reading and Understanding Text	Chapter 4
89.	B	Reading and Understanding Text	Chapter 4
90.	A	Reading and Understanding Text	Chapter 4

1. B. Hermia and Robin Goodfellow, a puck who causes much mischief, are characters in *A Midsummer Night's Dream*.

2. D. *The Giver, 1984,* and *The Lord of the Rings* are all science fiction novels.

3. C. *Fahrenheit 451* takes place in the future—in the 24th century.

4. D. *Night* is a memoir written by Elie Wiesel that offers a firsthand account of the Jewish people's horrific ordeal and his miraculous escape from death during the Holocaust.

5. A. Of the choices given, *Night* can best be described as personal writing, a form of writing meant to express innermost thoughts, feelings, and responses.

6. A. Tituba uses dialect from the area her family comes from. Scholars believe that Tituba, a slave in the Parris household, was most likely a slave from South America, not Africa.

7. B. A compound/complex sentence has two or more independent clauses and one or more dependent clauses.

8. D. Rhetoric is the effective use of language to persuade or please.

9. D. Reliable Internet sources should be checked for authorship, accuracy, purpose, and access (so that others can find the information again).

10. B. The proper MLA citation is B because it contains an underline for the book title and only the page number in parentheses since the author's name appears in the sentence.

11. D. Writers should consider the audience for their writing—who the intended reader is, what his or her background knowledge is, and how this piece might be purposeful beyond the classroom.

12. C. Shakespeare's Sonnet 18 compares a loved one to summer.

13. A. An anticipation guide is a series of open-ended questions intended to prepare students for the major themes or concepts in an upcoming reading assignment.

14. C. Miss Bell uses a replica of the Twin Towers as a concrete experience to start a discussion about 9/11 and activate students' prior knowledge prior to reading.

15. B. Mr. Audette is scaffolding instruction—offering students a model, guided practice, and independent practice with the support of a capable adult.

16. D. Johann Wyss wrote *The Swiss Family Robinson* in 1813.

17. B. In literature circles, students play key roles such as summarizer, word finder, passage master, and illustrator to make sense of their reading collaboratively.

18. D. A Venn diagram is a graphic organizer made up of overlapping circles and is best used to compare and contrast information.

19. A. This excerpt from *Gulliver's Travels* can best be described as prose in chronological sequence. The narrator tells the reader about his arrival in Lisbon, his welcoming at the Captain's home, and his efforts to be clothed properly and comfortably.

20. D. Jonathan Swift was born in 1667. *Gulliver's Travels* was first published anonymously in 1726.

21. C. A collective noun names a group or unit, such as *gaggle* of geese or *cache* of jewels.

22. B. The verb tense in this sentence is present perfect because the action (attending) began in the past but continues into the present.

23. A. In the omniscient point of view, the narrator is free to tell the story from any and all characters' perspectives.

24. C. The response screenplay: movie has an analogous relationship to score: concerto because a score is the text of a concert and a screenplay is the text of a movie.

25. B. A news article typically follows an inverted pyramid structure with the lead first, followed by details presented in the order of importance.

26. D. An editorial is a brief persuasive essay that expresses a viewpoint on a timely or important topic.

27. A. *Julie of the Wolves* is the story of a young Eskimo girl who experiences the changes inflicted upon her culture by outside forces.

28. C. S. E. Hinton wrote *The Outsiders* when she was 16 years old.

29. B. Ponyboy and Dallas are two of the main characters is the novel *The Outsiders*.

30. B. "All the world's a stage" is a metaphor comparing life to a play.

31. B. The mood of a literary work is the emotional state of mind or atmosphere created by the author.

32. D. Hughes captured the beauty of African American English Vernacular through his authentic and careful use of idioms and dialect.

33. C. In the publication stage of the writing process, a writer is least likely to use the Internet to search for writing ideas. This is more likely to occur in the prewriting stage.

34. A. The writing process is a recursive process in which the writer moves through the stages of writing in a unique sequence. The term *recursive* signifies that each writer's process is not linear—going directly from one prescribed stage to another—rather, the writing process is unique to each writer based on that writer's distinct needs.

35. D. Readers use three cueing systems: semantics, syntax, and structure. When a reader draws upon what he or she knows, the reader is using the semantic, or meaning, cueing system.

36. B. The root word *ceed* or *cede* means "to go" or "to yield."

37. C. Response journals are intended to enable students to construct meaning from their experiences and their reading of a text.

38. C. Writing teachers can best use writing workshop time to lead writing conferences with students.

39. C. The proper MLA citation of Dickens' *Great Expectations* is:

Dickens, Charles. Great Expectations. New York: Random House, 1907.

40. D. *Bartlett's Familiar Quotations* is the foremost print and online source of famous quotations.

41. A. In an appeal to authority, advertisers hire sports, television, film, and other celebrities to attest to the value of a product.

42. A. *Freight* and *receive* contain the vowel digraphs *ie* and *ei*. A vowel digraph is a pair of vowel letters used to create one sound.

43. B. Students who are nonfluent in English can read silently and comprehend with some proficiency before they can read aloud well; therefore, choice B is the least likely to be supportive for nonfluent English readers.

44. D. In *Bridge to Terabithia,* Jess has to overcome the loss of a friend. Of the choices available, the main conflict is person versus self.

45. A. The main character in *Holes* is Stanley Yelnats, whose name is a palindrome—a word that is the same when spelled backwards and forwards.

46. B. *Holes* is a story about bullying, lizards, and Camp Green Lake. The main character, Stanley Yelnats, is sent to Camp Green Lake as punishment for allegedly stealing a pair of sneakers. He is forced to dig a hole every day in the former location of Green Lake, and in those holes he finds yellow-spotted lizards.

47. D. *Holes* was written by Louis Sachar, the author of several young adolescent books, including the *Wayside School* series and the *Marvin Redpost* series.

48. C. Janie, a girl who was kidnapped as a child, is the main character in *The Voice on the Radio,* a companion novel to *The Face on the Milk Carton* and *Whatever Happened to Janie?*

49. A. Jim, a runaway slave, joins Huck Finn on his adventure down the Mississippi River.

50. A. Sentence A contains a dangling modifier—a modifier that fails to refer logically to the word it modifies. In this case, the teacher certification office did not take the Praxis II test.

51. D. Compound words are made up of two smaller words that together create new meaning.

52. A. During a peer conference, students read their writing to hear their ideas out loud and receive feedback from an initial audience. This is an appropriate revision-stage activity in which students re-see their writing in an effort to strengthen and change the piece.

53. C. In this advertisement, an appeal to tradition is being used.

54. C. *The Witch of Blackbird Pond* is a historical fiction novel that takes place in Connecticut in the late 1600s.

55. C. *The Glory Field* was written by Walter Dean Myers.

56. A. The narrator of *The Giver* is Jonas, a young boy chosen to keep all the memories of a society.

57. B. Primary sources are original documents, such as journals, diaries, laws, and maps.

58. C. Secondary sources are commentaries on primary sources.

59. D. *The Pigman* by Paul Zindel is the story of two high school sophomores who befriend Mr. Angelo Pignati, the Pigman.

60. A. A novel is best defined as an extended, fictional prose narrative.

61. D. Ponyboy in *The Outsiders* is the protagonist, or the central character in a narrative or drama.

62. B. Cause-and-effect texts are organized to show the relationship between events and their results.

63. B. The climax is the turning point in a story, when the problem is at its worst.

64. C. The prefix *self* is correctly followed by a hyphen.

65. C. Slang is informal speech made up of newly coined expressions or common words used in a new way.

66. D. Paterson opens *Bridge to Terabithia* with onomatopoeia, a literary device in which sound words are used.

67. B. Argument is a type of writing that tries to prove that something is true or convince the reader to see the writer's viewpoint.

68. C. One propaganda technique is to suggest that everyone is doing or believing something, so you should jump on the bandwagon, too.

69. D. In the first person point of view, the story is told from the perspective of one character.

70. D. This line from Clement C. Moore's *A Visit from Saint Nicholas* contains the simile "like a flash."

71. A. Round-robin reading aloud in class is a practice that often demotivates students.

72. B. "Shall I compare thee to a summer's day?" is the first line of a love sonnet.

73. C. To avoid plagiarism, students should summarize in their own words, cite quotations, and enclose borrowed words in quotation marks.

74. D. A euphemism is a polite way to discuss a topic that may bring about discomfort.

75. C. The verb *will attend* is in the future tense.

76. B. Subject writing includes writing interviews, accounts, or biographies to capture the meaning of the subject being written about.

77. A. Lincoln, one of the United States' great orators, used repetition in this quote to make his point effectively.

78. D. A well-written argument contains an assertion, a premise, and a conclusion.

79. D. "Dear Sir or Madam:" is an appropriate greeting in a business letter.

80. C. The words *belong* and *believe* contain one open syllable, *be-*.

81. B. When an author uses good diction, he or she chooses words that accurately convey the intended meaning and suit the occasion of the piece.

82. A. Hughes' poem "Harlem" is commonly referred to as "Dream Deferred." In this poem, the dream that is deferred, or put off, could be lost or destroyed. Lines such as "fester in the sun" and "stink like rotten meat" support this interpretation of the theme.

83. B. The topic sentence of this opening paragraph states that the president will speak candidly and decisively, as the people expect.

84. B. A supporting detail in this paragraph is "The president will speak the whole truth."

85. A. *Preeminently* means "most important" in the context of this speech.

86. C. Franklin Delano Roosevelt delivered his first inaugural address in 1933.

87. A. An English sonnet is traditionally written in iambic pentameter.

88. D. Elizabeth Barrett Browning wrote *Sonnets from the Portuguese,* a collection of 44 love sonnets to her husband, Robert Browning.

89. B. The poet uses an extended metaphor comparing her love to a garden.

90. A. The poet is asking her love to remain true to her.

Constructed Response I: Literary Analysis

Dickinson uses poetic form and homily to convey meaning in her poem "Success." This poem is comprised of three stanzas that are written in iambic trimeter, with an exception in the first two lines of the second stanza. This is a common technique in Dickinson's poetry; she often fluctuates meter between three and four stresses. The stanzas rhyme with an ABCD pattern; therefore, the second and fourth lines in each stanza are the only ones that rhyme. Dickinson makes a homiletic point—"Success is counted sweetest/By those who ne'er succeed." In other words, her primary message in the poem is that people tend to want most those things that they do not have. For example, she offers pairs of images that create an axiomatic truth: "To comprehend a nectar/Requires sorest need," and "As he, defeated, dying/On whose forbidden ear/The distant strains of triumph/Break, agonized and clear!" In other words, one must be in dire need to truly taste a nectar; a defeated, dying man better understands victory than a living army of soldiers capturing the victory flag.

Constructed Response II: Rhetorical Analysis

Dr. Martin Luther King, Jr., spoke persuasively and effectively as he addressed his large audience in Washington, D.C., in 1963. He used repetition, allusion, and metaphor to capture his listeners' attention and move all who heard him to action.

The orator began with an allusion to Abraham Lincoln's Gettysburg Address by stating, "five score years ago." Lincoln opened the Gettysburg Address with "four score and seven years ago." This time reference and the historical context of Lincoln's important speech that addressed the freeing of slaves in the United States provided the context for King's address.

King used repetition with the phrase "one hundred years later" to make the point that the time had come for change and to accentuate the dire circumstance of the African-American people of his day. This phrase built on the historical context of Lincoln's signing of the Emancipation Proclamation in the late 1800s. King described his people as experiencing segregation, poverty, discrimination, and marginalization.

Dr. King startled the listener when he stated in his second paragraph that "we must face the tragic fact that the Negro is still not free." He then used metaphor to make his point. Employing phrases such as "crippled by the manacles of segregation" and "the chains of discrimination," King evoked images of African Americans as modern-day slaves. He stated that the "the Negro is still languished in the corners of American society" in a similar way that slaves of yesterday were marginalized.

These first two paragraphs of Dr. King's "I have a dream" speech provided the historical context and rhetorical devices for his central message—that African Americans in the 1960s were enslaved by segregation and discrimination.

PART IV

CLOSING THOUGHTS

In this part, I have included a long-term and a short-term study timeline, resources to help you prepare efficiently and effectively for your Praxis II English Subject Area Assessment test, and a few last study tips.

A Few Final Tips

The purpose of this chapter is to offer you a few more test preparation tips and resources to help you achieve a passing score on your Praxis II English Subject Area Assessment test.

Registration

If your state requires more than one Praxis II test for certification, consider taking only one test per day. Taking a Praxis II English Subject Area Assessment test is a fast-paced, intense, and exhausting experience. Your test will be from one hour to four hours in duration. If you are required to take more than one test, you may want to exercise your option of spreading out your testing time to improve your performance.

Plan ahead. Presently, the Praxis II English Subject Area Assessment tests are available only in paper-and-pencil format, which requires registration a minimum of one month prior to the testing date. If you qualify for testing accommodations, then you will want to allow even more than one month for the registration process. Check the website www.ets.org/praxis for test dates, testing locations, accommodation requirements, and deadlines.

Remember, registration is less expensive and easier to complete online.

Some colleges or universities will provide a waiver for the fee for your Praxis II test. Talk to a financial aid officer to see if getting a waiver is a possibility for you.

Bring proof of registration, even if it's just a printout of your online registration confirmation.

If you're eligible for testing accommodations, complete the required documentation prior to registering for the test and mail it to ETS early. Be sure to double-check that the date on which you are planning to take the Praxis II test allows for testing accommodations. Also, be sure that accommodations are available at the testing location you request.

Studying

Don't wait until the last minute to study. Schedule study sessions the way you schedule other obligations, such as medical appointments and classes. Stick to your study plan.

Assess your strengths and weaknesses as a test-taker and student based on your past performance. If you are generally a strong test-taker, review this book's content and take the practice tests. If you are generally an anxious or not-so-strong test-taker, use this book to familiarize yourself with the format and content of the Praxis II tests and plan to use additional resources, such as English and education course textbooks, to thoroughly prepare for the test. If you experience test anxiety, you may want to seek the support of your university's or college's counseling services. ETS also offers a free guide about test anxiety that is available at www.ets.org.

This book has helped you experience the format of your test and determine the content you need to review. If you're not a great multiple-choice person, for example, study more of those questions. If you're struggling with reading comprehension, writing, or the fundamental English or language arts content, study and practice those sections to better prepare for your teaching licensure test.

Remember, all five of the practice tests in this book can help you prepare for the content of the Praxis II English Subject Area Assessment tests. If you complete only the practice test for the specific test you are required to take, you may want to at least review the English content covered on the four other practice tests. The format of the practice tests you review may differ from that of your test, but the broad content categories have overlapping principles and concepts. Some people have found that reading the answers and explanations for each practice test is an especially useful way to review content.

Exam Day

- Be sure to get a good night's sleep the night before your test.
- Eat a healthy, adequate breakfast.
- Remember your two forms of identification, pencils or pens, and proof of registration.
- Arrive at least 15 minutes early.
- Pass your Praxis II test!

Study Planning Guide

If You Have a Longer Time Line	
When	*What You Need to Do*
3 months (or more) before the Praxis II	Register for the Praxis II test that your state requires. Complete the paperwork for accommodations, if applicable. Complete the paperwork or speak with a financial aid officer about the possibility of a fee waiver, if applicable. Read the introduction and Part I of this book. Dust off your English language arts methods textbooks or borrow one from the library. More recent copies even include references to the Praxis II tests! Use your favorite Web browser to search for websites using keywords such as "Praxis II" and "English." Look for sites that contain PowerPoint presentations or the names of colleges or universities. Many of these sites are created by professors and offer a wealth of information to shore up your weaknesses and help you prepare for the content of the test. Bookmark these websites for future use.
2 months (or more) before the Praxis II	Make sure that you've registered for your test. Also, be sure to set aside proof of registration in a safe place—one that you'll remember! Read Parts I and II of this book to help you understand the format and content of the test. Use your favorite Praxis II websites—the ones you bookmarked last month—to help you prepare for the test. Take a look at the table of contents, glossary, and index of your education psychology textbook for even more information about the areas in which you are still learning.
1 month (or more) before the Praxis II	Take a test drive to the building in which you'll be taking your test. Time how long it takes and note the traffic conditions. Take the full-length practice tests in Part III of this book to simulate test-taking conditions and assess which areas you still need to study. Use your websites and English methods textbook to fill in any missing pieces of content.
1 week before the Praxis II	Set aside your proof of registration, a few #2 pencils with erasers, a couple of blue or black pens, and two valid forms of identification. Retake any or all of the full-length practice tests in this book. Review Part II of this book to refresh your memory on the test content.
The night before the Praxis II	Talk only to people who make you feel good and confident! Pack a water bottle and a small snack bag. Although you can't bring these things into the test session, you'll enjoy the brain refueling after the test. Go to bed early. Don't cram all night.

When	What You Need to Do
The day of the Praxis II	Relax. Take a deep breath. You've already put in lots of effort preparing for your Praxis II test. Eat a good breakfast. Remember to bring your water bottle, snack, proof of registration, IDs, and writing instruments. Arrive at the test center at least 15 minutes early.

If You Have a Shorter Time Line

When	What You Need to Do
1 month before the Praxis II	Register for the Praxis II test that your state requires. There are a late registration fee option and a standby option if you're registering within one month of the test. Complete the paperwork and submit it to ETS if you are eligible for accommodations. Talk to your financial aid officer to learn whether your school has a test fee waiver option. Read the introduction and Part I of this book.
3 weeks before the Praxis II	Read Parts II and III of this book. Take a test drive to the building in which you'll be taking your test. Time how long it takes and note the traffic conditions.
2 weeks before the Praxis II	Take the full-length practice tests in Part III of this book to simulate test-taking conditions and assess which areas you still need to study. Review the content outlines in Part II of this book to help shore up any areas whose content you are still learning.
1 week before the Praxis II	Set aside your proof of registration, a few #2 pencils with erasers, a couple of blue or black pens, and two valid forms of identification. Retake any or all of the pertinent full-length tests in this guide. Review Part II of this book to refresh your memory on the test content.
The night before the Praxis II	Talk only to people who make you feel good and confident! Pack a water bottle and a small snack bag. Although you can't bring these things into the test session, you'll enjoy the brain refueling after the test. Go to bed early. Don't cram all night.
The day of the Praxis II	Relax. Take a deep breath. You've already put in lots of effort preparing for your Praxis II test. Eat a good breakfast! Remember to bring your water bottle, snack, proof of registration, IDs, and writing instruments. Arrive at the test center at least 15 minutes early.

Resources

This chapter provides a list of resources that you may find helpful as you prepare for the content of your Praxis II English Subject Area Assessment test.

Suggested References

The suggested references in this section might help prepare you for the English content of the Praxis II, and might prove helpful in your English classroom one day soon.

Abrams, M. H., & Greenblatt, S. (Eds.) (2006). *The Norton Anthology of English Literature* (8th ed.). New York: Norton.

American Psychological Association (2001). *Publication Manual of the American Psychological Association* (5th ed.). Washington, DC: Author.

Baym, N. (Ed.) (1999). *The Norton Anthology of American Literature* (5th ed.). New York: Norton.

Calkins, L. M. (1994). *The Art of Teaching Writing*. Portsmouth, NH: Heinemann.

Dornan, E. A., & Dawe, C. W. (2003). *The Brief English Handbook: A Guide to Writing, Thinking, Grammar, and Research* (7th ed.). Boston: Longman.

Gates, H. L., & McKay, N. Y. (Eds.) (2004). *The Norton Anthology of African American Literature* (2nd ed.). New York: Norton.

Gibaldi, J. (2003). *MLA Handbook for Writers of Research Papers* (6th ed.). New York: Modern Language Association.

Hacker, D. (2003). *A Writer's Reference* (5th ed.). Boston: Bedford/St. Martin's.

Harris, T. L., & Hodges, R. E. (Eds.) (1995). *The Literacy Dictionary: The Vocabulary of Reading and Writing*. Newark, DE: International Reading Association.

Raffel, B. (1994). *How to Read a Poem*. New York: Penguin Group.

Ramazani, J., Ellman, R., & O'Clair, R. (Eds.) (2003). *The Norton Anthology of Modern and Contemporary Poetry* (3rd ed.). New York: Norton.

Robb, L., Klemp, R., & Schwartz, W. (2002). *The Reader's Handbook: A Student Guide for Reading and Learning*. Wilmington, MA: Great Source.

Willis, H., & Klammer, E. (1986). *A Brief Handbook of English* (3rd ed.). New York: Harcourt Brace Jovanovich.

Literary Works

This list gives you a sense of the range of works included on the Praxis II: English Subject Area Assessment tests. It is not exhaustive; these works may or may not appear on your actual exam.

Beowulf (unknown author)

Things Fall Apart, Chinua Achebe

The House of the Spirits, Isabel Allende

I Know Why the Caged Bird Sings, Maya Angelou

Pride and Prejudice, Jane Austen

Go Tell It on the Mountain, James Baldwin

The Good Earth, Pearl S. Buck

The House on Mango Street, Sandra Cisneros

Heart of Darkness, Joseph Conrad

The Red Badge of Courage, Stephen Crane

Great Expectations, Charles Dickens

Narrative of the Life of Frederick Douglass, Frederick Douglass

Invisible Man, Ralph Ellison

The Great Gatsby, F. Scott Fitzgerald

Anne Frank: The Diary of a Young Girl, Anne Frank

The Miracle Worker, William Gibson

Lord of the Flies, William Golding

A Raisin in the Sun, Lorraine Hansberry

The Scarlet Letter, Nathaniel Hawthorne

A Farewell to Arms, Ernest Hemingway

The Odyssey, Homer

Their Eyes Were Watching God, Zora Neale Hurston

The Turn of the Screw, Henry James

The Metamorphosis, Franz Kafka

The Woman Warrior, Maxine Hong Kingston

Annie John, Jamaica Kincaid

The Giver, Lois Lowry

The Crucible, Arthur Miller

Death of a Salesman, Arthur Miller

House Made of Dawn, N. Scott Momaday

1984, George Orwell

Animal Farm, George Orwell

The Catcher in the Rye, J. D. Salinger

Romeo and Juliet and other plays and sonnets, William Shakespeare

Ceremony, Leslie Marmon Silko

The Grapes of Wrath, John Steinbeck

The Joy Luck Club, Amy Tan

Roll of Thunder, Hear My Cry, Mildred D. Taylor

The Hobbit, J. R. R. Tolkien

The Adventures of Huckleberry Finn, Mark Twain

The Color Purple, Alice Walker

Ethan Frome, Edith Wharton

Night, Elie Wiesel

Our Town, Thornton Wilder

The Glass Menagerie, Tennessee Williams

A Streetcar Named Desire, Tennessee Williams

Native Son, Richard Wright

The Pigman, Paul Zindel

Internet Resources

Bartleby.com: Great Books Online: www.bartleby.com

Diana Hacker's Rules for Writers, 5th edition: www.dianahacker.com/rules/instructor/dev_clar.html

Electronic Texts for the Study of American Culture at the University of Virginia: xroads.virginia.edu/~HYPER/hypertex.html#s

Graphic Organizers at SCORE: www.sdcoe.k12.ca.us/SCORE/actbank/torganiz.htm

Wikipedia, a great online encyclopedia: www.wikipedia.org